The Mark and the Knowledge

THE MARK
AND THE
KNOWLEDGE

**Social Stigma
in Classic American Fiction**

Marjorie Pryse

Published by the Ohio State University Press
for Miami University

Library of Congress Cataloguing in Publication Data

Pryse, Marjorie, 1948–
    The mark and the knowledge

    Includes index.
    1. American fiction—History and criticism.
2. Social problems in literature. 3. Characters and characteristics in literature. I. Title.
PS374.S7P7   813'.009'27   78-23229
ISBN 0-8142-0296-9

Contents

Acknowledgments

I would like to express my appreciation to Professors Harry Berger, Jr., and Michael Cowan at University of California, Santa Cruz. Professor Cowan directed the Ph.D. dissertation that served as the basis for this book. Professors Priscilla W. Shaw and Thomas A. Vogler read the manuscript in its early stages and offered valuable suggestions.

I am deeply grateful for the assistance of Alan Cheuse, who read the work in its final form and offered suggestions throughout.

I also thank *American Literature* and *Studies in Short Fiction* for permission to reprint sections of this book that appeared in article form. A condensed version of chapter six appeared as "Ralph Ellison's Heroic Fugitive" in *American Literature,* March 1974, Copyright 1974 by Duke University Press. *Studies in Short Fiction* published part of chapter four as "Race: Faulkner's 'Red Leaves,'" Spring 1975.

For their patience and encouragement through the years, I owe special thanks to my parents.

The Mark and the Knowledge

And God said, "I have put the mark on him and now
I am going to put the knowledge."

And old Doc Hines said, "Do you think you are a
nigger because God has marked your face?"
"Light in August"

1

The Transcendental Imagination: The Mark as Focus

Every unique object in the physical world bears some visible or invisible mark by which it may be distinguished from its closest kind. Without contradicting the founding fathers who made an American literature possible, Americans from the time of the first explorers have considered themselves unique; we have not interpreted the equality of all men to mean that all men are identical. Even such individual and original difference, however, holds no semantic meaning apart from the concept of similarity. When contemporary linguists refer to the "marked" case, they imply the existence of a logically bounded semantic or syntactic context within which a particular word or construction achieves its relative distinction. When Kenneth Burke formulated his *Grammar of Motives,* he argued that "to tell what a thing is, you place it in terms of something else. This idea of locating, or placing, is implicit in our very word for definition itself: to *define,* or *determine,* a thing, is to mark its boundaries."[1]

But marking involves more than classifying objects and distinguishing among individuals; it describes a process by which we not only learn about each other but also communicate that knowledge. This process, what I've termed "marking," involves both noticing and attributing. Therefore, in asking the paradoxical yet familiar question, what is "American" about American literature, we may consider that the exploration of the new world and the literature that recorded that exploration (roughly from Cooper onwards) have marked trails that turn the literary critic into a pathfinder. The notch on the tree that reads "American" tells us not that we have arrived at the end but that we have not lost the trail. When explorers, historians, and inheritors all join in a search for an American identity (which the act of defining America as a democracy did not resolve), they indicate, by marking, that the concept of similarity (among individuals who join together in order to form a community) has no social or political meaning apart from the concept of difference.

The fiction of social and metaphysical isolation, as I will define it in this study, provides the context within which American literature ·becomes "American." Of course, even this distinction is only relative, for studies of outcast and scapegoat individuals have abounded since the Old Testament. Americans did not invent the theme of social difference, and yet the marked character—solitary, excommunicated, expatriate—becomes a significant concern for our best nineteenth- and twentieth-century novelists. What relationship exists between the artist and the social outcast in American fiction or between the social phenomenon of lynching and the creation of a literary work? If a novel does more than reflect and report, if it becomes not simply the record of a search for American identity but a means of searching, then the novel itself becomes an American problem: how to write one? how to read one?

In my study of American fiction, I have been intrigued by the novelist's frequent choice of the mark or brand as his central symbol. A survey that includes Stephen Crane's Henry Fleming in *The Red Badge of Courage* and Henry Johnson in "The Monster," Edith Wharton's Ethan Frome, Henry James's John Marcher, Sherwood Anderson's Wing Biddlebaum and other characters in *Winesburg, Ohio,* Fitzgerald's Jay Gatsby, Hemingway's Jake Barnes, Flannery O'Connor's "grotesques," and marked outsiders in Mark Twain and Richard Wright only begins to suggest the range of the American novelist's concern with stigma. It might prove illuminating to examine each of these works and others in order to demonstrate the significance of the theme that links them; certainly a literary historian could write a comprehensive study of social deviance in the American novel. My method in this book, however, has been to choose a few representative texts that clearly emerge, on any list of major American novels, as studies of marking, and then to interpret the fictional societies each work creates. In each of these texts—Hawthorne's *The Scarlet Letter,* Melville's *Moby-Dick,* Faulkner's *Light in August,* and Ellison's *Invisible Man*—the principle of exclusion by which a community creates and affirms its own identity finds its artistic correspondence in the process of selecting names and symbols by which the fictional narrator expresses and transcends social and metaphysical isolation.

The recurrent focus on marked characters may profitably be described as both the method and the consequence of the American transcendental imagination. In each of these four novels, the narrator's attempt at aesthetic resolution depends on, and derives from, the social, religious, and political transcendence of the outcast figure. I have chosen the phrase "transcendental imagination" deliberately, because, although the philosophical foundations of American transcendentalism remained nebulous, even for those central figures in the movement—Emerson, Thoreau, and Bronson Alcott—who articulated them the most clearly,[2] the attempt of the transcendentalists to provide religious and philosophical solutions for social and historical problems becomes one characterizing mode of the American consciousness after Emerson as well. American fiction has its roots in transcendentalism.

It has become a critical commonplace to state that the concerns of the early nineteenth-century writers center on the relationship between the individual and society. In particular, as Emerson suggests, the transcendentalist viewed solitude as a solution to the problems of society. In his essay, "The Transcendentalist," he characterizes the representative man as aloof and withdrawn from community. "This retirement," he states, proceeds not "from any whim on the part of these separators" but "is chosen both from temperament and from principle; with some willingness too, and as a choice of the less of two evils."[3]

The idea that the transcendentalist chose his isolation willingly does not imply that he escaped society's notice. On the contrary, in spite of the seriousness that the transcendentalists attributed to their withdrawal from society, they became, as Emerson describes it, "still liable to that slight taint of burlesque which in our strange world attaches to the zealot." Thus the label "transcendentalist" carried the force of social stigma: "The Philanthropists inquire whether Transcendentalism does not mean sloth; they had as lief hear that their friend is dead, as that he is a Transcendentalist; for then is he paralyzed, and can never do anything for humanity." As early as the transcendentalist movement, then, the American understanding of social stigma included a metaphysical dimension. A philosopher's or a writer's ideas might be irregular enough to merit labeling him in consequence. By ending his essay with some moderating words on hermits, Emerson suggests a need for tolerance for the "one or two solitary voices in the land, speaking for thoughts and principles not marketable or perishable."[4] Society ought to be large enough, he seems to be saying, to accommodate a few eccentrics.

In the case of the hermit, whose isolation from society results from mutual agreement, the psychological stigma of exclusion becomes inconsequential and even amusing. For the individual who wishes to remain part of his community, however, to solve its problems without losing his citizenship, social stigma defines the boundaries within which he must confine his individuality. This individual becomes the province of the American novelist, and as we read the fiction of the past two centuries, we discover that society has not been large enough for a long time to include its cripples, its artists, its dissenters, and its minorities, all of whom share, if not physical marks or brands, evidence of social and metaphysical difference apparent to the discerning eye.

Unlike the American transcendentalist who withdrew from society in order to establish a more principled relationship with it, the individual who tries to live within society's boundaries may risk involuntary isolation from community. From the Old Testament on, society has ritually characterized its response to such individuals by identifying them and excluding them as scapegoats of one kind or another. What is interesting as a general observation is that both individual withdrawal and social exclusion create caricatures either physically or symbolically marked by their transformation from individuals into representative men. Furthermore, these figures express, and by expression attempt to resolve, the hidden conflicts and internal contradictions of individual and collective human behavior.[5]

The American experience of internal contradiction, namely, that we are a society of equal individuals, may be historically and nationally explored in our treatment of the Negro. As Ralph Ellison implies in *Shadow and Act,* what was romantic and transcendental about early and mid-nineteenth-century American literature was a "conception of the Negro as a symbol of Man." This conception receded, post-Reconstruction, into what Ellison describes as a general repression of the American consciousness. For Ellison, evidence of this repression—that social problems have not been transcended but simply ignored as a result of civil war—may be found in the absence of social reality in the "realism" of the late nineteenth century, with the exception of Stephen Crane. It was not until the "emergence of the driving honesty and social responsibility of Faulkner,"[6] according to Ellison, that an awareness of ongoing civil war returned to the American literature. This civil war may be seen, in psychological terms, as the American fight "against our own religious doubts, the insecurity of our own political position, and the one-sidedness of our own national viewpoint."[7]

The American Negro has held from the time of his first enslavement the social position of national scapegoat. In this sense Ellison is correct in identifying the Negro's social and psychological as well as physical segregation as a symbol. Yet the scapegoat psychology is really an inversion of the transcendental view that solitude might contribute to a solution of society's problems. The latter is an attempt to achieve social integration without the formation of "shadow" consequent to lynch laws and witch trials.[8] But the attempt at metaphysical transcendence, a concomitant problem for the transcendentalist, fails because there is no equivalent in Western religion to the vehicle of the ritual scapegoat. The characteristics of this vehicle—that it is tangible, literal, and visible—find no analogy in Western metaphysics except the Easter passion, in which, although Christ died for us, we must accept the guilt for his crucifixion without experiencing the cathartic joys of joining his accusers. The bread made flesh serves as our only tangible contact with the crucified victim, and the Puritans refused to accept literal transubstantiation. Thus social exclusion served one function of religious ritual for the Puritans and their descendants. Social exclusion, dramatized most clearly in our historical treatment of the Negro, has provided American community with transcendent catharsis.

For Emerson, the world existed as expanding circles, as correspondences, as analogy; and the power of the analogist lay in his ability to create his own world, thus affirming his organic relationship with the universe without relying on ritual. In his journals Emerson writes: "It seems to be true that the more exclusively idiosyncratic a man is, the more general & infinite he is, which though it may not be a very intelligible expression means I hope something intelligible. In listening more intently to our own reason, we are not becoming in the ordinary sense more selfish, but are departing more from what is small, & falling back on truth itself & God. For it is when a man does not listen to himself but to others, that he is depraved & misled."[9] The asocial individual—the hermit—creates an entire world by becoming the only person in it, and he locates the source of divinity within his own spirit. In Quentin Anderson's terms, "In the particular cultural circumstances Emerson's imaginative leap was decisive; he not only said himself, but made it possible for others to say, that the more clearly distinctive the voice of the celebrant, the more unmistakably does he attest the divine in him."[10] Transcendence depended on self-realization.

Emerson's own parenthetical remark, that his statement "may not be a very intelligible expression," explains the logician's frustration with Emerson's conclusions about the nature of reality and his dismissal of Emerson's analogical method. The logical contradiction inherent in these conclusions is that the particular limits our perception of the universal and must be transcended; at the same time it becomes the analogic vehicle for doing so. The transcendence of the particular is not possible without the existence of the particular. Thus, as Quentin Anderson writes, "transcendentalism is a carefully measured madness, which admits its aberration when ordering coal. It does not sustain; it is occasional like the revival."[11]

The Eastern philosopher's reevaluation of Emerson would be more charitable. Eastern philosophy, one influence among many on American transcendental thought, postulates a logic in analogy that is as "true," as useful in the pursuit of knowledge as Western rationalism. In the analogical pursuit, as the romantics and the transcendentalists have tried to show us, subjective knowledge (as opposed to objective or scientific knowledge) is accompanied by moments of integration between the perceiver and his world.[12] These moments amount to experiences of enlightenment in the form of self-realization—precisely the enlightenment that becomes the goal of Eastern means of gaining knowledge.

But Emerson lacked what the Indian philosophy incorporates in its analogical pursuit—a technique (some form of yoga, for example). And it is the emphasis on technique, on individual practice of some method for increasing perception and achieving knowledge, that, had the American transcendentalists articulated it, would at the very least have lent method to that "carefully measured madness." In the absence of a sustaining methodology, in the chasm between scientific "enlightenment" and romantic organicism, transcendentalism became, as Perry Miller points out, primarily a religious or a philosophical movement rather than a literary one.[13]

In the light of other influences on American transcendentalism, perhaps Miller's distinction is too rigid. The metaphysical poetry of Donne and Herbert, for example, created in literary forms the structure of the practice of religious meditation. Closer to home, the Puritans viewed meditation as a rigorous method of self-examination, following Thomas Hooker in *The Application of Redemption* (1657), and the American poet Edward Taylor wrote his *Preparatory Meditations*[14] as the "last heir of the great tradition of English meditative poetry that arose in the latter part of the sixteenth century." Although Taylor was born and educated in England, Louis Martz asserts that his *Meditations* reflect the condition of the American poet conversing with God in the wilderness, in a "peculiar mixture of the learned and the rude, the abstract and the earthy, the polite and the vulgar";[15] and as a result, Taylor created an "American" work. To the extent that transcendentalism was already part of the English literary tradition in the late sixteenth century, then, it was also part of the early American Puritan literary tradition.

In her introduction to *The Metaphysical Poets,* Helen Gardner writes that "the metaphysical manner of setting a subject, 'hammering it out,' and then 'shutting it up' is closely allied to the method of religious meditation and . . . many metaphysical poems are poetical meditations." Thus, even Donne's secular poems may be termed metaphysical "in its true sense, since they raise, even when they do not explicitly discuss, the great metaphysical question of the relation of the spirit and the senses." She emphasizes the "concentration" of metaphysical poetry—"The reader is held to an idea or a line of argument"—and its development of the conceit. "All comparisons discover likeness in things unlike: a comparison becomes a conceit when we are made to concede likeness while being strongly conscious of unlikeness."[16]

In their emphasis on method, Emerson, Thoreau, and Melville emerge from the tradition of English metaphysical poetry. Emerson's doctrine of the "over-soul" derives from his attempt to create metaphysical correspondences to express "the relation of the spirit and the senses." Melville's notion of "trying-out" his theme in *Moby-Dick* may be likened to the metaphysical poets' penchant for what Gardner calls "hammering out" their subject, and in the first chapter of the novel, Ishmael explicitly refers to the white whale as one of the "wild conceits that swayed me to my purpose."[17] And Thoreau's *Walden* is a carefully constructed analogy between natural life cycles and daily processes, a work that Stanley Cavell goes so far as to describe as scripture.[18]

Cavell's statement that "a writer in meditation is literally a human being awaiting expression"[19] may recall one of the passages from *Walden* in which Thoreau implicitly refers to the cycle of meditation and expression as the prelude to his own creation:

> In the morning I bathe my intellect in the stupendous and cosmogonal philosophy of the Bhagvat Geeta, since whose composition years of the gods have elapsed, and in comparison with which our modern world and its literature seem puny and trivial; and I doubt if that philosophy is not to be referred to a previous state of existence, so remote is its sublimity from our conceptions. I lay down the book and go to my well for water, and lo! there I meet the servant of the Bramin, priest of Brahma and Vishnu and Indra, who still sits in his temple on the Ganges reading the Vedas, or dwells at the root of a tree with his crust and water jug. I meet his servant come to draw water for his master, and our buckets as it were grate together in the same well. The pure Walden water is mingled with the sacred water of the Ganges.[20]

In a concluding remark, Cavell states, "I do not wish to claim that Thoreau anticipated the Civil War; and yet the *Bhagavad Gita* is present in *Walden*—in name, and in moments of doctrine and structure."[21]

Cavell's comparison is useful in extending his own correspondence of *Walden* as scripture, for the particular "despair" that the hero of the Indian epic confronts is civil war: Arjuna does not wish to take arms against his relatives, the Kurus, and calls on Lord Krishna for aid. The aid Krishna gives is contained in verse 48 of the second part of the *Gita*: "Established in Yoga, perform action."[22] With this verse, Krishna begins to expand the subject of the epic, whereby self-consciousness is attained by practicing a technique of meditation (loosely referred to as "yoga") and alternating meditation with "karma" (work or activity). Thus Cavell can conclude that in *Walden* as in the *Bhagavad Gita,* "the way of knowledge and the way of work are one and the same."[23]

In a consideration of the mechanics of social exclusion—marking as a prelude to self and social knowledge—it is useful by analogy to examine the principles of yoga, the generic name for meditation techniques that have been associated with Eastern philosophy for centuries. The only technique I am familiar with firsthand is the one taught by Maharishi Mahesh Yogi (known in this country as "transcendental meditation"). In this technique, a variant of a type of yoga known as "mantra yoga," the meditator is given a mantra (a Sanskrit word or phrase) by a teacher and shown how to use this mantra as a focus of sound and thought that produces the subjective effect of "diving" within consciousness until, at some point, waking consciousness is "transcended" (in Maharishi's terms[24]), the meditator may lose the mantra for a short period, and for the duration of the transcendence, the individual sits in "bliss consciousness," "satori," the presence of the Absolute, the oceanic universal, "pure awareness," or "pure being," as the state has been variously described.

It is significant that mantras are specific sounds, or signs, that may not be translated into English or any other language because they have no referential meanings in Sanskrit. They are what the linguist would term "content-free" symbols. Theoretically, the mind can only transcend the content-bound thoughts of the waking state when it becomes absorbed in a thought that contains such a symbol. But the mantra is a literal sign; it may be spelled, spoken, and communicated. To the moment of transcendence during meditation, it remains literal, part of the world of physical signs and symbols. As I understand what Maharishi calls "transcending," the meditator focuses on the literal mantra (or "mark") until the boundaries of the symbol dissolve and the meditator experiences a state of mind that for American readers must resemble Thoreau's description of sublimity at Walden Pond.

In the absence of a technique like the one Maharishi proposes for the meditator, American transcendentalism failed to provide a physical vehicle by which its adherents could attain Thoreau's "sublimity." It is worth conjecturing that, had the transcendentalists succeeded, they might have eliminated the seeming inevitability of the witch trial or the lynch mob from our history. Like the community in the scapegoat ritual, the meditator in mantra yoga chooses a physical vehicle to contain his impurities. By focusing on this vehicle during the meditation, he transcends his individuality. Like the mantra, the scapegoat bears the burden of communal evil—the marking agents assert that he is not part of them, that they are not responsible for the evil he carries. However, ritual social purification, unlike meditation, has only a temporary effect, and thus, as Sir James Frazer wrote, "a general clearance of evils is resorted to periodically."[25]

The subjective experience of transcending during meditation may be compared to the catharsis of ritual purification, the temporary effect of the scapegoat ritual. But unlike the social enactment, in which for the physical vehicle—the human scapegoat—ritual death is real death, in mantra yoga, as I have explained, the mantra is content-free. Only the teacher, by tradition, knows the effects of the mantra; the student is told only that the mantra will be a life-supporting vehicle for him to achieve periodic transcendence and to evolve towards personal enlightenment. Such a tradition releases the meditating individual from a need for Puritan self-analysis by assuming that if he has not attained enlightenment, his analysis would be faulty; and at the same time, it locates the presence of evil as well as the possibility of salvation within the individual, theoretically eliminating the need for social scapegoats. In this last respect, it differs considerably from the Puritan tradition of meditation, which, content-bound in both its epistemology and its theology, places the burden of moral judgment on the human memory and locates specific evils in marked individuals.

F. O. Matthiessen writes, "The tendency of American idealism to see a spiritual significance in every natural fact was far more broadly diffused than transcendentalism. Loosely Platonic, it came specifically from the common background that lay behind Emerson and Hawthorne, from the Christian habit of mind that saw the hand of God in all manifestations of life. . . ."[26] The recurring social and individual emphasis on "the mark" in American fiction provides a focus for exploring consciousness that may be interpreted as similar in intention to the mantra in mantra yoga, to the victim as physical vehicle in the scapegoat ritual, and to the "particular" or the "relative" in the transcendentalist system. Early nineteenth-century transcendentalism may be viewed, then, as just one manifestation of the American search for self-consciousness, and its literary significance described as the formal attempt to find natural correspondences for metaphysical truths by means of a "transcendental meditation."

In American fiction, the focus on physically or metaphorically marked characters replaces the "concentration" of metaphysical poetry; but as epistemology, the scarlet letter, the whale, the racial identity of Christmas, and the theme of invisibility all hold the reader to a single "idea or line of argument." In addition, the four novels of my study may all be described as religious meditations, in the sense that, as I will show in subsequent chapters, the narratives are "preparatory," like Edward Taylor's poems, for transcending the American dialectic—the conflict between equality and identity. These four works portray individuals in conflict with their communities. Yet the narrators and the narrative designs of each novel suggest that there exists a system of metaphysical, social, and artistic correspondences in which becoming the enlightened American, achieving American community, and creating the American novel require following the same marked trail. The novelist searches for symbols, the penitent discovers sins, and the lynch mob chooses victims; the American epistemology becomes a cyclical pattern of marking, analyzing until the limits of the analysis are transcended, then returning to re-mark and re-view.

Hester Prynne, Ishmael and Pip, Joe Christmas, Hightower, Byron Bunch and Lena Grove, and Invisible Man all oppose prescribed forms in the communities they inhabit. They possess, in Hawthorne's terms, a law to themselves. Others, either unable to exist outside the canons of social convention (Arthur Dimmesdale), or unwilling to do so (Percy Grimm), contribute to the creation of an American social religion, where law and theology become identical forces, subjecting humanism and spirituality to strict definition and excluding metaphysical paradox. In portraying the conflict between the individual and the community, Hawthorne, Melville, Faulkner, and Ellison reveal the transformation inherent in the Puritan sensibility by which metaphysics becomes "social physics," but is accompanied by no less fervor.

The Puritans interpreted metaphysics as the study of God and everything in the physical world as a manifestation of God's will. In their divine interpretation, marks symbolized God's imprint on the world, his presence as the wrathful avenger or the granter of grace. The impulse to mark within the Puritan consciousness expressed a pervasive metaphysical insecurity that cannot tolerate paradox or ambiguity, desires not that God's will be grace but that God's will be known, and forces this "knowledge" by assigning labels (Adultery, Evil, Negro) to individuals (Hester Prynne, Moby Dick, Joe Christmas) who then serve as scapegoats in modern enactments of ancient rituals. The path to self-knowledge for the Puritans and their heirs lies in the creation of a social symbolism—a system of marks and brands. The subject matter of the American novelist reflects the symbolizing process of his own art as well as his historical consciousness.

I have chosen to include a discussion of two stories by William Faulkner in this book because in them Faulkner clearly establishes his awareness of the relationship between the social and the metaphysical. The social outcast becomes a vehicle for the inclusive community to create, however erroneously, a sense of its own identity and union, as Faulkner indicates in "Dry September"; yet social exclusion and metaphysical isolation may become corresponding existential situations, as the body servant in "Red Leaves" realizes. For the marking agents in these stories (Jefferson and the Indian community), marking out specific individuals is intended as catharsis (the social equivalent of individual transcendence), a means of strengthening the social center. Such community action, however, leads to further blindness and a perversion of spirituality; it is only the outcast individuals, carrying the social burden, who achieve transfiguration—who literally transform the "figure" by which they are marked into a state of quasi-social, quasi-spiritual transcendence.

Marius Bewley states, "If we except Calvinism which, as an active theology, had already given way before the growing popularity of Transcendentalism at the time Hawthorne began to write, America inherited no great theological system with which to order experience."[27] Certainly Faulkner and Ellison, however, share the transcendental consciousness of Hawthorne and Melville, and convey it in their fictional worlds. The principles of social definition by exclusion, and solitude as a solution to social problems, which Hawthorne and Melville explore and for which, as I have indicated, Emerson was a major spokesman, become social substitutes for theology in Faulkner and Ellison. The transcendental epistemology incorporates the attempts of both Joe Christmas and Invisible Man to transform personal knowledge into social action, to achieve social and political change by transforming the mark-as-brand (for Invisible

Man's literary predecessors) into the mark-as-password to social identity.

As I understand the concept of marking, and as the preceding discussion should indicate, Western logic plays a very small role in tracing the effects of the transcendental imagination on the American consciousness. In fact, as Hawthorne, Melville, Faulkner, and Ellison demonstrate, and as I will illustrate in the chapters to follow, the novelist, who works analogically, is able to perceive as well as to articulate the relationship between social and metaphysical isolation in American culture. Because the process of making symbols, and even of using language itself, is analogous to the process of noticing and recording by which I have defined marking, the novelist has it within his power to create a work that will both correspond to the Emersonian universe and become yet another expanding circle, part of the natural world and bounded by it, yet at the same time containing it. As Harry Levin writes, "language was related to perception through the doctrine of correspondences. For the writer who accepted the Emersonian metaphysic, there was no choice but to be a symbolist."[28] This awareness, which makes the novel part of the world and yet the physical vehicle for transcending it, defines the transcendental imagination of our greatest fiction writers. Symbol making converts social problems into aesthetic and metaphysical ones; and if the resulting fictions transform the "bad art" of the social marking agents into the materials for symbolism, their creators are only attempting to construct a scaffold, a masthead, a high tower, or a Harlem ladder that will bridge the social and the metaphysical.

I have loosely followed Emerson's own blueprint in constructing my study of the marking process in American fiction. Analogy justifies digression. One of the dangers in writing a thematic criticism is the tendency to use novels as logical "evidence" to prove a point by inductive reasoning. Yet just as the mathematician can never reach infinity by induction without calling on intuition, so the literary critic must also work intuitively sooner or later in order to transcend the linear limits of Western reason. I have chosen to rely on my own transcendental imagination sooner perhaps than many of my readers will feel comfortable with, but I have done so with the goal of any work of literary criticism in mind: I have wanted to construct a chart that may increase the reader's understanding of novels that are already familiar, yet continue to fascinate us because we can never fully apprehend their meaning except by finding new critical analogies.

As a result, although I have indicated here the usefulness of examining "the mark" in a reading of American literature, I later subordinate social and theological interpretations to specific narrative and thematic concerns in the novels, and, in doing so, must claim an absurdity inherent in the entire study. The logical ending point in a discussion of markedness involves not a conclusion but rather another question—what would a study of the concept of non-markedness involve? For I have assumed that certain characters *are* marked and that we may study them. Writing a book on the topic tends to overemphasize the very phenomenon, tends to "mark" it, unfortunately, as the only significant approach to American literature. But as Erving Goffman points out in *Stigma,* "The occasionally precarious and the constantly precarious form a single continuum, their situation in life analyzable by the same framework . . . it is not to the different that one should look for understanding our differentness, but to the ordinary. The question of social norms is certainly central, but the concern might be less for uncommon deviations from the ordinary than for ordinary deviations from the common."[29] And as Invisible Man states, "Perhaps I like Louis Armstrong because he's made poetry out of being invisible." Perhaps it is also possible to make literary criticism out of the visibility of stigma and symbol without losing sight of the mystery that remains undefined. The concept of markedness obscures as well as reveals, for the marked individual, for his community, and above all, for the reader who would be an interpreter of signs.

Notes

1. Kenneth Burke, *Grammar of Motives* (New York: Prentice-Hall, 1945), p. 24.

2. See Perry Miller's introduction to *The Transcendentalists* (Cambridge, Mass.: Harvard University Press, 1950). Howard Vincent, in *The Trying-Out of Moby-Dick* (Carbondale, Ill.: Southern Illinois University Press, 1965), writes, "Transcendentalism in New England is difficult to describe. . . . Transcendentalism had many faces, but whether the term was used to describe a philosophy of individualism, a religious attitude towards life, a collection of individual lunacies, or man's intuitive understanding of Truth, it was fundamentally, to quote Emerson . . ., 'a protest against usage, and a search for principles.' No more definite than that, Transcendentalism may be briefly labeled as 'an enthusiasm, a wave of sentiment, a breath of mind,' as its chief historian, Frothingham, described it; while Santayana summed it up best of all: 'Transcendentalism is an attitude or a point of view rather than a system'" (pp. 154–55).

3. Ralph Waldo Emerson, "The Transcendentalist," in *The Complete Works of Ralph Waldo Emerson,* The Concord Edition, 12 vols. (Cambridge, Mass.: Harvard University Press, 1903), 1:342.

4. Ibid., pp. 354–59.

5. In *The Golden Bough* (London: Macmillan, 1955), Sir James Frazer wrote that the idea that we can "transfer our guilt and sufferings to some other being who will bear them for us . . . arises from a very obvious confusion between the physical and the mental, between the material and the immaterial" (9:1). When the victim is a human sacrifice, the scapegoat becomes the individual who possesses a birthmark or other distinguishing physical characteristic, which the group interprets as a sign from the gods. "Evils are invisible and intangible; and, on the other hand, there is a

visible and tangible vehicle to carry them away. And a scapegoat is nothing more than such a vehicle" (9:224).

6. Ralph Ellison, *Shadow and Act* (New York: Random House, 1964), pp. 68 ff.

7. Erich Neumann, *Depth Psychology and a New Ethic*, trans. Eugene Rolfe (London: Hodder & Stoughton, 1969), p. 52.

8. Neumann describes a process by which the negative part of both the individual and the collective psyche becomes purified in ritual projection of the shadow— "making evil conscious through making it visible and by liberating the unconscious from this content through projection" (Ibid., pp. 51–52). He predicts, "It will continue to be necessary for the collective to liberate itself by exploiting the psychology of the scapegoat so long as there are unconscious feelings of guilt which arise, as a splitting phenomenon, from the formation of the shadow. It is our subliminal awareness that we are actually not good enough for the ideal values which have been set before us that results in the formation of the shadow" (Ibid., p. 45).

9. *The Journals and Miscellaneous Notebooks of Ralph Waldo Emerson*, ed. William H. Gilman and Alfred R. Ferguson (Cambridge, Mass.: Harvard University Press, 1960), 3:199. Emerson's essay "The American Scholar" expands on this statement, encouraging each man to be himself "an university of knowledges. . . . We have listened too long to the courtly muses of Europe" (*Complete Works*, 1:113).

10. Quentin Anderson, *The Imperial Self: An Essay in American Literary and Cultural History* (New York: Random House, 1971), p. 13.

11. Ibid., p. 47.

12. Harry Levin writes, in *The Power of Blackness: Hawthorne, Poe, Melville* (New York: Knopf, 1958): "Transcendentalism, shifting its base from the inscrutable to the scrutiny, still retained the premise that matter was the mere external manifestation of spirit. Revelation was no longer based on dogma, but upon the mystical intuition or the poetic insight that could scrutinize the welter of appearances and discern the presence of hidden realities. To read those hieroglyphics, to interpret the analogies whereby the soul of man might link itself with the physical world, such was the imaginative challenge that Emerson's *Nature* held for the generation that grew up with it . . ." (p. 14).

13. Miller, p. 9.

14. The poems were written from 1682 to 1725; for first complete publication, see *The Poems of Edward Taylor*, ed. Donald E. Stanford (New Haven: Yale University Press, 1960).

15. This quotation and the one preceding are from Martz's foreword to Stanford, pp. xxxv–xxxvi.

16. Helen Gardner, introduction to *The Metaphysical Poets* (Baltimore: Penguin, 1957), pp. 17–27.

17. Herman Melville, *Moby-Dick*, ed. Harrison Hayford and Hershel Parker (New York: Norton, 1967), p. 16.

18. Stanley Cavell, *The Senses of Walden* (New York: Viking Press, 1972).

19. Ibid., p. 58.

20. Henry David Thoreau, *Walden and Civil Disobedience*, ed. Owen Thomas (New York: Norton, 1966), p. 197.

21. Cavell, p. 115.

22. Maharishi Mahesh Yogi (trans.), *On the Bhagavad-Gita: A New Translation and Commentary* (Baltimore: Penguin, 1969), pp. 135 ff.

23. Cavell, p. 116.

24. My references to Maharishi and to transcendental meditation are taken from notes made during the Humboldt, California, lectures (August 1972). His particular interpretation of Eastern philosophy and scriptures is recorded in his translation of *The Bhagavad-Gita*.

25. Frazer, p. 224.

26. F. O. Matthiessen, *American Renaissance* (London: Oxford University Press, 1941), p. 243.

27. Marius Bewley, *The Eccentric Design: Form in the Classic American Novel* (New York: Columbia University Press, 1957), p. 190.

28. Levin, p. 15.

29. Erving Goffman, *Stigma* (Englewood Cliffs, N.J.: Prentice-Hall, 1963), p. 127.

2

The Scarlet Letter: **Social Stigma and Art**

The Scarlet Letter establishes marking as epistemology. As Hawthorne's Surveyor/narrator discovers the "rag of scarlet cloth" in "The Custom-House," then proceeds to write his romance, he demonstrates how the process of noticing, or marking in the sense of observing, holds him to a "single idea or line of argument" and leads to an analysis of the letter's meaning that transcends its significance either as artifact, when he finds it in the Custom-House, or as physical stigma, when he tells the tale he reads in the "sheets of foolscap." In order to tell the tale, the narrator must transcend his focus on the letter, which is tangible for him in "The Custom-House," so that in a sense, *The Scarlet Letter,* by its very existence, attests to both the process and the effects of marking.

In the analysis that follows, I interpret Hawthorne's fictional community with this process in mind. The Surveyor/narrator in "The Custom-House" establishes the hermeneutics by which the reader must come to terms with the romance. To mark Hester Prynne the way the Boston community does is to define her, or to attempt to do so. Her stigma defines the boundaries within which she must confine her individuality. Therefore Hester expresses the hidden conflicts and internal contradictions of Puritan behavior. However, when she dresses Pearl in the colors of her stigma, she reveals her own ability to resolve those conflicts. For Hester's isolation is social. Within the confines of her proscriptions, she finds personal strength and spiritual peace that transcend the material and social exigencies of her life. Dimmesdale, by contrast, expresses the metaphysical insecurity of his community. What I will describe, using a term from sociology, as Dimmesdale's social "discreditability" is akin to the religious pressure he feels to determine whether or not he is among "the Elect." His feelings of social discreditability create the spiritual uneasiness of someone predestined to be included with "the Damned."

In creating an analogy between Dimmesdale's inner conflict and the external conflict Hester Prynne feels as she confronts the Boston community, Hawthorne reveals the transformation by which metaphysical insecurities can manifest themselves as social actions. The "law" Hester and Dimmesdale broke threatens the very identity of their community. Further, as I will show, in his creation of Chillingworth, Hawthorne attempts to answer the question of the artist's role in a community whose identity is informed by the paradoxical reliance on the revealed meaning of marks and signs in the face of uncertainty, their absolute mortal inability to know what has been preordained.

Hawthorne has found a symbol that contains his search in the romance much as Hester's stigma defines the parameters of her existence in the community. Hawthorne engages in a search if not for what is peculiarly American about the Puritan community, then at least for what insights an understanding of that community can provide. His narrator focuses on the scarlet letter as both a physical object and a tangible symbol in the construction of his allegory until its symbolic meaning is transcended, the allegory falls away, and the reader, like Hester, Dimmesdale, Chillingworth, the Puritan community, and the narrator himself, is left with what Hawthorne's penultimate chapter titles "the revelation" of the scarlet letter. Hawthorne derives his aesthetic resolution by transcending the social, religious, and political themes in his fiction. Analogously, our own analysis of *The Scarlet Letter* explores that process by which marking leads to clearer knowledge of who and what we are.

I

Hawthorne chooses to introduce *The Scarlet Letter* with an essay that seems to be but indirectly linked with the tale that follows.[1] He states a twofold intention: to establish his authority as editor for the romance; and to give a "faint representation" of his mode of life as a Surveyor of the Customs.[2] "The Custom-House" itself must be read in light of the romance it accompanies, just as, in turn, the introductory essay illuminates some of Hawthorne's narrator's concerns in *The Scarlet Letter*.

In "The Custom-House," Hawthorne relates finding a "rag of scarlet cloth," which, "on careful examination, assumed the shape of a letter. It was the capital letter A." He described his initial curiosity: "My eyes fastened themselves upon the old scarlet letter and would not be turned aside. Certainly, there was some deep meaning in it, most worthy of interpretation, and which, as it were, streamed forth from the mystic symbol, subtly communicating itself to my sensibilities, but evading the analysis of my mind" (p. 31). In prefacing the novel with "The Custom-House" essay, Hawthorne chooses to establish the occasion of finding the letter as the point of inception of the tale.[3] More is at stake here than the writer's history of the genesis of his work. Indeed, "The Custom-House" is actually part of the novel; *The Scarlet Letter* opens with Hawthorne's somewhat prurient gaze: "My eyes . . . would not be turned aside." We must regard the essay not as autobiography but rather as Hawthorne's conscious fabrication of an introduction to his romance.

Hawthorne explicitly states in the opening pages that his narrator stands at some distance from himself, and that his narrator's concerns will govern the structure of *The Scarlet Letter*. He claims that there are limits in the extent to which "an author, methinks, may be autobiographical, without violating either the reader's rights or his own" (p. 4). Such limits do not approach full autobiographical disclosure. "The truth seems to be, however, that, when he casts his leaves forth upon the wind, the author addresses, not the many who will fling aside his volume, or never take it up, but the few who will understand him, better than most of his schoolmates and lifemates" (p. 3). Hawthorne's limited narrator thus confronts one of the predominant concerns of the characters in the tales—who yearn for fellowship, yet fear that others will penetrate too far into their mystery. The Unpardonable Sin for the converts in "Young Goodman Brown" is to become "more conscious of the secret guilt of others, both in deed and thought, than they could now be of their own."[4] Hawthorne's narrator wants "to find out the divided segment of the writer's own nature, and complete his circle of existence by bringing him into communion with it"; at the same time, he wants to position a veil, to create limits of autobiography, that will serve to prevent "violation" of "the reader's rights and his own."

The narrator's attempts recall another of Hawthorne's characters, Mr. Hooper in "The Minister's Black Veil." In this tale, the "simple black veil, such as any woman might wear on her bonnet," allows the minister to change himself into something awful, only by hiding his face.[5] The artificial physical boundary the minister creates between himself and the people around him he intends as a symbol of the invisible separation that exists between them already. But it isolates him completely, separates him further from community, even though, on his deathbed, he consoles himself by viewing "on every visage a Black Veil."[6] Certainly the narrator of "The Custom-House" does not intend such separation as makes of the minister a monster. And yet, without exploring the complexities of isolation that his arbitrary limits impose, he chooses, like the minister, to set up a tangible, physical emblem between himself and the narrative he is about to relate.[7]

Hawthorne begins his exploration of the relationship between the townspeople and the mark with which they brand Hester by considering the corresponding relationship of narrator to symbol in "The Custom-House."[8] More than Hawthorne's other novels, *The Scarlet Letter* approaches the problems of the working artist in terms of the physical mark or sign that both provides him with an analogical focus for his isolation and enforces that isolation. Studying the progression of the narrator's concerns in "The Custom-House" prepares the reader for social complications of marking that the ensuing narrative then considers.[9]

Up to the moment in which he finds the letter, the narrator describes the gourmandise of the Custom-House officers. The Custom-House is the place for tales—not of shipwrecks or the world's wonders, but of the morning's breakfast, or tomorrow's dinner. The old Inspector likes to recount his past indulgences: "I have heard him smack his lips over dinners, every guest at which, except himself, had long been food for worms" (p. 19). He is fascinated with their fecundity in the face of old age and decay, and describes the Collector as a man "yet capable of flinging off his infirmities like a sick man's gown . . . and starting up once more a warrior" (p. 21). The General has a fondness for the "sight and fragrance of flowers," and the narrator writes: "The heat that had formerly pervaded his nature, and which was not yet extinct, was never of the kind that flashes and flickers in a blaze, but, rather, a deep, red glow, as of iron in a furnace" (p. 21).

He associates gourmandise with living a full life—for the Inspector has enjoyed much roast meat, twenty children, and three wives—but he finds that it also may be achieved during the indolence of sinecure. This pastoral view of sinecure initially leads Hawthorne's narrator to accept the job as Surveyor. Thus he comments, early in the essay, on the "strange, indolent, unjoyous attachment for my native town, that brought me to fill a place in Uncle Sam's brick edifice" (p. 12), and on the figure of the federal eagle, whose wing seems at the beginning of his tenure to shelter and protect, although her claws become her more significant attributes after he is fired. Further explaining his willingness to return to Salem, the narrator, in another reference to sustenance and tangibility, claims that "even the old Inspector was desirable, as a change of diet, to a man who had known Alcott" or Brook Farm, Emerson, Ellery Channing, Thoreau, Hillard, or Longfellow (p. 25). His exposure to the transcendentalists has led him to "relish" more contact with the material world, and eating becomes the analogue for this contact that suits him best in the essay.

The narrator's fondness for the excessive sensuality of these old men, before he realizes at the end of the essay that their indolence is also a form of impotence, yields to his description of his own experience of physical sensation on finding the "rag of scarlet cloth." While he meditates, fascinated, on the origins and meaning of the scarlet letter, he "happens" to place it on his own breast. "It seemed to me,—the reader may smile, but must not doubt my word,—it seemed to me, then, that I experienced a sensation not altogether physical, yet almost so, as of burning heat; and as if the letter were not of red cloth, but red-hot iron. I shuddered, and involuntarily let it fall upon the floor" (p. 32). In this moment, the narrator comes closest in the essay to experiencing, himself, the sensuality of the Inspector or the furnace glow of the Collector's red "heat." In a turn of his own analogy, he emphasizes for the reader the significance of his experience by musing on what the Weighers and Gaugers must have thought of his hours spent pacing the floor, in contemplation of the letter. "They probably fancied that my sole object—and, indeed, the sole object for which a sane man could ever put himself into voluntary motion—was, to get an appetite for dinner" (p. 32). Yet he neither increases his appetite nor comes to terms with the letter. "My imagination was a tarnished mirror" (p. 34). Thus he realizes that as long as he stays in the Custom House, he won't be able to write.[10]

His lengthy descriptions of gourmandise and sensuality now serve to emphasize the narrator's isolation, when he finds himself unable to indulge in it. "It was a folly, with the materiality of this daily life pressing so intrusively upon me, to attempt to fling myself back into another age; or to insist on creating the semblance of a world out of airy matter, when, at every moment, the impalpable beauty of my soap-bubble was broken by the rude contact of some actual circumstance" (p. 37). In retrospect he realizes that "the fault was mine. The page of life that was spread out before me seemed dull and commonplace, only because I had not fathomed its deeper import" (p. 37). But whether or not at some future date the fragments he remembers will "turn to gold upon the page," "I had ceased to be a writer of tolerably poor tales and essays, and had become a tolerably good Surveyor of the Customs. That was all" (pp. 37–38). Thus, when he is politically "guillotined," as he terms it, he likens the experience to that of a man who wants to commit suicide and, before he has the chance, is timely murdered.

In order to come to terms with the physical world, he has to remove himself from it, to spiritualize his burden, to make of his experience "a bright transparency," and not end up, like the old Inspector, making "the dinner-hour the nucleus of the day" (p. 40). His "decapitation" serves as his withdrawal from the world of physical sensations so that he states, "Henceforth it ceases to be a reality of my life. I am a citizen of somewhere else" (p. 44). Yet in ending he contrasts his own calmness throughout the procedure with the "blood thirstiness that is developed in the hour of triumph" for the victors. "There are few uglier traits of human nature than this tendency . . . to grow cruel, merely because they possessed the power of inflicting harm" (pp. 40–41).

II

With such an introduction, in which gourmandise becomes blood thirst, in which the eagle's wing becomes the blade of the guillotine, and for which the physical, tangible rag of scarlet cloth becomes both the vehicle of sensation and the emblem of separation and literary inadequacy, it is not surprising that the mark or brand in *The Scarlet Letter* becomes both a pathway to understanding (bringing the narrator into communication with his own divided segment, as it similarly acts to unite the townspeople) and a mark of separation not unlike the Minister's Black Veil. Thus the place to begin a discussion of the romance is its title and the narrator's initial exploration of the significance of the scarlet letter.

Titles are markings, signposts; and they can also be misleading. In my high school English class, we equated the scarlet letter with what it "stood for"—adultery—and read Hawthorne completely as a moral road sign. We took our places as spectators among the Puritan community and either did not notice (or it was not "pointed out" to us) that the narrator's own concerns in the novel move quite beyond the literal and allegorical meaning the scarlet letter has for the townspeople.

The critical equivalent to this "moral road sign" interpretation of *The Scarlet Letter* is to read the novel as a study of guilt and isolation.[11] Yet Hawthorne's narrator reveals in "The Custom-House" that what intrigues him about the letter he finds is its mystery, not an experience it referentially portrays. He discounts the actual sensual moment he experienced and, throughout the romance, focuses on the inherent meaning of the letter.[12] Hawthorne distinguishes between stigma and moral guilt; and he interprets the letter as an external mark or brand rather than as a referential reflector. As A. N. Kaul writes, *The Scarlet Letter* "deals not with the sin of adultery but with the diverse repercussions on human relationships resulting from the consciousness of this sin."[13] And thus, as Richard Chase points out, "the adultery which sets everything going happens before the book begins."[14] From the imaginary moment of its conception in "The Custom-House," *The Scarlet Letter* is birthmarked.

The romance opens with "a throng of bearded men" assembled in front of the prison door. As they wait, the reader is placed among them: we wait for something to emerge; it is clear that we are not permitted an interior view. The aesthetic distance this "waiting" produces allows the reader to share the narrator's ambivalence. We want to look, and yet we do not want to look too closely. The ambivalence inherent in the narrator's stance resembles the prurient fetishism with which he fingered the cloth in "The Custom-House." There he allowed his mind to engage compensatorily in the mechanism of reading the written history of the letter, which at first escaped his notice. In the narrative, the initial aesthetic distance prevents both narrator and reader from engaging in those "burning" sensations that the tangible letter produced.

The narrator also stands at a historical remove, further distancing the reader, and suggests an irony that recurs throughout. He states, "The founders of a new colony, whatever Utopia of human virtue and happiness they might originally project, have invariably recognized it among their earliest practical necessities to allot a portion of the virgin soil as a cemetery, and another portion as the site of a prison" (p. 47).[15] The disjunction between "human virtue and happiness" and "practical necessity" sets up a paradox in the opening chapters, when the magistrates demand that Hester confess the identity of her accomplice. As Michael Davitt Bell writes, "This contradiction between the supposed advocacy of liberty and the actual denial of it produced the central tension that informs the historical romance of New England."[16] The demands the magistrates make on Hester deny her liberty. The stigma they force upon her thus expresses the paradox Hawthorne presents to the reader, and by means of aesthetic and historical distance throughout the opening scene, the narrator views the crowd while the crowd itself focuses on the scarlet letter. The reader stands back with the narrator, viewing the letter as a mark, not of moral transgression, but rather of community reaction. From the beginning, then, the novel studies the social effects of marking—how it affects the victim, Hester; and how the accusers and observers, the governors and townspeople, differently interpret it.[17] Hawthorne examines the multitude of perspectives a reader may adopt towards his narrator, his major characters, and his predominant symbol.[18]

The goodwives gathered around the scaffold interpret the mark as both tangible and symbolic punishment, and they generally agree that it is not severe enough. One woman states, "'At the very least, they should have put the brand of a hot iron on Hester Prynne's forehead . . . little will she care what they put on the bodice of her gown!'" A second replies, "'let her cover the mark as she will, the pang of it will be always in her heart.'" And a third, described as the "ugliest as well as the most pitiless of these self-constituted judges," states, "'What do we talk of marks and brands, whether on the bodice of her gown, or the flesh of her forehead? . . . This woman has brought shame upon us all, and ought to die!'" (p. 51). The town beadle, who "represented in his aspect the whole dismal severity of the Puritanic code of law" (p. 52), states that "iniquity is dragged out into the sunshine" (p. 54) when Hester emerges from her prison. As the members of the crowd express their understanding of the brand, it is evident that they share their interpretation of the stigma as a punishment that involves public spectacle.

The earlier work that most clearly anticipates Hawthorne's theme of marking as a stigma that brings punishment and disgrace to the bearer is "The Birthmark," the first tale in *Mosses*. In this story, Aylmer the alchemist marries a woman whose beauty is marred only by a small birthmark on her face, in the imprint of a tiny hand. Aylmer's attitude towards the mark destroys by degrees his recognition of Georgiana's beauty—and he determines to erase it from her face. "'No, dearest Georgiana, you came so nearly perfect from the hand of Nature that this slightest possible defect, which we hesitate whether to term a defect or a beauty, shocks me, as being the visible mark of earthly imperfection.'"[19] The mark, making visible that imperfection, becomes a mark of shame. As the narrator comments, "It was the fatal flaw of humanity which Nature, in one shape or another, stamps ineffaceably on all her productions, either to imply that they are temporary and finite, or that their perfection must be wrought by toil and pain."[20]

Unlike the Boston townspeople, the marking agents for Hester's brand, Aylmer cannot claim responsibility for the birthmark, but his inability to live with it suggests more about his own "earthly imperfection" than Georgiana's. "Yet, had Aylmer reached a profounder wisdom, he need not thus have flung away the happiness which would have woven his mortal life of the selfsame texture with the celestial. The momentary circumstance was too strong for him; he failed to look beyond the shadowy scope of time, and, living once for all in eternity, to find the perfect future in the present."[21] Aylmer invests the mark with its significance, thus transforming an ordinary birth defect into a metaphysical allegory. At the same time, his attempt to erase the mark symbolizes his "strong and eager aspiration towards the infinite."[22] In *The Scarlet Letter,* the same eagerness leads the townspeople to disregard Hester as a symbol of human imperfection and to view her instead as the actual flaw. She possesses their "birthmark," which must be revealed, in an attempt to erase it in themselves.[23]

When Hester emerges from the prison, the narrator extends the range of meaning her brand connotes. Her face, "besides being beautiful from regularity of feature and richness of complexion, had the impressiveness belonging to a marked brow and deep black eyes" (p. 53). In this context, the word "marked" associates Hester's forehead with the brow of Cain; and biblically marked, the feature denotes either a curse or a blessing. At the same time, the scarlet letter is magical or mythological. "It had the effect of a spell, taking her out of the ordinary relations with humanity, and inclosing her in a sphere by herself" (p. 54).

The secular, theological, and mythological overtones of the mark become intertwined for the Puritans, "a people amongst whom religion and law were almost identical" (p. 50).[24] Thus Hester assumes a saintliness in spite of her criminality and the reader discovers that "those who had before known her, and had expected to behold her dimmed and obscured by a disastrous cloud, were astonished, and even startled, to perceive how her beauty shone out, and made a halo of the misfortune and ignominy in which she was enveloped." Furthermore, "to a sensitive observer, there was something exquisitely painful in it" (p. 53). The narrator sympathizes with this pain: "There can be no outrage, methinks, against our common nature, . . . no outrage more flagrant than to forbid the culprit to hide his face for shame; as it was the essence of this punishment to do" (p. 55). He views this enforced revelation of shame as an outrage because it violates an individual's privacy; it probes too deeply into the soul; and it encourages morbid curiosity in the spectators.

In spite of her social exclusion, Hester remains an object of curiosity; the invasion of her privacy is accompanied by a barrier to intimacy. The townspeople view her mark as punishment; the governors, as a witness to divine revelation; the narrator, as an object of manifest outrage; and Hawthorne and his reader, as a literal mask that obscures rather than reveals, a mystery that contains the paradox of "exquisite pain." And in addition to her social stigma, Hester also bears the burden of the novel's symbolism. "Giving up her individuality, she would become the general symbol at which the preacher and moralist might point, and in which they might vivify and embody their images of woman's frailty and sinful passion" (p. 79). Thus the narrator further marks Hester, speculating on her position as a social outcast and ignoring her personal history and character.[25]

III

By remaining within the geographical limits of the Puritan settlement when her punishment does not force her to do so, Hester expresses "a fatality, a feeling so irresistible and inevitable that it has the force of doom, which almost invariably compels human beings to linger around and haunt, ghostlike, the spot where some great and marked event has given the color to their lifetime; and still more irresistibly, the darker the tinge that saddens it" (pp. 79–80). The brand that "marked" Hester's future, "has given the color" to her life, also gives it significance and meaning. But the narrator chooses to explore Dimmesdale, instead of Hester, in order to discover this meaning.[26] At the same time, he avoids labeling the relationship that exists between the two characters. He states that Hester felt compelled to remain near someone "with whom she deemed herself connected in a union, that, unrecognized on earth, would bring them together before the bar of final judgment" (p. 80), and asks, "Had Hester sinned alone?" (p. 86), yet he suspends an immediate answer to the question. The suspense that he creates enables him to explore the relationship between Hester and Dimmesdale, and between private behavior and social sin, the complexities of which their past history as adulterers would not explain. To narrowly define their relationship in the same way that the townspeople mark Hester would obscure the deeper and more abstract symmetry that emerges between their respective social situations. Hester and Dimmesdale are linked for Hawthorne, and both the reader's and the narrator's understanding of one character depends on understanding both. The complementary contrast between Hester's mark and Dimmesdale's "unmarked" involvement in the crime they commit against society, between Hester's externalization of her stigma and Dimmesdale's internalization of it, between public and private guilt, provides the novel with its dialectic and captures Hawthorne's imagination.

In *Stigma* Erving Goffman reviews the classical situation of the Greek scapegoat and provides a model of social exclusion that clarifies Hawthorne's dialectic. In modern society, according to

Goffman, stigma refers to the "situation of the individual who is disqualified from full social acceptance."[27] His social "crime" may be only an undesirable differentness, a departure from the "normal" expectation. Goffman does not directly comment on the branding inherent in Puritan punishment, but his analysis clearly defines the motivations behind such action. "The term stigma and its synonyms conceal a double perspective: does the stigmatized individual assume his differentness is known about already or is evident on the spot, or does he assume it is neither known about by those present nor immediately perceivable by them? In the first case one deals with the plight of the *discredited,* in the second with that of the *discreditable*."[28] In Goffman's terms, Hester Prynne has already been discredited, whereas Dimmesdale is only potentially discreditable. As *The Scarlet Letter* indicates, it is easier for an individual to manage being discredited, where the stigma is immediately visible to all members of the community, than with the constant possibility of becoming discredited—the state of being discreditable, Dimmesdale's state. Hester must learn to live with her punishment, but Dimmesdale cannot escape constantly redefining the crime and attempting to punish himself.[29]

We may compare Goffman's description of the physically stigmatized individual with Hawthorne's portrait of Hester. The narrator writes, "it now and then appeared to Hester . . . that the scarlet letter had endowed her with a new sense. She shuddered to believe, yet could not help believing, that it gave her a sympathetic knowledge of the hidden sin in other hearts. She was thus terror-stricken by the revelations that were thus made" (p. 86). Further, "in all her miserable experience, there was nothing else so awful and so loathsome as this sense" (pp. 86–87). Goffman writes, "We tend to impute a wide range of imperfections on the basis of the original one, and at the same time to impute some desirable but undesired attributes, often of a supernatural cast, such as 'sixth sense,' or 'understanding.'"[30] That Hawthorne's narrator should impute to Hester such a "new sense" suggests the extent to which the Puritans re-create Hester when they label her. She resembles the converts in "Young Goodman Brown," who, because of the "sympathy" of their "human hearts for sin," experience a new ability to perceive the evils of others.[31] But unlike Goodman Brown, who, without accepting final conversion, is nevertheless "turned away" from Faith by the meeting in the forest, Hester avoids the gloom of her occasional understanding. "Be it acccepted as a proof that all was not corrupt in this poor victim of her own frailty, and man's hard law, that Hester Prynne yet struggled to believe that no fellow mortal was guilty like herself" (p. 87). Hester has been given the power to tell her accusers who they are, yet she denies this power.[32]

Conversely, Dimmesdale, turning inward as a result of Hester's branding, "longed to speak out, from his own pulpit, at the full height of his voice, and tell the people who he was" (p. 143). His tendency, "more than once," is to discredit himself fully before his congregation, to say to them, "'I, your pastor, whom you so reverence and trust, am utterly a pollution and a lie!'" (p. 143). He thinks, like the Reverend Hooper in "The Minister's Black Veil," that he cannot tell them what he is without telling them what they are; and his "vague confessions" simply extend the compassion and admiration he receives from his listeners. Therefore, the narrator writes, "above all things else, he loathed his miserable self" (p. 144).

The effect of keeping his secret hidden, of internalizing his own guilt, removes Dimmesdale from the tangible world. He keeps nightly vigils, during which "visions seemed to flit before him," and in spite of the fact that Dimmesdale knows they are not tangible, yet "they were, in one sense, the truest and most substantial things which the poor minister now dealt with" (p. 145). The effect of this hypocrisy, as the narrator terms it, is to deprive his reality of its substance. Because Dimmesdale contains within himself, or thinks he does, the power to ease his chronic discreditability by public confession, as he continually fails to do so, he creates a barrier between himself and reality.[33] That reality has public and social dimensions that he cannot face; his only reality becomes a self-created one. "To the untrue man, the whole universe is false,—it is impalpable,—it shrinks to nothing within his grasp. And he himself, in so far as he shows himself in a false light, becomes a shadow, or, indeed, ceases to exist. The only truth that continued to give Mr. Dimmesdale a real existence on this earth, was the anguish in his inmost soul, and the undissembled expression of it in his aspect" (pp. 145–46). In metaphysical terms, Dimmesdale tries to define his own scarlet letter, to create his own meaning, in effect to create his own world, and places even Hester at a distance; no other human being exists in the world Dimmesdale creates for himself, and thus there are no elements in it of compassion, objectivity, or absolution.[34]

The inherent contradiction in his attempt results from the effects of internalizing a symbol that possesses only public and social significance. The scarlet letter only operates as a stigma when it may be seen. The letter on her breast, visible and public, focuses the effect of Hester's stigma; she does not define it, but rather, it defines her. This visual manifestation of her separateness has the effect of freeing Hester from her initial guilt. Thus, at the end of seven years, the governors of the town recommend her letter be removed, and she herself feels liberated from it during her encounter with Dimmesdale in the forest—she casts it aside into the bushes.

Ironically, Dimmesdale's own discreditability, as time passes, becomes a permanent barrier between himself and the community. Discreditability contains within itself the seeds of self-perpetuation. It is clear that such is the case from the opening of the novel, for the townspeople attribute mystery as well as meaning to the scarlet letter—Hester wears a blatant token of her secret actions (her adultery) in part *because* she has been secretive (refusing to reveal the father of her child). Hester's punishment must be as manifest as possible because it then reduces the Puritans' awareness of mystery.

Assigning a label attaches significance to an action or a tendency in a character that has previously escaped naming or notice. For the Puritans, assigning the label of the scarlet letter suggests their necessity to be able to equate content with form, thereby controlling content. The name "adultery" becomes a container for those passions in Hester that led to her initial encounter with Dimmesdale. It becomes equally a form that contains, controls, those same passions in the Puritans themselves. Just as Hester lives peacefully with her stigma because it is visible, so the Puritans manage hidden and formless emotions by externalizing them in a sign. Assigning a label does more than control meaning, however; it also obscures it. The act of externalization reflects the Puritan refusal to recognize.[35] Hester unconsciously exploits this refusal when she dresses Pearl—the child of her wildness—in the costume of her stigma, red cloth trimmed with gold thread.[36] Thus the Puritan view of the human condition contains a central paradox, that signifying should obscure significance.

The scaffold itself, for Hester in the novel's opening scene, and for Dimmesdale later, symbolizes the revelation of mystery. Dimmesdale in particular associates the physical structure of the scaffold with the public recognition that will ease his "ugly" evenings of self-torture and substanceless visions. He thus climbs the scaffold on which Hester stood seven years previously because "there might be a moment's peace in it." His vigil there fails to bring him peace because "the town was all asleep. There was no peril of discovery" (p. 147).

It is not surprising that Dimmesdale might think such a vigil would ease his mind, given the substanceless state of the mental world he has constructed for himself. Thus, for a moment, it is as if he exposes the whole world, the whole of his world, to his secret:

> And thus, while standing on the scaffold, in this vain show of expiation, Mr. Dimmesdale was overcome with a great horror of mind, as if the universe were gazing at a scarlet token on his naked breast, right

over his heart. . . . Without any effort of his will, or power to restrain
himself, he shrieked aloud; an outcry that went pealing through the
night, and was beaten back from one house to another, and reverber-
ated from the hills in the background. . . .
"It is done!" muttered the minister, covering his face with his hands.
"The whole world will awake, and hurry forth, and find me here!"
But it was not so. (p. 148)[37]

Dimmesdale continues to stand on the scaffold while another cler-
gyman passes by. Again, for a moment, Dimmesdale feels himself
discovered. He imagines himself remaining in his place at dawn,
when the whole world would find him. Only Hester and Pearl appear, however, and join him on the scaffold at his request. When he
takes Hester's hand, "there came what seemed a tumultuous rush of
new life, other life than his own, pouring like a torrent into his
heart" (p. 153). Hester revitalizes Dimmesdale, she supports him
momentarily, yet this support only confirms his isolation. "With the
new energy of the moment, all the dread of public exposure, that had
so long been the anguish of his life, had returned to him" (p. 153).

By cutting himself off from the possibility of publicly accepting his
own complicity in Hester's crime, Dimmesdale fails to share the
control the townspeople achieve by their insistence on revealed
meaning. This control creates a social structure that supports the
individuals within it.[38] By transforming truth into "the veriest
falsehood," Dimmesdale deprives himself of the moral and psychological support inherent in the Puritan system. "In no state of society would he have been what is called a man of liberal views; it
would always be essential to his peace to feel the pressure of a faith
about him, supporting, while it confined him within his iron
framework" (p. 123). He does not discover the full force and extent of
society's conventions until he has broken them, then set himself
apart from that society by hiding his transgressions. In this way he
finds himself without support, since the very attempt of his
parishioners to give him aid in the form of a physician becomes the
external force that contributes to his deterioration.

Even Hester relies on this support. The narrator states when Hester emerges from her confinement that her "first unattended
footsteps from the threshold of her prison" are possibly more tortur-
ous than the agony of public spectacle because "the very law that
condemned her—a giant of stern features, but with vigor to support,
as well as to annihilate, in his iron arm—had held her up, through
the terrible ordeal of her ignominy" (p. 78). Only a strong individual
can survive when the support is gone; and thus, although Hester
falters in her first steps from the prison, she survives. Hester's

strength even in her excommunication derives partly from the community, for by remaining she serves a social function. She achieves an uncomfortable place in the social structure but a place nevertheless. The meaning of her mark is the social role she plays—that of the moral outcast.[39]

Dimmesdale continues to derive his sustenance from Hester even at his death. In the last scaffold scene, he makes his public confession: "With a convulsive motion, he tore away the ministerial band from before his breast. It was revealed! But it were irreverent to describe that revelation. For an instant the gaze of the horror-stricken multitude was concentrated on the ghastly miracle; while the minister stood with a flush of triumph in his face, as one who, in the crisis of acutest pain, had won a victory." But he cannot sustain, alone, his moment of triumph. "Then, down he sank upon the scaffold! Hester partly raised him, and supported his head against her bosom." She asks him, "'Shall we not meet again?'" His last words mock her question. He tells her, "'Hush,'" reminds her of "'the law we broke,'" and as he continues, his attention turns back again, finally, on himself: "'God knows; and He is merciful! He hath proved his mercy, most of all, in *my* afflictions. By giving *me* this burning torture to bear upon *my* breast! By sending yonder dark and terrible old man, to keep the torture always at red-heat! By bringing *me* hither, to die this death of triumphant ignominy before the people! Had either of these agonies been wanting, *I* had been lost forever! Praised be his name! His will be done! Farewell!'" (pp. 255–57, my italics).

The allegorical tone of the revelation of the letter in the third scaffold scene pushes the reader towards a simplistic interpretation of Dimmesdale's "salvation" or "crucifixion." When Dimmesdale calls God's witness to his own sins and forgives his enemy (Chillingworth), he intensifies the crucifixion atmosphere of the scene, but his last words dispel it. And Hawthorne refuses, in his last chapter, to definitively comment on Dimmesdale's death. The appearance of allegory, on the contrary, adds to the complexities of Hawthorne's tale; it provides even more of a mask on the mystery by reinforcing that mask with the very elements of social structure his novel tries to penetrate; Dimmesdale publicly confesses his sin before a world that does not distinguish between law and religion, and Hawthorne does not clarify whether the crime the minister has committed is social or spiritual.

In the tales, the allegory often seems clearer. Perhaps this is because the alignment of narrative sympathies is not as complex as it becomes in *The Scarlet Letter*. As a type of the self-infested socially diseased character, Roderick Elliston seems clearly a Dimmesdale figure. In "Egotism; Or, The Bosom Serpent," Hawthorne writes,

> All persons chronically diseased are egotists, whether the disease be of the mind or body; whether it be sin, sorrow, or merely the more tolerable calamity of some endless pain, or mischief among the cords of mortal life. Such individuals are made acutely conscious of a self, by the torture in which it dwells. Self, therefore, grows to be so prominent an object with them that they cannot but present it to the face of every casual passer-by. There is a pleasure—perhaps the greatest of which the sufferer is susceptible—in displaying the wasted or ulcerated limb, or the cancer in the breast; and the fouler the crime, with so much the more difficulty does the perpetrator prevent it from thrusting up its snake-like head to frighten the world; for it is that cancer, or that crime, which constitutes their respective individuality.[40]

Elliston has a clearer knowledge of the path to his own salvation than Dimmesdale does. Whereas Dimmesdale associates religious confession with the tie that will heal his humanity, Elliston tells Herkimer, the friend, when he asks whether there exists a remedy for this "loathsome evil," "'Yes, but an impossible one. . . . Could I for one instant forget myself, the serpent might not abide within me. It is my diseased self-contemplation that has engendered and nourished him.'"[41] Elliston's "salvation" comes from his wife Rosina, who in a moment of "hope and unselfish love," tells him to forget himself, and as he does so, the "bosom serpent" can be heard moving off through the grass. The ending of *The Scarlet Letter* contrasts decidedly with the ending of the tale, for although Dimmesdale succeeds momentarily in confessing his stigma, which had been the cure he prescribed for himself, he does so in such a way as to compromise the moment by claiming God's grace. Thus, he rejects the only real aid that could "save" him in this moment—if we read it in the light of "Egotism"—to respond to Hester's implicit plea for Dimmesdale to forget himself.[42]

IV

The end of the novel leaves uncertain more than Dimmesdale's salvation. The nature of his crime and the extent of his own complicity in it also remain ambiguous. To understand this uncertain ambiguity, we may again examine Hawthorne's introductory essay to *The Scarlet Letter*. In "The Custom-House," the narrator is expelled from his job as Surveyor of the Customs as a matter of political reform. His description of this reform is curious in light of Dimmesdale's attempt to turn the scaffold—the structure of public punishment—into a cross. He talks about the "political guillotine"—also a structure of punishment—that has "decapitated" the Surveyor in him. Whatever basis there may be for the narrator's "unceremonious ejectment" (and he suggests that he may have been lax in performing his duties, preferring to roam among mankind rather than confine himself to political activity), he implies also that any breach of political faith would have been construed with theological severity. Thus political activities become "narrow paths" from which he chooses to diverge, and by his expulsion, he earns "the crown of martyrdom." In addition, as I mentioned earlier, the narrator describes his release as the good fortune "of a person who should entertain an idea of committing suicide, and, altogether beyond his hopes, meet with the good hap to be murdered" (p. 42); Dimmesdale shares the psychological lassitude characteristic of the narrator and finds himself fortunate enough to die after he has made his public confession. The narrator of "The Custom-House" is not altogether displeased "to observe the blood thirstiness that is developed in the hour of triumph" by his political enemies; and he observes, "The moment when a man's head drops off is seldom or never, I am inclined to think, precisely the most agreeable of his life. Nevertheless, like the greater part of our misfortunes, even so serious a contingency brings its remedy and consolation with it" (p. 41).

The narrator has been released from his own inability to write amid the sensual and material atmosphere of the Custom House. He comes to blame as well the political structure of which he is a part for the torpor of his own imagination.

> An effect—which I believe to be observable, more or less, in every individual who has occupied the position—is, that, while he leans on the mighty arm of the Republic, his own proper strength departs from him. He loses, in an extent proportioned to the weakness or force of his original nature, the capability of self-support. ... The ejected officer ... may return to himself, and become all that he has ever been. But this seldom happens. ... Conscious of his own infirmity ... he forever afterwards looks wistfully about him in quest of support external to himself. (pp. 38–39)

Dimmesdale's need for the support of social and theological structure, and his inability to remove himself from it in order to test his own renewal, earn the sympathies of the ejected Surveyor/narrator, whose subsequent exploration of the meaning in the scarlet letter is tinged with his own experience. The death of Dimmesdale becomes a martyrdom; and Hawthorne chooses the allegory of romance, a mode that ironically obscures more than it reveals.[43]

The Scarlet Letter, seen from the perspective of the narrator's concerns in "The Custom-House," thus becomes a consideration of the relationship between the individual and his sociopolitical and sociotheological roles. The individual who possesses a freely ranging imagination that does not adhere to the "narrow paths" of political and theological vision may find himself ejected, like the Surveyor. Dimmesdale's weakness merits the sympathy of the narrator because of its universality but also because Dimmesdale's inability to accept his sensibility and his materiality resembles the narrator's own. For the narrator seeks, in the atmosphere of the Custom House, a change of diet from Emersonian spirituality; he finds it, momentarily, in the sensation the scarlet letter produces when he marks himself by placing the letter on his own breast; and he returns to it, in imagination, during his meditations on the letter.

His inability to revive it again, by purely metaphysical speculation, leads him to sympathize with Hester's intellectual coldness. Hester's life turns "in a great measure, from passion and feeling, to thought" when she is marked out from the rest of her society. But "the world's law was no law for her mind," and thus she contemplates an abstract and individual revolution:

> Men of the sword had overthrown nobles and kings. Men bolder than these had overthrown and rearranged—not actually, but within the sphere of theory, which was their most real abode—the whole system of ancient prejudice, wherewith was linked much of ancient principle. Hester Prynne imbibed this spirit. She assumed a freedom of speculation, then common enough on the other side of the Atlantic, but which our forefathers, had they known it, would have held to be a deadlier crime than that stigmatized by the scarlet letter. . . .
> It is remarkable, that persons who speculate the most boldly often conform with the most perfect quietude to the external regulations of society. The thought suffices them, without investing itself in the flesh and blood of action. (p. 164)

How do we understand a passage like this after reading "The Custom-House"? That the narrator wants to believe that the sphere of theory is the "real" world? That freedom of speculation incites more serious revolutions than "the flesh and blood of action"? Hawthorne's treatment of Dimmesdale, if these are simply rhetorical questions, may be read as a justification of his own methods. He permits the "thought" to suffice, without releasing the "flesh and blood" that, from time to time in *The Scarlet Letter*, suggests its presence just beneath the surface. Hawthorne thus controls the passions inherent in his subject and leads Henry James to remark: "Puritanism, in a word, is there, not only objectively as Hawthorne tried to place it there, but subjectively as well. Not, I mean, in his judgment of his characters in any harshness of prejudice, or in the obtrusion of a moral lesson; but in the very quality of his own vision, in the tone of the picture, in a certain coldness and exclusiveness of treatment."[44]

V

The manipulation of content in Hawthorne's recurrent meditations on the form of the scarlet letter is most evident and most problematic in the narrator's treatment of Roger Chillingworth. Chillingworth is, as many critics have pointed out, a type of the artist figure in Hawthorne's studies of the artist in isolation.[45] But Chillingworth has failed as an artist; his very creation negates the life he attempts to portray. Like Aylmer in "The Birthmark," Rappaccini in "Rappaccini's Daughter," Ethan Brand, and Owen Warland in "The Artist of the Beautiful," Chillingworth commits the unpardonable sin of the artist who denies or destroys life by transforming it into art.

During Chillingworth's first interview with Hester, the narrator describes him as a person with special visual powers.

> "Believe me, Hester, there are few things,—whether in the outward world, or, to a certain depth, in the invisible sphere of thought,—few things hidden from the man who devotes himself earnestly and unreservedly to the solution of a mystery. Thou mayest cover up thy secret from the prying multitude. Thou mayest conceal it, too, from the ministers and magistrates, even as thou didst this day, when they sought to wrench the name out of thy heart, and give thee a partner on thy pedestal. But, as for me, I come to the inquest with other senses than they possess. I shall seek this man, as I have sought truth in books; as I have sought gold in alchemy. . . . Sooner or later, he must needs be mine!" (p. 75)

Like the stigmatized Hester, Chillingworth possesses "other senses" than those of ordinary human perception. He can discern the non-manifest invisible thoughts and secrets of men. Whereas Hester shuns this sense, however, Chillingworth cultivates it, and in the forest meeting between Hester and Dimmesdale at the end of the novel, Dimmesdale points the moral of Chillingworth's story: "'That old man's revenge has been blacker than my sin. He has violated, in cold blood, the sanctity of a human heart'" (p. 195). By the alignment of the narrator's sympathies with Hester and Dimmesdale in this scene, Dimmesdale's judgment becomes the reader's as well. The curious and problematic aspect of this sympathy, however, is that the chapters that focus on Chillingworth before he assumes the role of daemonic agent in Dimmesdale's suffering treat him with some compassion. He is described, in effect, as a counterpart of the narrator himself.

The ability to discern the nonmanifest, to determine the meanings hidden in visible signs, is the province of the good artist as well as the evil one, and such curiosity initially motivated the narrator's attraction to the "rag of scarlet cloth." When the reader meets Chillingworth for the second time (in chapter nine, "The Leech") it is clear that the narrator himself has suspended his judgment of the physician. Both good and evil tendencies are inherent in the narrator's description. "His first entry on the scene, few people could tell whence, dropping down, as it were, out of the sky, or starting from the nether earth, had an aspect of mystery, which was easily heightened to the miraculous. He was now known to be a man of skill; it was observed that he gathered herbs, . . . like one acquainted with hidden virtues in what was valueless to common eyes" (p. 21). The source of his arrival, whether from the sky or "the nether earth," becomes a subject of mystery for the townspeople. Nevertheless, again, Chillingworth possesses special vision, and what he finds in his probing, which (the narrator elsewhere describes) Chillingworth accompanies with "a cautious touch, like a treasure-seeker in a dark cavern" (p. 124), are the "hidden virtues in what was valueless to common eyes."

In addition, as part of his artist's power, Chillingworth possesses a clear vision of relationship *between* the manifest and the non-manifest. During one discussion with Dimmesdale, late in their acquaintance, Chillingworth describes some weeds he once found growing on the grave of a dead man. "'They grew out of his heart, and typify, it may be, some hideous secret that was buried with him, and which he had done better to confess during his lifetime. . . . These black weeds have sprung up out of a buried heart, to make manifest an unspoken crime'" (p. 131). Here Chillingworth resembles the narrator of the *Twice-Told Tales* or *Mosses* in drawing his moral. The narrator of *The Scarlet Letter* also resembles Chillingworth, in his own exploration of the relationship between manifest and nonmanifest forms, between the complementary public and private effects of stigma on Hester and Dimmesdale.

The relationship that develops between Dimmesdale and Chillingworth provides the artist-physician with his eventual opportunities for discerning the invisible—at the minister's expense. However, in its initial stages the friendship grows out of mutual respect and attraction. The narrator states, "This learned stranger was exemplary, as regarded at least the outward forms of a religious life, and, early after his arrival, had chosen for his spiritual guide the Reverend Mr. Dimmesdale" (p. 120). In spite of the narrator's comment on the "outward forms," which qualifies the sincerity of Chillingworth's spiritual life, the passage does not indicate that Chillingworth, on his arrival, conceals evil intentions in his attraction for Dimmesdale. The narrator describes the relationship that develops between them as symbiotic—"these two men, so different in age, came gradually to spend much time together" (p. 123).

In spite of Dimmesdale's lack of what the narrator calls "liberal views," he enjoys Chillingworth's presence; they mutually attract each other. The passage that describes Dimmesdale's fascination is complex and intriguing from a critical point of view. After the narrator suggests that Dimmesdale needs the "iron framework" of theology to insure his peace of mind, he adds:

> Not the less, however, though with a tremulous enjoyment, did he feel the occasional relief of looking at the universe through the medium of another kind of intellect than those with which he habitually held converse. It was as if a window were thrown open, admitting a freer atmosphere into the close and stifled study, where his life was wasting itself away, amid lamplight, or obstructed day-beams, and the musty fragrance, be it sensual or moral, that exhales from books. But the air was too fresh and chill to be long breathed, with comfort. So the minister, and the physician with him, withdrew again within the limits of what their church defined as orthodox. (pp. 123–24)

The language of this unusual passage, "tremulous" and "freer atmosphere," suggests that Dimmesdale finds a potential liberation from his guilt in the "occasional relief" of his attachment to Chillingworth. It is not necessary to use twentieth-century language to describe this freedom; Hawthorne's own phrase, "the flesh and blood of action," accurately describes the sensibility Dimmesdale briefly encounters. Chillingworth and Dimmesdale approach an intimacy in their frankness that threatens the minister; for Dimmesdale, the air is "too fresh and chill," possibly because it is removed from his accustomed confines, and he forces the withdrawal (in the narrator's own language) into the "orthodox."

Hawthorne does not make the nature of this intimacy explicit, although the "withdrawal" of the friendship into conventional bounds is accompanied by Dimmesdale's and Chillingworth's joint move into a pious widow's house, the walls of which are decorated with a tapestry representing "the Scriptural story of David and Bathsheba, and Nathan the Prophet, in colors still unfaded, but which made the fair woman of the scene almost as grimly picturesque as the woe-denouncing seer" (p. 126). The Biblical story of David and Bathsheba is one of adultery; Nathan the prophet chastises David while he is king concerning his conduct in sending Uriah, Bathsheba's husband, off to the wars to be killed so that his adultery will not provoke God's wrath.[46] Thus the tapestry is an emblem of the human situation in *The Scarlet Letter*. Implicit in Hawthorne's presentation of this detail, however, the only one of its kind in *The Scarlet Letter*, is also David's earlier history, his homosexual relationship with Jonathan. Dimmesdale's attraction for Chillingworth, if not homosexual in origin, at least contains the seeds of a human intimacy that frightens him. Thus Chillingworth's initial admiration for Dimmesdale, when forced back within what the church defines as orthodox, becomes twisted, and he assumes the role, not of Jonathan, but of the "woe-denouncing seer."

After *The Scarlet Letter* passes its concluding scaffold scene, Hawthorne's narrator once again takes up the subject of this relationship between Chillingworth and Dimmesdale. The narrator condemns Chillingworth's actions, saying that "This unhappy man had made the very principle of his life to consist in the pursuit and systematic exercise of revenge; and when, by its completest triumph and consummation, that evil principle was left with no further material to support it,—when, in short, there was no more devil's work on earth for him to do, it only remained for the unhumanized mortal to betake himself whither his Master would find him tasks enough, and pay him his wages duly" (p. 260). After making this point, however, the narrator recommends mercy in the reader's judgment of Chillingworth:

> It is a curious subject of observation and inquiry, whether hatred and love be not the same thing at bottom. Each, in its utmost development, supposes a high degree of intimacy and heart-knowledge; each renders one individual dependent for *the food of his affections and spiritual life* upon another; each leaves the passionate lover, or the no less passionate hater, forlorn and desolate by the withdrawal of his object. Philosophically considered, therefore, the two passions seem essentially the same, except that one happens to be seen in a celestial radiance, and the other in a dusky and lurid glow. In the spiritual world, the old physician and the minister—mutual victims as they have been—may, unawares, have found their earthly stock of hatred and antipathy transmuted into golden love. (pp. 260–61, my italics)

Once again the narrator uses the metaphor of sustenance, as in his earlier use of "flesh and blood," to describe the symbiosis of love and the parasitic thwarting of hatred.

F. O. Matthiessen's discussion of Chillingworth is particularly relevant in this context. He writes, referring to the chapter "The Leech and His Patient," "The irony of the title lies in the fact that though the old physician knows Dimmesdale's bodily weakness to be due to a deeper sickness of the spirit, and though he is determined to discover its cause, he is actuated not by the hope that he may suggest a cure, but that he may suck out his patient's very vitality."[47] In the portrait of Chillingworth, the reader discovers that revenge may turn into a perverse but life-sustaining force for the avenger. The connotations of "blood-thirsty" become transformed into those of "blood thirst," thirst for the "flesh and blood of action," of experience—similar to the need for a "change of diet" that led

Hawthorne's narrator to serve as Surveyor, similar to the lack of materiality in Dimmesdale's life that led him into his intimacy with Chillingworth, similar to the adultery that serves as a prelude to the romance and leads to the townspeople's perverse exclusion of Hester Prynne.

In this connection, it is enlightening to compare Chillingworth and Dimmesdale. For like Chillingworth, Dimmesdale also depends for his own sustenance on another human being—Hester. And during at least two crucial moments in his life, he receives the strength he needs—the first during the midnight scaffold scene that I have already discussed; and the second during his encounter with Hester in the forest, after which he returns to town a new man, filled with renewal of energy that enables him to write, in a burst of inspiration, an Election Day sermon that turns out, ironically, to have as its subject "the relation between the Deity and the communities of mankind" (p. 249). Unlike Chillingworth, however, Dimmesdale is not condemned by the narrator; if anything, the narrator excuses his "Remorse" and "Cowardice" (p. 148) because they are human failings. Chillingworth's morbid curiosity alone ranks with the devil.

The objective evidence for excusing Dimmesdale and condemning Chillingworth is not conclusive. This confuses the reader. In addition to the blood thirst that both share, the narrator indicates that, during one interview at least, Chillingworth specifically offers Dimmesdale a cure for his spiritual illness that is not a leech cure—the public confession. "With somewhat more emphasis than usual," suggesting that for once, at least, Chillingworth speaks earnestly and truthfully, he tells the minister that men who hide their guilt "'fear to take up the shame that rightfully belongs to them. . . . Trust me, such men deceive themselves!'" (p. 133). He points out that Hester's public acceptance of her shame has made her sufferings less intense than Dimmesdale's burden of the "mystery of hidden sinfulness" (p. 135). Dimmesdale refuses to continue this discussion with the physician and leaves the room "with a frantic gesture" (p. 137).

With all of the objective indications, then, that Chillingworth is not, at least at the inception of his crime, himself the pure embodiment of evil; and with the equally objective evidence that Dimmesdale shares the burden of guilt in his own deterioration, the question thus becomes more insistent—how does Chillingworth become transformed into the devil the narrator states he is (p. 170), and why, since the evidence for this remains inconclusive?

The technical answer to the first part of the question, *How*, is relatively straightforward. The narrator describes Chillingworth, from his first appearance in the novel, as a deformed individual, physically marked, just as Hester Prynne is marked, to immediate visual perception. Chillingworth's features are those "of a person who had so cultivated his mental part that it could not fail to mould the physical to itself, and become manifest by unmistakable tokens." He also has a deformed back (p. 59). In addition, he is a man of mystery, and his "darkness," physically as well as biographically, becomes Hawthorne's tool. When it becomes clear that a man has not been sent by God, the Puritan instinctively concludes his link with Satan. In *The Scarlet Letter*, the complexities of Chillingworth's relationship with Dimmesdale do not become part of the public domain; only the narrator explores them. Thus, the Puritanic progression of the final judgment of Chillingworth suggests the narrator's intervention, the narrator's own shifting of sympathies.

Why these sympathies shift is apparent, I think, in the scene in which Chillingworth reveals his own demonism. There are two significant evasions of revelation in the novel. The first, withholding Dimmesdale's association with Hester, as I have discussed, provides the scaffolding on which the narrator builds his symmetric study of marked and unmarked individuals. The second evasion, withholding knowledge of what Chillingworth finds on Dimmesdale's breast, is more difficult to justify.

The narrator prepares the scene for revelation by permitting the reader a privileged view of Chillingworth. He describes the physician's manner, in which he hypocritically hides his "mysterious and puzzled smile" from the minister:

> This expression was invisible in Mr. Dimmesdale's presence, but grew strongly evident as the physician crossed the threshold.
> "A rare case!" he muttered. "I must needs look deeper into it. A strange sympathy betwixt soul and body! Were it only for the art's sake, I must search this matter to the bottom!" (pp. 137–38)

The passage suggests that the narrator, as well, is about to manifest something to the reader, "were it only for the art's sake." As Chillingworth approaches Dimmesdale, however, the reader's view is forced back. We continue to see Chillingworth, but not what Chillingworth himself sees. Chillingworth at this moment becomes the only intimate witness to the ghastly elements in Dimmesdale's soul.

It is certainly true that the narrator eventually gives the reader a good indication, although he does not ultimately commit himself, that what Chillingworth finds is a letter "A" etched on Dimmesdale's breast. By that time, however, Dimmesdale has pointed to Chillingworth as the emblem of evil, and the narrative power of this moment of Chillingworth's revelation has been superseded by the third scaffold scene. Clearly, then, Hawthorne's narrator is not, in the private moment with Chillingworth, interested in Dimmesdale. He has allowed the physician to approach the minister out of his initial artistic curiosity, but at the moment of revelation, withdraws. Instead he focuses on Chillingworth's expression—and on the artist's narrow escape. The narrator writes,

> After a brief pause, the physician turned away.
> But with what a wild look of wonder, joy, and horror! With what a ghastly rapture, as it were, too mighty to be expressed only by the eye and features, and therefore bursting forth through the whole ugliness of his figure, and making itself even riotously manifest by the extravagant gestures with which he threw up his arms towards the ceiling, and stamped his foot upon the floor! Had a man seen old Roger Chillingworth, at that moment of his ecstasy, he would have had no need to ask how Satan comports himself when a precious human soul is lost to heaven, and won into his kingdom.
> But what distinguished the physician's ecstasy from Satan's was the trait of wonder in it! (p. 138)

The scene suggests an explanation for Hawthorne's choice of his own mode and genre—allegory and romance. In "The Custom-House," his narrator had written, "A better book than I shall ever write was there; leaf after leaf presenting itself to me, just as it was written out by the reality of the flitting hour, and vanishing as fast as written, only because my brain wanted the insight and my hand the cunning to transcribe it" (p. 37). But "these perceptions have come too late," and the transcription of "the reality of the flitting hour" is not the narrator's *métier*. Instead, he withdraws from the materiality and sensuality of life at the Custom House, and is timely ejected—not into a more realistic world, but into a world of romance (just as the reader is abruptly "ejected" into the tale that follows). And in *The Scarlet Letter*, the narrator's narrow escape asserts the ascendancy of romance over materialism. In this moment he refuses, avoiding the unpardonable sin of the tales, to explore Dimmesdale's most intimate secrets, focusing instead on the dangers of the chasm, which may lead the unsuspecting artist into the devil's kingdom.

In the short sketch "Monsieur du Miroir," Hawthorne considers this chasm as the "impenetrable mystery" that separates the narrator from his own reflection. He writes of the man in the mirror, "the chief that I complain of is his impenetrable mystery, which is no better than nonsense if it conceal anything good, and much worse in the contrary case."[48] F. O. Matthiessen reflects, "What moved him in 'Monsieur du Miroir' was the related contrast between superficial appearance and hidden truth, between the pale features of the man reflected in the mirror and the tormented life that was locked up in his heart."[49] The narrator refutes the efficacy of exploring the reflection, of probing behind what he calls the man's "delusive garment of visibility."[50] Yet he does explore it, for the space of the sketch, and the fictional situation depicts a moment of potential self-exploration and self-revelation. "Monsieur du Miroir" suggests that a similar self-exploration process takes place in *The Scarlet Letter*, that like the man in the mirror, Chillingworth also becomes the narrator's reflection, and when the revelation becomes too painfully intimate, he withdraws his sympathies from Chillingworth, who becomes the figure the casual reader remembers—the man who cries, at Dimmesdale's death, "'Thou has escaped me!'"[51]

Thus, "incited . . . by the propensities of a student of human nature"[52] to explore the hidden meanings behind the scarlet letter, the narrator of Hawthorne's romance ends also by looking in a mirror. He stated in the sketch, "So inimitably does he counterfeit that I could almost doubt which of us is the visionary form, or whether each be not the other's mystery, and both twin brethren of one fate in mutually reflected spheres."[53] The mirror analogue appropriately describes, not the relationship between the rag of scarlet cloth accompanied by the sheets of foolscap the narrator finds and the tale he then proceeds to construct, but rather a relationship between the narrator of "The Custom-House" and the narrator of *The Scarlet Letter*. If Chillingworth is a type of the artist, the artist certainly resembles Chillingworth as well. As "The Custom-House" shows, both are motivated by blood thirst, although Hawthorne's reflection on this, in the romance, leads him to withdraw his narrative curiosity just on the verge of material revelation. In *The Scarlet Letter*, the narrator chooses allegory, unlike his demonic counterpart within the narrative, who would lay bare Dimmesdale's soul if he could. In support of his own withdrawal, he states: "'There can be, if I forebode aright, no power, short of the Divine mercy, to disclose, whether by uttered words, or by type or emblem, the secrets that may be buried with a human heart. The heart, making itself guilty of such secrets, must perforce hold them, until the day when all hidden things shall be revealed'" (p. 131). In spite of his concern for social roles in the novel, he is not interested in disclosing the secrets in Dimmesdale's heart—or his own. He does not have that much "blood thirst." Hawthorne's very choice of allegory characterizes his subject as ultimately introspective—directed toward protecting the individual from the community.

In his choice of mode, however, he reveals a great deal about himself. As Baskett has suggested, from the moment when Hawthorne places the scarlet letter on his breast he becomes "the figure of the Alienated Artist."[54] However, although it is true that many of Hawthorne's artists, not simply the narrator of *The Scarlet Letter*, are isolated from society,[55] and although A. N. Kaul is probably correct when he writes that Hawthorne "saw in art itself the true answer to this dilemma" because "art could be a form of communion without conformity,"[56] what *The Scarlet letter* demonstrates is that Hawthorne is more interested in isolation than in communion, if by communion Kaul means mutual revelation and confession among the members of a community. Hawthorne focuses on the letter as a means of attaining self-knowledge; he chooses allegory rather than the "flesh and blood of action." As Fogle writes, "Allegory gives point and reference and therefore is in itself a guarantee of purpose; it affords a principle to which the action of narrative may be referred and around which the action may be organized."[57] In these terms, Hawthorne's own use of allegory becomes analogous to the Puritan practice of meditation and the physics of social exclusion. All three require recurrent focus on the mark in order to achieve transcendent knowledge. Yet allegory allows Hawthorne to achieve an artistic resolution of social and metaphysical problems and still keep his distance from the material world.

In *The Scarlet Letter*, then, Hawthorne integrates the use of marking as social, artistic, and metaphysical method for both the artist/outcast and his excluding community. The difference between viewing the novel as a study of marking and viewing it more traditionally as a study of isolation from society[58] is to see Hawthorne's art not simply as historical romance and certainly not as naturalistic reflection of the world (that would require "flesh and blood") but rather as an epistemological process in and of itself. It is also to seize upon this epistemology as one component of "American" literature. Hawthorne links but does not equate his search for the significance in a symbol with the Puritan quest for revelation of guilt and exclusion of the stigmatized offender. In so doing, he uncovers the close relationship between social stigma and art for the Puritan community. Harry Henderson alludes to this process in *Versions of the Past:* "What is at first taken by the community as a sort of algebraic sign for a quality of the personality . . . is transformed almost immediately by the author from the allegorical to the symbolic level. To an imagination dominated by literal readings of natural and social phenomena, nothing could be more subversive than symbolism."[59] If Hester manages her own version of American revolution while living within the confines of her stigma, Hawthorne establishes a working definition of American identity while withdrawing behind the protective walls of his allegory. It is part of the

American temper, he seems to be saying, to learn about the world by marking it, then establishing it as American by excluding what is marked.

The difference between the community's use of stigma to strengthen its social identity and the artist's use of the mark as a focus for symbolistic inquiry is clear: the Salem witch trials, the lynching of Negroes in the South, and the struggle of minorities of all kinds for two centuries are emblematic of the deep metaphysical insecurity we have inherited from the Puritans. In the struggle for identity, both in the sense of who we are and how much we are alike, American communities have not tolerated deviance. What is destructive to our country, however, has created viable ground in which our literature has flourished. By the same method, the American fiction writer has focused often on stigma, as if this were the aberrant and abortive result of American attempt at community.

As Hawthorne indicates, markedness is an indicator of an individual's visibility and thus his potential isolation from community; it is also, as I will show in subsequent chapters, one technique American writers following Hawthorne continue to use in their progressively complex studies of the changing American identity. Hawthorne's concern with social stigma explores the Puritan's attempt to make the nonmanifest manifest. Following Hawthorne, Melville examines the correspondence between the physical world and the metaphysical one. Faulkner's analogous concern returns to the social realm of public and private experience and in Ellison, the parameters of correspondence are social visibility and invisibility. For each of these writers, however, what is at stake is what it means to be American. As Charles Feidelson writes, "The symbolistic outlook involves much more than the stylistic device which is ordinarily called 'symbolism'; the physics of symbolistic literature depends on its metaphysics . . . the theory of symbolism is really a theory of knowledge."[60] I would only add to this, following my study of *The Scarlet Letter*, that a study of American symbolistic literature involves a study of stigma. As I will attempt to show in my analysis of *Moby-Dick*, Melville, though he is not explicitly concerned with American sociology, has seized upon marking as the epistemology particularly suited to Ishmael, the American orphan, in his search for who he is.

Notes

1. Austin Warren, in his introduction to *Nathaniel Hawthorne, Representative Selections* (New York: American Book Co., 1934), stated that "The Custom-House" is

"a curiously unsuitable introduction to the masterpiece" (p. xviii). Critics in recent years have tended to disagree with this assessment of the relationship between the essay and the romance. See, for example, Frank MacShane, "The House of the Dead: Hawthorne's Custom House and *The Scarlet Letter*," *New England Quarterly*, 35 (March 1962); Marshall Van Deusen, "Narrative Tone in 'The Custom-House' and *The Scarlet Letter*," *Nineteenth-Century Fiction*, 21 (June 1966); Dan McCall, "The Design of Hawthorne's 'The Custom House,'" *Nineteenth-Century Fiction*, 21 (March 1967); or Paul John Eakin, "Hawthorne's Imagination and the Structure of 'The Custom-House,'" *American Literature*, 43 (November 1971). Eakin points out that Hawthorne is "as fully a literary creation as any of his characters, and the essay . . . shares the leading properties of his fiction" (p. 347).

Charles Feidelson, in *Symbolism and American Literature* (Chicago: University of Chicago Press, 1953), states that "every character, in effect, reenacts the 'Custom House' scene in which Hawthorne himself contemplated the letter, so that the entire 'romance' becomes a kind of exposition of the nature of symbolic perception" (p. 10). Copyright 1953 by the University of Chicago. All rights reserved. All excerpts from this work are reprinted by permission. And Sam Baskett, in "*The* (Complete) *Scarlet Letter*," *College English*, 3 (February 1961), writes: "For Hawthorne himself in a sense is the major character in the romance as well as in the sketch; and in both parts of the book the theme is the same: the relation of the individual to whatever the society, irrespective of its nature, in which he finds himself" (p. 325).

2. *The Scarlet Letter*, The Centenary Edition (Columbus: Ohio State University Press, 1962), p. 4. All further references to this work in this chapter appear in the text.

3. In noting that Hawthorne "in point of fact came upon his subject quite otherwise," Charles Feidelson does not distinguish between the author of the essay and its narrator (*Symbolism and American Literature*, p. 9).

4. *Hawthorne's Works*, The Riverside Edition (Boston: Houghton Mifflin, 1883), 2:104.

5. *Works*, 1:53.

6. Ibid., p. 69.

7. Harry Henderson, in an excellent chapter on Hawthorne in *Versions of the Past: The Historical Imagination in American Fiction* (New York: Oxford University Press, 1974), writes of "The Minister's Black Veil" that it is "at least in part a commentary on the final *cul-de-sac* of Puritan introspection and exclusiveness" (p. 101). Among the many commentators on Hawthorne, I find Henderson one of the most useful. As my own discussion of Hester and Dimmesdale that follows later in this essay will suggest, Hawthorne perceived the relationship between theological cast of mind and social behavior that characterized the Puritan community. Henderson seems to be implying here that the black veil, like the scarlet letter, is a literal manifestation of the spiritual stigmata the Puritan searched for during introspective meditation. My own discussion of *The Scarlet Letter* develops this idea more fully.

8. More is at stake in the romance and its accompanying essay than either a discussion of solitude and society or the relationship between fiction and history, themes that Hawthorne develops again in *The House of the Seven Gables*. And in spite of the Brook Farm model for *The Blithedale Romance* and the discussions early in that novel of the transcendentalism that guides Zenobia in forming the colony, this third of what Henry James termed Hawthorne's "American novels" deals with the failure of an idea, not the creation of a symbol. In *Seven Gables*, the artist figures, Clifford and the daguerreotypist Holgrave, bear little relationship to the narrator; the subject is art, not the process of creating it, except as daguerreotype becomes a symbol of aesthetic process. And in *Blithedale*, although Miles Coverdale certainly suffers the burden of isolation imposed on him by Zenobia, Priscilla, and Hollingsworth, he ends by blaming his preoccupation with the romance on his "love" for Priscilla rather than viewing it as a comment on the isolation of the artist.

9. F. O. Matthiessen comments on "the continual correspondences that [Hawthorne's] theme allowed him to make between external events and inner significances." The "external events" I am most concerned with in this study involve the social behavior of the Puritan community. In an interesting choice of phrase, Matthiessen calls these "continual correspondences" Hawthorne's "transcendental habit" (*American Renaissance* [London: Oxford University Press, 1941], p. 275).

10. That indolence is also a form of historical ignorance is Henderson's theme in *Versions of the Past:* "The man and the nation lacking a meaningful understanding of

their past are like the old Inspector . . ., who recalled only certain gourmandizing exploits 'while all the subsequent experience of our race, and all the events that brightened or darkened his individual career, had gone over him with as little permanent effect as the passing breeze'" (p. 95).

11. See Edwin T. Bowden, *The Dungeon of the Heart: Human Isolation and the American Novel* (New York: Macmillan, 1961), or Gordon Roper, "Sin and Isolation," in *A Scarlet Letter Handbook*, ed. Seymour L. Gross (San Francisco: Wadsworth, 1960).

12. Charles Feidelson describes what he calls "the central theme of the sketch . . . the theme implicit in the vignette of Hawthorne poring over the scarlet letter. . . . That self-portrait . . . amounts to a dramatic definition of the following 'romance' and of the author's relation to it. The author's *donnée*, as James would call it, is neither Imagination nor Actuality *per se* but a symbol whose inherent meaning is *The Scarlet Letter*" (p. 9).

13. A. N. Kaul, *The American Vision: Actual and Ideal Society in Nineteenth-Century Fiction* (New Haven: Yale University Press, 1963), p. 147.

14. Richard Chase, *The American Novel and Its Tradition* (Garden City, N.Y.: Doubleday, 1957), p. 70.

15. See Kaul for a general discussion of the complexities of Hawthorne's historical view.

16. Michael Davitt Bell, *Hawthorne and the Historical Romance of New England* (Princeton: Princeton University Press, 1971), p. 13.

17. John E. Becker comments on the novel's first chapter, prefacing the scene in which Hester appears before the crowd, in a way that is relevant to my argument in this study: "The first chapter acts as the prelude to a meditation, it is a 'composition of place.' It is vividly pictorial and yet completely static. It does not start the action; it starts a process of reflection and prepares us for many moments ahead when we will be forced to suspend our interest in the story, focus our attention on a symbol or symbolic tableau, and meditate" (*Hawthorne's Historical Allegory: An Examination of the American Conscience* [Port Washington, N.Y.: Kennikat Press, 1971], p. 90). What I have described as Hawthorne's aesthetic distance does remove the reader from direct unmediated perception of the novel's drama. The "process of reflection" that Becker describes accurately depicts the way in which the mark provides the reader with a focus for "meditation." We may view each separate interpretation or perspective on the letter as yet another opportunity for the reader to "focus our attention . . . and meditate" on the letter's meaning.

18. The tendency of critics in the past has been to interpret a single stance as Hawthorne's own; and thus, interpretations of the novel are various and widely divergent. The spirit of mystery that intrigues Hawthorne in "The Custom-House," and the range of perspectives his narrator provides the reader in the opening two chapters, indicate a *deliberate* inconsistency. See Charles Child Walcutt, "*The Scarlet Letter* and Its Modern Critics," in *Twentieth Century Interpretations of The Scarlet Letter*, ed. John C. Gerber (Englewood Cliffs, N.J.: Prentice-Hall, 1968) for a survey of critical positions on the novel. Hyatt H. Waggoner, in *Hawthorne: A Critical Study* (Cambridge: Harvard University Press, 1963), states further, "What seems to me to need doing at this point in the development of Hawthorne criticism is to show *why* the work is more enigmatic than Hawthorne's other finished romances, even though there is a sense in which one would think it ought to be clearer. It ought to be clearer because it has less action and more exposition devoted to analysis of meaning. Expository writing is a way of 'telling,' narration a way of 'showing.' If symbolism is always more ambiguous than allegory and art contains a functional ambiguity that would be a defect in logical statement, why is this novel, which leans so heavily on statement, so ambiguous?" (pp. 126–27). Waggoner tries to answer his own question by showing that "Hawthorne . . . is letting his images do most of the work for him" (p. 127), but it seems to me that Waggoner's question is more interesting than his attempt to answer it. The novel *is* ambiguous, and ambiguity is part of Hawthorne's subject. As Feidelson writes, "Hawthorne's subject is not only the meaning of adultery but also meaning in general; not only *what* the focal symbol means but also *how* it gains significance" (p. 10). And in the opening scene, the letter gains significance *as* an object that requires interpretation.

19. *Works*, 2:48.

20. Ibid., p. 50.

21. Ibid., p. 69.

22. Ibid., p. 61.

23. Harry Henderson views Hawthorne as a "holist" within his own understanding of what that word means. A holistic view of culture, as Henderson defines it, creates "an illusion of a whole civilization or culture, in which each institution or characteristic of a society might be seen as integral to the total culture" (p. 18). Furthermore, "For the holist, it is manners and mores which are significant. . . . The holist sees society as a seamless web of relationships" (p. 36). Therefore Hester's stigma is integral to the Boston community, "in which all surface manifestations of behavior carry social significance" (p. 115). For the townspeople, Hester is not a symbol; she is rather the embodiment of their own sin. The effect of their perspective forces the interconnection between private and public worlds. Henderson states later, "The distinction between the inner and outer spheres of human existence is such a pivotal intuition of Hawthorne's writing that it is difficult to overestimate its impact on the holist frame, in which the interlocking surfaces *are* 'society.' A character's position within or outside this matrix dictates the content and pattern of his thought" (p. 116). By assigning Hester her particular stigma, the magistrates are attempting to establish not only Hester's position within the community but also the "content or pattern" of her thought. By interpreting her stigma, the townspeople are trying to understand their own position as well. They are part of the same "matrix." Thus Henderson views the opening scene as "as dramatic a 'private' and 'public' concern as one can imagine" (p. 115).

Two additional comments from other critics shed light on this point. Baskett writes, "The scarlet letter itself is a vivid emblem of the Puritan belief that no individual action occurs outside the purview of the theocratic society" (p. 323). To say this is to concur implicitly with Henderson, because the townspeople's attempts at interpretation establish their "purview" of Hester's action. Becker, in *Hawthorne's Historical Allegory*, goes so far as to describe Hester's punishment as "an allegorical celebration of the Puritan way of life. In public punishment, the culprit is the representative of forces which are undermining society. The people assemble into a hierarchically structured group in order to accomplish a ritual destruction of the criminal force. This may be done by the destruction of the criminal or, less radically, by so torturing the criminal that, symbolically at least, the crime is considered removed both from his heart and the hearts of the gathered assembly" (p. 95). Becker is commenting on the scapegoat ritual here. For the Puritans, however, at least for the townspeople in the opening scene, Hester's stigma is not a symbolic punishment. The Puritans are not ritualistically self-conscious, as Becker implies. Hester's crime, her punishment, and the resulting expulsion of evil from their midst are all real.

24. Many critics have discussed the significance of this quotation. Among them Becker states, "In contrast to society in any other place or at any other time, Puritan society cannot distinguish between offenses against society and offenses against God. Within such a world, the individual conscience, the 'heart,' has no distinct place" (p. 91). Henderson writes, "One of Hawthorne's most telling criticisms of New England Puritanism is conveyed by his portrayal of it as a civilization which believed that its obsession with forms and appearances brought it closer to 'pure' religion" (p. 115). Joseph Schwartz, in "Three Aspects of Hawthorne's Puritanism," *New England Quarterly*, 36 (June 1963), comments, "From Hawthorne's point of view the Puritan way of life, their denial of civil liberty for others, and their theology combined to give an unfavorable aspect to the national character. It created a social system, based upon an identification of law and religion, that trammeled itself as it did the people who lived under it" (p. 207). When the religious practice of such a community involves searching for stigmata as part of meditation, it is not surprising that Hester's legal punishment should resemble a social religion. However, as Henderson writes, "To the nineteenth- or twentieth-century mind the concept of a civilization attempting to realize transcendental ideals by reinforcing the formal matrix of society is highly ironical" (pp. 115–16).

25. As Marius Bewley writes, "In the last analysis, Hawthorne is not interested in Hester's private drama. She exists magnificently in the art as the focus of tangled moral forces, but she is herself as much of a symbol as the scarlet letter which she wears on her breast" ("Psychology and the Moral Imagination," in Gerber, p. 39). And as Becker comments on the additional burden Hawthorne gives Hester: "We see both the allegorical Hester created by the Puritans and Hawthorne's Hester, more real,

more mimetic, yet still a character in an allegory. . . . But her very resistance to the Puritan allegory will make her an allegorical figure within Hawthorne's allegory. The scar of the Puritan punishment marks Hester for life; her resistance twists her into a figure of resistance" (p. 98).

26. "The story, indeed, is in a secondary degree that of Hester Prynne; she becomes, really, after the first scene, an accessory figure; it is not upon her the *dénoûment* depends. . . . The story goes on, for the most part, between the lover and the husband." See Henry James, *Hawthorne* (New York: Collier, 1966), p. 100.

27. Erving Goffman, *Stigma* (Englewood Cliffs, N.J.: Prentice-Hall, 1963), preface.

28. Ibid., p. 4.

29. As Quentin Anderson expresses it, "Hester's punishment is to Dimmesdale's suffering as public infamy is to private shame" (*The Imperial Self: An Essay in American Literary and Cultural History* [New York: Random House, 1971], p. 67).

30. Goffman, p. 5.

31. *Works,* 2:103.

32. As Anderson expresses it, "Hester herself is made to perceive a sense of guilty participation in the faces of some of those she encounters, as if she were the embodiment of acts and impulses they do not confess" (p. 69).

33. For another discussion of Dimmesdale's need for confession, see George E. Woodberry, "The Dark Side of the Truth," in Gross, where he states: "Absolution, so far as it is hinted at, lies in the direction of public confession, the efficacy of which is directly stated, but lamely nevertheless; it restores truth, but it does not heal the past" (pp. 16–17).

34. As Anderson comments, "the response of Dimmesdale to his sense of transgression is to attack his own body; the response of the townspeople is to attack the separated member, the bearer of the stigma, the extruded evil" (p. 69). Anderson implies here that Dimmesdale's self-flagellation is analogous to the Puritan stigmatization. In effect, Hawthorne is demonstrating in Dimmesdale the pervasiveness of Puritan theology within the individual conscience. Just as the Boston community's attempt to exclude marked individuals is analogous to the Puritan meditation, conversely Dimmesdale himself may be viewed as the single embodiment of Puritan community. He is, to anticipate Melville, "the world in a man-of-war."

35. Hawthorne's portrait of the Puritan inability to tolerate mystery that has not been made manifest suggests a cultural cast of mind. In a related observation concerning Bellingham and Wilson in the novel, Henderson writes: "Though they are history-makers and role-enforcers, they have no insight into the inner life. For Hawthorne, the separation of 'heart and head' was not the chief fault of the history-makers of New England; it was, rather, their inability to imagine a human reality behind the masks of society, an imaginative, not an emotional, failure" (p. 118).

36. Becker sees Hester's action as an individual one: "Hester stands forth in defiance of that society. She has taken the symbol which was to make her another allegorical figure in the Puritan allegorical world and, by force of an almost violent art, has turned it into an expression of her own defiant individuality" (p. 94). My own interpretation of Hester's management of her stigma is more akin to what Henderson terms the holistic view of Puritan society.

37. See Marius Bewley, *The Eccentric Design: Form in the Classic American Novel* (New York: Columbia University Press, 1957), pp. 161–74, for an excellent discussion of the midnight scaffold scene and Dimmesdale's public expiation.

38. In an interesting discussion of allegory in *The Scarlet Letter,* Becker comments: "A society whose public ritual is made to extend in this way beyond the ritual arena and the ritual moment into daily life, is a society so committed to allegory that it has become not a mode of expression but a mode of life. The correspondence between concrete events and eternal truths becomes a presupposition of life itself" (p. 96). It is this very presupposition that allows the Puritans their "control" and emphasizes their intolerance for mystery or ambiguity or paradox.

39. Baskett makes a point about "The Custom-House" that suggests Hawthorne's affinities with Hester. "Hawthorne's growing, if unwilling, understanding that, despite his desire for withdrawal from an uncongenial 'system,' he must somehow establish a significant, self-nurturing relation with it, is intensely signified when he places the scarlet letter on his breast" (p. 327). Hester must also establish such a relation with a similarly "uncongenial" system.

40. *Works,* 2:309.

41. Ibid., p. 319.

42. Kaul talks about several stories ("Wakefield," "The Man of Adamant," "Egotism") in which people alienate themselves from society: "These are thus the stories of a peculiar destiny: of an alienation which arises from cold selfishness, from deluded piety, and from egotistical individualism, and which leads in all cases to a corruption of the human personality and the break-down of normal social relations within the community. They are the parables of a culture in which the Puritan absorption with the self has shaded off into the democratic ideal of the individual's self-sufficiency" (p. 158).

43. Joel Porte, in *The Romance in America: Studies in Cooper, Poe, Hawthorne, Melville, and James* (Middletown, Conn.; Wesleyan University Press, 1969), comments on Hawthorne's experience: "All the major characters in *The Scarlet Letter,* including Hawthorne himself, aspire to the condition of the romancer—a position of spiritual depth and understanding earned through sympathy with or experience of pain. The price of attaining such a bad eminence is worldly danger: 'decapitation' for Hawthorne when he is removed as Surveyor of the Customs and thus permitted to return to writing, or pariahdom for Hester. . . . *The Scarlet Letter,* in short, can be read as an allegory of art" (pp. 98–99).

44. James, p. 101.

45. See Millicent Bell, for example, who points out that the "peculiar faculty of Chillingworth" is "peculiarly akin to the artist" (p. 74). Henderson calls Chillingworth "the searcher of the inner man just as Bellingham and Wilson are the censors of the outer" (p. 117). Henderson's comparative study of Dimmesdale and Chillingworth is also interesting here: "Dimmesdale's tragedy is that he cannot be secure in either his faith or his role. His faith is impotent before social imperatives. Chillingworth, like a charlatan, assumes new roles with ease. For him, man is made by art, not by faith. . . . In the social ascendancy of Dimmesdale over Chillingworth Hawthorne epitomizes a New World which eschewed art to choose a faith it could not live with" (p. 121).

46. See 2 Samuel 12.

47. Matthiessen, p. 306.

48. *Works,* 2:183.

49. Matthiessen, p. 258.

50. *Works,* 2:194.

51. In support of my idea that Hawthorne sees much of himself in Chillingworth, Kaul talks about the fact that the pursuit of art "could become an obsession, a means of isolation from the world rather than a mode of communication with it. When this happens, when art is unrelated to human sympathy, its 'diabolism' . . . becomes a fact in Hawthorne's moral vision" (p. 164). Chillingworth is thus an example of an artist whose "art" becomes "unrelated to human sympathy."

52. *Works,* 2: p. 182.

53. Ibid., p. 195.

54. Baskett, p. 326.

55. Critics have made this point about the isolation of Hawthorne's artists. A. N. Kaul, for example, talks about the "spiritual death" that results from "conformity to certain kinds of society. . . . [Hawthorne's artists] live in a society which combines the Puritan mistrust of art with the emphasis on practicality and utility of both the early New England code and latter-day American life. It is a society in which the artist has no recognized place unless it be the one traditionally reserved for the Black Man" (p. 166). And R. K. Gupta, in "Hawthorne's Treatment of the Artist," *New England Quarterly,* 45 (March 1972), pp. 65–80, states: "In the case of the artists, loneliness is imposed by society. The artists do not themselves deliberately reject human brotherhood. . . . They are isolated because of society's failure to understand them and value their achievement."

56. Kaul, p. 167.

57. Richard Harter Fogle, *Hawthorne's Fiction: The Light & The Dark* (Norman: University of Oklahoma Press, 1964), p. 42.

58. This is one standard interpretation of the novel. Marius Bewley writes, for example, *"The Scarlet Letter* is a study of isolation on the spatial plane . . . the

conflict between Hester and the community is the most poised statement Hawthorne ever made of the tension between solitude and society" (p. 174). R. W. B. Lewis, in "The Controlled Division of Sympathies," in Gross, writes: "Hawthorne felt . . . that the stuff of narrative consisted in the imaginable brushes between the deracinated and solitary individual and the society or world awaiting him. . . . In *The Scarlet Letter* not only do the individual and the world, the conduct and the institutions, measure each other: the measurement and its consequences are precisely and centrally what the novel is about" (p. 26). And Quentin Anderson states: "Hawthorne saw human selves as fostered in a net of relations, finding their meaning and value only through those relations" (pp. 60–61).

59. Henderson, pp. 116–17.
60. Feidelson, pp. 49–50.

3

Moby-Dick: **Social Physics and Metaphysics**

The Scarlet Letter studies social stigma and yet, by means of allegory, maintains a curious distance from the world, from the "flesh and blood of action." Melville's novel embraces that "flesh and blood," yet seems ostensibly about anything but social stigma. As I will discuss in this chapter, Ishmael has already learned White-Jacket's lessons and therefore Ishmael combats metaphysical rather than social isolation. Then why include a study of *Moby-Dick* in a book about social stigma in American fiction?

Moby-Dick becomes an implicit reflection on social stigma by focusing on the vision that results from Ishmael's social invisibility. His vision is not social, but his invisibility is. Thus Melville implies that wisdom for the American, symbolized in part by the omniscience Ishmael achieves as narrator, requires his social invisibility. This makes Melville akin to the transcendentalists because, in going to sea, Ishmael escapes the landed concerns of his society, which include social hierarchy and social stigma.

At the same time, as I will indicate in the discussion that follows, Ishmael carries with him the Puritan tendency to focus on objects in the material world that are physically marked. In so doing, he manifests the Puritan epistemology in which social behavior is analogous to the inner scrutiny of meditation but at the same time he removes himself from the community within which the Puritans of Hawthorne's novel create and contain their identity. For Ishmael does not need to exclude other human beings from the world in order to discover who he is. He turns not to stigma but to symbolism. Unlike Ahab, who attributes malice to the inscrutable and then pursues it in the manifest form of the white whale, thereby demonstrating his own Puritanism, Ishmael is content to focus on those qualities of the physical world that are marked in order to transcend to an understanding of the ineffable, the absolute world of "land-lessness."

Ahab's pursuit is analogous to Hester's initial branding in the sense that Ahab, like the Puritans, searches for meaning inherent in physical stigma (for Ahab, of course, the stigma is his ivory leg). Yet Ahab is also like Dimmesdale. He is discreditable like the minister; he cannot reveal the true nature of his pursuit of the whale to the "community" of men aboard the *Pequod*. The search for knowledge in such a context of discreditability, for Dimmesdale and for Ahab, can produce metaphysical isolation. Ishmael attempts to overcome such isolation.

Much more than Hawthorne's narrator, Ishmael is "struck" by markings. As a sailor, Ishmael focuses on Ahab's marked quest in order to achieve self-consciousness and narrative omniscience. As a narrator, Ishmael focuses on things that are marked in order to achieve symbolic significance for his narrative. Art itself becomes Ishmael's substitute for the social scapegoat the Puritans needed. And Melville escapes the allegorical level Hawthorne remains mired in because, unlike Hawthorne, Melville allows his own narrator to participate in the real action of the narrative as a sailor on board the *Pequod*.

Melville achieves both the "flesh and blood of action" and Ishmael's "transcendental imagination" precisely *because* Ishmael is a character as well as a narrator in his fiction. Hawthorne pushes toward creating a narrator who is a "character" in the tale by introducing *The Scarlet Letter* with "The Custom-House," but he does not achieve the resolution between "the Actual and the Imaginary" or fact and fancy or the physical and the metaphysical that Melville does. Melville's triumph is his ability to envision conflicting views—and conflicting worlds—at the same time. Melville is able to balance unity with multiplicity—the realm of the absolute with the finite relative world. As Feidelson writes, "The whale is simultaneously the most solid of physical things and the most meaningful of symbols. The voyaging intellect of Ishmael interacts with the material world to generate symbolic meaning."[1] Ishmael's tolerance for mystery, for "landlessness," finds no analogue in *The Scarlet Letter*. Whereas Hawthorne is uncomfortable with duality, Ishmael relishes it.

Therefore Melville's fear that "without some hints touching the plain facts," some readers "might scout at Moby-Dick as a monstrous fable, or still worse and more detestable, a hideous and intolerable allegory" is actually a jest. "Going a-whaling yourself" allows Ishmael the "flesh and blood of action" and therefore *Moby-*

Dick moves beyond what the medieval philosophers considered the allegorical level of meaning. Melville's novel is purely analogical. *Moby-Dick*'s analogies allow Melville to transcend Hawthorne's "mere" allegory and Ishmael's attempt to "contain" his experience within his narrative becomes much more convincing than Hawthorne's literal choice of the scarlet letter as a "container" for symbolic significance.

Ishmael's narrative provides Melville with a physical "container" for symbolism. Yet that symbolism is open to interpretation. As Feidelson expresses it, "the entire book, which constitutes [Melville's] reading [of the universe], is only 'a draught—nay, but the draught of a draught.' The reader inherits the job. *Moby-Dick* is a developing meaning. 'I put that brow before you. Read it if you can.'"[2] Ishmael's narrative demonstrates the effects the Puritans hoped for from their epistemology yet failed to reach because they lacked Melville's transcendental imagination. Had the Puritans been able to embrace the "power of blackness"[3] instead of attempting to contain it in social stigma, they might have succeeded in sharing Ishmael's "clean tabernacles of the soul."

Both Hawthorne and Melville are concerned with subjective knowledge. However, whereas Hawthorne doesn't think it should be made objective for all the world to glimpse, Melville feels compelled to reveal it. Therefore, although Melville is not explicitly concerned with stigma in the social sense, the range of markedness is even greater in *Moby-Dick* than in *The Scarlet Letter*. Melville is not content merely to discern the signs of universal meaning; he creates them and allows the act of perception, for Ishmael, to become epistemology. For it is by looking, by noticing, that Ishmael, as a type of the American fictional narrator, "marks" the significance of objects in the world and transcends, however temporarily, metaphysical isolation. And it is by focusing on Ishmael that the reader can do the same. Ishmael serves as the reader's "marker" in the same way that Ahab is the mark Ishmael follows in his quest for the "grand hooded phantom."

I

Marius Bewley writes, "We are sometimes inclined to lose sight of the elementary fact that the whole complex movement of *Moby-Dick* originates in Ahab's inability to resign himself to the loss of a leg."[4] If Bewley is correct, then *Moby-Dick* becomes, like *The Scarlet Letter,* a study of physical branding. But unlike Hawthorne, who directs the reader's attention to the "rag of scarlet cloth" in "The Custom-House," Melville opens *Moby-Dick* not with Ahab or the story of

Ahab's crippling, but with Ishmael. And Ishmael is marked not by a physical stigma but by his isolation from the universe. He suffers a case of the spleen, describes grimly the "damp, drizzly November in my soul," and knows it is "high time to get to sea as soon as I can" whenever "my hypos get such an upper hand of me."[5] In contrast with the prefatory pages of the narrative, in which Melville's "sub-sub" has marked "whatever random allusions to whales he could anyways find in any book whatsoever, sacred or profane" (p. 2), Ishmael lacks precisely what the "Extracts" seem to contain—a point of reference.

The critical controversy surrounding this novel emerges from Melville's separation between Ishmael's metaphysical quest and Ahab's revenge pursuit of the whale. In nineteenth-century terms, Emerson's dichotomy between the materialist, "who takes his departure from the external world, and esteems a man as one product of that," and the idealist, who "takes his departure from his consciousness, and reckons the world an appearance,"[6] simplifies to an extreme the duality of Ahab and Ishmael. However, within the text, the separation becomes further complicated as a problem of narration. Is it Ishmael's experience "some years ago" with Ahab's voyage that now, in the present tense of the opening sentence, leads him to tell the story? Or do ontological dilemmas lead him to interweave his narrative of metaphysical correspondences and his fascination with Ahab's pursuit? If Ahab motivates the novel, then Ishmael's search becomes his attempt to understand the thematic significance of Ahab's voyage. If the novel results from Ishmael's a priori ontological meditations, just as Ishmael attempts to rid himself of the "hypos" in his soul by going whaling, then the "marking" in the novel—by no means limited to Ishmael's portrayal of Ahab, but including Queequeg, Pip, Moby Dick, and Ishmael himself—becomes the narrator's means of resolving his "hypotheses" about the universe by constructing metaphysical correspondences. In this second view, whaling becomes Ishmael's "reading" of the universe, one interpretation of the reality he constructs; the quest and the telling become synonymous activities for the narrator.

Melville struggled with similar narrative problems prior to writing *Moby-Dick;* in form if not in intensity, *White-Jacket* creates a narrative design that Melville then adapts to his larger theme. *White-Jacket,* more explicitly than the later novel, is a narrative occasion as much, if not more, than the record of a voyage, even though the narrator remains humorously faithful to his form: "But, though not a few good chapters might be written on this head, I must again forbear; for in this book I have nothing to do with the shore further than to glance at it, now and then, from the water; my man-of-war world alone must supply me with the staple of my matter; I have taken an oath to keep afloat to the last letter of my narrative."[7] The novel allows Melville discursive exposition on the structure of the man-of-war, the activities within, and an allegorical representation between the shipboard world and the landed one; the ship becomes a theater, a chapel, a college, and a social state, as well as the implied extension of White-Jacket's own individual conflict—he, too, is a man-of-war. Yet the relative weakness of *White-Jacket* is built into the novel from the beginning; for the voyage is one, not in search of adventure or vengeance, but simply "homeward bound." Not until *Moby-Dick* does the literal correspondence between life on land and life at sea reach thematic integration.

But it is curious that, in finding the physical vehicle (whaling) that will sustain a voyage with physical as well as metaphysical purpose, Melville leaves behind the particular focus that allows the earlier novel its moments of metaphysical intensity. Ishmael, unlike White-Jacket, is not a scapegoat. In the earlier novel, the narrator's jacket, with all of its other idiosyncrasies, has the misfortune to be white among a black-coated crew. If White-Jacket could only command enough black paint to discolor the coat, he feels he would escape both the assaults of the elements and those of his fellow sailors. But the paint is denied to him; and his resultant visibility makes him the scapegoat of social dis-ease. In addition, the lack of consistent integration between Ishmael's roles as sailor and narrator is decidedly not a problem in *White-Jacket*. When White-Jacket the sailor climbs onto the mast, White-Jacket the narrator falls off. And the sailor/narrator's moment of arraignment at the mast by Captain Claret (chap. 67), one of the dramatic climaxes of the earlier novel, contrasts markedly with the absence of any face-to-face encounter between Ishmael and his captain, Ahab.

Thus, in a study of marked characters in American fiction, it makes sense to consider White-Jacket; and less immediate sense to deal with Ishmael. Yet Melville's distinction between the earlier novel, whose narrator is visibly marked in his fictional world, and *Moby-Dick,* whose narrator is marked only for the reader, emphasizes a transition between what I term in my chapter title social physics and metaphysics. In the earlier novel, the narrator explores the artist's perception of his social role; White-Jacket achieves vision after he transcends his social visibility. In *Moby-Dick,* Ishmael combats not social but metaphysical isolation. In a sense, White-Jacket is a more primitive Ishmael; and from this point of view, Ishmael has already learned White-Jacket's lessons.[8]

Hester Prynne and White-Jacket are scapegoats, marked by their social groups. In a social situation, where the character has become visibly manifest, to recognize the mark (Hester's letter, the white jacket, Ahab's leg) does not constitute a visionary act. Therefore, the very visibility of the narrator's social identity in *White-Jacket* limits his vision; he has been named by his crewmates and has accepted that social definition of himself. His white jacket serves as his psychological and emotional defense in a way that both protects him, because he can blame the jacket, and limits him, because he accepts the narrow definition of his differentness. He achieves moments of vision, and certainly perceives the allegory in his situation that the other men on the *Neversink* do not; but he clothes his observations in physical form until the moment of his symbolic "rebirth" at the end, when out of necessity he cuts himself loose from his jacket to keep from drowning in its limitations. As *White-Jacket* indicates, the mark itself limits the marked man's knowledge of himself and he becomes, as in Hawthorne, a literal manifestation of the marking community's own obscured self-knowledge, their particular form of limited vision.

In *Moby-Dick,* the lack of social marking agents complicates the question of marking. Who marks Queequeg? Moby Dick? Pip? Ahab? Ishmael? The narrator suggests that social stigma is a landed concern that Ahab, in particular, avoids by going to sea. On land, Ahab must "dissemble" his madness and motives, so that "when with ivory leg he stepped ashore at last, no Nantucketer thought him otherwise than but naturally grieved, and that to the quick, with the terrible casualty which had overtaken him. . . . Had any one of his old acquaintances on shore but half dreamed of what was lurking in him then, how soon would their aghast and righteous souls have wrenched the ship from such a fiendish man!" (pp. 161–62). Ishmael recognizes Ahab's dissembling, in the chapter "Moby Dick," and implies that, on land, Ahab might have become, in Goffman's terms, socially discredited. In the novel, however, Ahab's brand becomes both a narrative and a metaphysical focus, not a social one; as do Queequeg's markings, the White Whale's hieroglyphs and legends, and Pip's madness. These markings and legends do not escape the notice of the *Pequod*'s crew, but the whalemen avoid interpretation as surely as they avoid mutiny.[9]

Further, not even Ishmael bears a social mark. Although his opening sentence suggests that he is marked in the Biblical sense and cast out to wander, only Ishmael himself—and the reader—recognizes his alienation. Within the novel, he enjoys a privileged and private view without being, himself, visible. Queequeg is the only other crew member of the *Pequod,* after Peleg and Bildad leave the ship, who even acknowledge a relationship with Ishmael; certainly Ahab does not. Thus, although Ishmael is clearly marked for the reader by virtue of his name, he possesses an anonymous invisibility aboard ship.

That the crew should not recognize Ishmael's stigma would seem to reflect that the focus of the novel for the narrator is personal rather than social. In itself, Ishmael's marking does not place him beside Hester Prynne, or beside Joe Christmas or Invisible Man, whom I discuss in later chapters; and yet, in the novel's juxtaposition with *White-Jacket* and *The Scarlet Letter,* we must consider him marked even more than those other fictional bearers of social stigma. It goes almost without saying, for the reader who is familiar with *White-Jacket,* that visibility leads to social exclusion. Ishmael, in achieving the invisibility of a White-Jacket finally stripped of the jacket, also moves beyond the limitations of White-Jacket's vision, and Melville's succeeding novel thus reflects on social stigma by focusing on a character whose social identity has been all but obliterated by anonymity, whose vision results, as surely as Hester's visibility resulted, from the social blindness of his fellow sailors.

Moby-Dick becomes, in part, Ishmael's meditation on the relationship between vision and visibility. In his meditative moments at the masthead, Ishmael possesses a self-consciousness that White-Jacket's social exclusion imposed on him, but that Ishmael voluntarily chooses. White-Jacket complains that whereas other crewmen escaped detection, "their identity undiscoverable—my own hapless jacket forever proclaimed the name of its wearer. It gave me many a hard job, which otherwise I should have escaped . . . how easy, in that mob of incognitoes, to individualize *'that white jacket,'* and dispatch him on the errand."[10] The errands to which he refers often send him "to communicate some slight order to the captains of the tops." White-Jacket thus, he implies, spends more time ascending aloft than the other crewmen; and so even in *White-Jacket,* the masthead becomes associated with meditation and vision. The narrator writes, "I am of a meditative humor, and at sea used often to mount aloft at night, and, seating myself on one of the upper yards, tuck my jacket about me and give loose to reflection."[11] White-Jacket's visibility increases his opportunities for meditation; and from such an altitude, encased in the jacket, which the narrator wears as protection from the cold, he is pitched into the sea at the end of the novel and almost drowned. Only by ripping the jacket open with his knife, "as if I were ripping open myself,"[12] does he escape death by water—or by the hands of his own comrades, who mistake the jacket for some white shark about to make an end to him, and fill it with harpoons an instant after the narrator frees himself from it. The harpooning of the jacket and White-Jacket's narrow escape establish paradigms that Ishmael in *Moby-Dick* self-consciously explores.

II

Ishmael's resolve to go to sea reverses both the *Neversink*'s journey and classical quest narrative. The *Neversink* and Homer's Odysseus are homeward bound, whereas Ishmael's quest initially has no goal, except as this goal romantically "looms" in the distance, just beyond the horizon of thought; fog or darkness shrouds, distorts, and exaggerates its form. Although according to *The Oxford English Dictionary* the origin of the verb "loom" is unknown, the word's suggestion of impending occurrence or lurking in shadows indicates that whether or not some earlier form may have derived from the Latin *lumen*, or *light*, "loomings" connotes a potential dawning. Related words, *to lumine*, for example, or *illumine*, and the Latin *luminare, heavenly body*, all suggest qualities of light and reflected light. Ishmael must go to sea "whenever my hypos get such an upper hand of me" in order to escape the "lunacy" or reflected light of his "loomings."[13] Further, the primordial connotations of "loomings" indicate, throughout the quest that follows, that the origins of the quest are more important to Ishmael initially than some known goal. For he comes to define his own goals, and in so doing, defines a romantic theme: the rejection of theology and the substitution of personal myth.[14]

It is clear from the beginning that Ishmael feels driven, compelled, to the sea. At first glance, Ishmael suggests that the sea is an escape: "This is my substitute for pistol and ball. With a philosophical flourish Cato throws himself upon his sword; I quietly take to the ship." In his next thought, however, he implies that the sea itself embodies the same desire in every man: "There is nothing surprising in this. If they but knew it, almost all men in their degree, some time or other, cherish very nearly the same feelings toward the ocean with me" (p. 12). He cites the water-gazers, the land-bound tradesmen, as evidence that "almost all men," whether or not they consciously know it, share some subjective experience that motivates them to act, and states, "Yes, as every one knows, meditation and water are wedded for ever" (p. 13).

The meditative act is one kind of reflection for Ishmael, also involving a looming, a dawning of light. Thus he explains the story of

Narcissus, "who because he could not grasp the tormenting, mild image he saw in the fountain, plunged into it and was drowned." The image Narcissus sees is that of his own "self" reflected in the water; but it is also all of nature, as Ishmael explains. "But that same image, we ourselves see in all rivers and oceans." The image of nature reflected in the sea and the reflection of self viewed in meditation are one and the same thing. "It is the image of the ungraspable phantom of life; and this is the key to it all" (p. 14).

The looming moment is the one just prior to visual manifestation, just before the phantom assumes form. It is the earliest impulse of the oceanic nonmanifest to become a wave of creation; and thus the verbal force of "loomings" suggests a prelude to action. Ishmael sees and motivates in one nebulous compulsion: going to sea is his meditation; the nature of self-reflection is the recreation and display of creation; and mystery, all that he does not understand, initially motivates him. Ishmael explains this compulsion as "an everlasting itch for things remote. I love to sail forbidden seas, and land on barbarous coasts" (p. 16). Going to sea thus securely "grounds" the former landsman, but in a more satisfying way; the meditative act fulfills a basic need in water gazers; and the ocean of forms and patterns incorporated in the novel reflects the intensity of the light the narrator achieves. *Moby-Dick* is Melville's attempt to construct a many-faceted "scope," an instrument of vision. As Charles Feidelson expresses it, "The first chapter of *Moby-Dick* is the statement of a point of view. Ishmael opens his narrative by identifying voyage with vision: the field of man's vision is the sea . . . the sensibility of the individual man opens onto the ocean. . . . Beneath the jocular tone these initial paragraphs create an effect of irrepressible need. The attraction of the mind to the sea is life itself as a quest for knowledge."[15]

Ishmael's response to the oil painting on the wall in the Spouter-Inn characterizes in small his approach to knowledge in the novel. He describes what he sees:

> But what most puzzled and confounded you was a long, limber, portentous, black mass of something hovering in the centre of the picture over three blue, dim, perpendicular lines floating in a nameless yeast. A boggy, soggy, squitchy picture truly, enough to drive a nervous man distracted. Yet was there a sort of indefinite, half-attained, unimaginable sublimity about it that fairly froze you to it, till you involuntarily took an oath with yourself to find out what that marvellous painting meant. Ever and anon a bright, but, alas, deceptive idea would dart you through.—It's the Black Sea in a midnight gale.—It's the unnatural combat of the four primal elements.—It's a blasted heath.—It's a Hyperborean winter scene.—It's the breaking-

up of the ice-bound stream of Time. But at last all these fancies
yielded to that one portentous something in the picture's midst. *That*
once found out, and all the rest were plain. But stop; does it not bear a
faint resemblance to a gigantic fish? even the great leviathan himself?
(p. 20)

The irony of the multitude of his farfetched interpretations of the
painting is emphasized by the conspicuous lack of any theological
interpretation—for, with regard to the pervasive symbolism of the
rest of the novel, a reader might wonder why Ishmael does not also
think of the Trinity, or the three crosses of the Crucifixion. But the
dramatic "stop" Ishmael puts to the process of interpretation
suggests his substitution of whaling for theology: it is a democratic
theme, whose legends have not yet been imbued with religious significance, and whose factual lore has not even been properly interpreted. "In fact, the artist's design seemed this: a final theory of my
own, partly based upon the aggregated opinions of many aged persons with whom I conversed upon the subject. The picture represents
a Cape-Horner in a great hurricane; the half-foundered ship welter-
ing there with its three dismantled masts alone visible; and an
exasperated whale, purposing to spring clean over the craft, is in the
enormous act of impaling himself upon the three mast-heads" (pp.
20–21). Ishmael's own interpretation is very funny, and seems to be
quite as arbitrary as the interpretations he rejects.

In light of the correspondence he discovers in the sea as a symbol
of the source of knowledge, Ishmael's choice to interpret the "nameless yeast" of the painting as a seascape becomes less arbitrary. He
has already recognized that whaling is a poetic conceit: "in the wild
conceits that swayed me to my purpose, two and two there floated
into my inmost soul, endless processions of the whale, and, midmost
of them all, one grand hooded phantom, like a snow hill in the air"
(p. 16). And in narrating *Moby-Dick* Ishmael retrospectively orders
the process by which, as a young man, he came to focus on whaling
as a vehicle for resolving the miscellaneous struggles of consciousness before it becomes conscious of itself, finds a voice, and identifies
a quest. Marking becomes his literary method as well as his epistemological technique for arriving at self-consciousness.[16]

Moby-Dick begins at the beginning of Ishmael's quest, not in
medias res. Ishmael the storyteller has learned from Ishmael the
man: the process of achieving symbolic significance originates in
concrete detail. Thus, although Ishmael suspects that his quest for
origins will lead him to pursue the "snow hill in the air," he also
realizes that his more immediate problems concern food and lodg-
ing. He does not disregard the practical goals of the whaling indus-

try that resulted in the opulence of the houses in New Bedford; there are material gains from "light" as well as philosophical ones. Motives for founding the garden in the new world—for planting parks "upon this once scraggy scoria of a country" (p. 38)—were economic as well as religious.

Neither does Ishmael allow economy to replace theology (he has his own substitute—he is willing to accept any "lay" for a berth on the *Pequod* and a chance to pursue metaphysical phantoms), and on his first morning in New Bedford, he begins his landed leave-taking by visiting a chapel. His decision to seek a congenial berth in a whaling ship has led him to consider his grave. Yet he dissociates his metaphysical curiosity from his own death.

> Yes, there is death in this business of whaling—a speechlessly quick chaotic bundling of a man into Eternity. But what then? Methinks we have hugely mistaken this matter of Life and Death. Methinks that what they call my shadow here on earth is my true substance. Methinks that in looking at things spiritual, we are too much like oysters observing the sun through the water, and thinking that thick water the thinnest of air. Methinks my body is but the lees of my better being. In fact take my body who will, take it I say, it is not me. (p. 41)

Ishmael's attempt at self-conviction here mixes false bravado and genuine innocence and parodies Emersonian Platonism; at the same time, he tries to interpret the significance of Father Mapple's masthead pulpit: "there must be some sober reason for this thing; furthermore, it must symbolize something unseen. Can it be, then, that by that act of physical isolation, he signifies his spiritual withdrawal for the time, from all outward worldly ties and connexions?" (p. 43). Ishmael finds that the "act of physical isolation" must "symbolize something unseen" and thereby explains his fascination for things that are marked—isolated from their own kind. This fascination leads Ishmael to accept Queequeg as a bedfellow: "With much interest I sat watching him. Savage though he was, and hideously marred about the face—at least to my taste—his countenance yet had a something in it which was by no means disagreeable. You cannot hide the soul" (pp. 51–52). And it leads him to choose the grotesquely inlaid and antiquely marked *Pequod* as his literal whaling vehicle.

Within his transcendental epistemology, by which Ishmael aligns himself with other marked objects and creatures and attempts spiritual withdrawal, the contrast of dialectical opposition becomes his point of view, his reminder of his own mortality and its inner spiritual essence. Lying in bed with Queequeg, having overcome his initial aversion to the cannibal's tattoos, he understands the essence of dialectical self-consciousness:

> truly to enjoy bodily warmth, some small part of you must be cold, for there is no quality in this world that is not what it is merely by contrast. Nothing exists in itself. If you flatter yourself that you are all over comfortable, and have been so a long time, then you cannot be said to be comfortable any more. . . . For this reason a sleeping apartment should never be furnished with a fire, which is one of the luxurious discomforts of the rich. For the height of this sort of deliciousness is to have nothing but the blanket between you and your snugness and the cold of the outer air. Then there you lie like the one warm spark in the heart of an arctic crystal. (p. 55)

Later in the novel, he states, "as for me, if, by any possibility, there be any as yet undiscovered prime thing in me . . . then here I prospectively ascribe all the honor and the glory to whaling" (p. 101). The "prime thing" and the "warm spark" that the narrator hopes to discover finds its physical correspondence in the whaler's search for sperm oil, for "the whaleman, as he seeks the food of light, so he lives in light. He makes his berth an Aladdin's lamp, and lays him down in it; so that in the pitchiest night the ship's black hull still houses an illumination" (p. 355). The light and spiritual heat Ishmael comes to associate with sperm oil, landlessness, and masthead reverie form the corresponding physical "cure" for his metaphysical problem, his soul's "drizzly November." He leaves behind his landed Presbyterianism: "meditation and water are wedded forever."

In my introductory chapter, I discussed the relationship between Eastern meditation techniques and American transcendentalism. There are moments at the masthead where Ishmael seems to achieve a state of "transcendence" that resembles Eastern enlightenment, and in retrospect, Father Mapple's pulpit loses some of its queerness. Ishmael calls himself "a dreamy meditative man" (p. 136), and he confesses that from his vantage point a hundred feet above the decks, he "kept but sorry guard," having "the problem of the universe revolving in me" (p. 139). He describes the masthead experience in Emersonian terms:

> but lulled into such an opium-like listlessness of vacant, unconscious reverie is this absent-minded youth by the blending cadence of waves with thoughts, that at last he loses his identity; takes the mystic ocean at his feet for the visible image of that deep, blue, bottomless soul, pervading mankind and nature; and every strange, half-seen, gliding, beautiful thing that eludes him; every dimly-discovered, uprising fin of some undiscernible form, seems to him the embodiment of those elusive thoughts that only people the soul by continually flitting

through it. In this enchanted mood, thy spirit ebbs away to whence it came; becomes diffused through time and space. ... (p. 140)

He later writes, "in that dreamy mood losing all consciousness, at last my soul went out of my body" (p. 241). The experience becomes a common one—"that unaccountable drowsiness which ever would come over me at a midnight helm" (p. 354).

The Eastern influence does not pervade the surface of the novel, and as theology Ishmael rejects it as he rejects all theologies, but its presence is unmistakable.[17] In one passage, marked by the peculiarly humorous tone Ishmael adopts whenever he speaks directly of spiritual philosophies, Christian or pagan, he talks about the Indian *Vedas*, "or mystical books, whose perusal would seem to have been indispensable to Vishnoo before beginning the creation, and which therefore must have contained something in the shape of practical hints to young architects, these Vedas were lying at the bottom of the waters; so Vishnoo became incarnate in a whale, and sounding down in him to the uttermost depths, rescued the sacred volumes. Was not this Vishnoo a whale-man, then? even as a man who rides a horse is called a horseman?" (p. 306). The word *veda*, in Sanskrit, means *knowledge*; thus the *Vedas* refer both to the eternal truth that, by its nature, is timeless, and to the earliest cognized form of this knowledge by the epic poet Veda Vyasa about 5,000 years ago.[18] Melville deals with both the philosophical and the literal notion of the *Vedas*. Literally, he jokes about "Vishnoo" rescuing "the sacred volumes." Although Vishnu names a particular Hindu deity, this deity is itself just one manifestation in Eastern philosophy of three essential forces of life, or *gunas*. These forces are contained in the interplay between *sattva, rajas,* and *tamas*, roughly the forces that express creation, put it forth and maintain it, and serve to retard or destroy its growth.[19] Vishnu manifests the *rajas guna*, and thus, in Melville's analogy, represents the force in creation that provides the initial spur to put forth; thus he "rescued" the *Vedas*.

The conceptual connection between this *rajas* force and the whale's activities clarifies Ishmael's own compulsion for landlessness. Ishmael describes "Vishnoo," incarnate in a whale, "sounding down in him to the uttermost depths." The whale's activity of "sounding" or diving provides Ishmael's own link in the analogy between ocean gazing and meditation.[20] The noun "sound" and the verb have different origins, according to *The Oxford English Dictionary*. The noun originates from the Latin *sonus*, or *melody*, and the verb from the Old English *sund*, or *sea*. The associative link between the two may possibly be that *sound* results from vibrations striking the eardrum, but not from diving. Diving in water does produce sensation in the eardrum, however; and the verb *sound* may associate these two vibratory effects. Physics has demonstrated that sound travels through water in physical waves. Ishmael expresses his knowledge of an "inner ear" that deepens ordinary hearing as "inner vision" suggests more than ordinary sight. "Is it not curious, that so vast a being as the whale should see the world through so small an eye, and hear the thunder through an ear which is smaller than a hare's? But if his eyes were broad as the lens of Herschel's great telescope; and his ears capacious as the porches of cathedrals; would that make him any longer of sight, or sharper of hearing? Not at all.—Why then do you try to 'enlarge' your mind? Subtilize it" (p. 280). It is therefore interesting to note that sounds—particular words or "mantras"—are used extensively as literal vehicles for "diving" in Indian meditation techniques.[21] Without possessing knowledge of these Eastern techniques, Ishmael still finds the most life-supporting vehicle available to him, which for Ishmael the whaleman is the pursuit of the whale (if only he could be pursued at the depths he sounds) and for Ishmael the narrator the established cognition and realization of his quest as a metaphysical conceit.

A. N. Kaul writes, Ishmael "comes very close to regarding [the universe] as one indivisible totality—a vast ambiguity of man, fish, and the elements, of good and evil. But while such an insight bears remarkable affinity to the viewpoint of oriental metaphysics, Ishmael achieves it not through oriental contemplation but through sustained action. Though he does not pursue Moby-Dick out of vengeance, yet pursue him he must if he is to comprehend him and to resolve the problem of the universe."[22] Ishmael's moments on the masthead are analogous to "oriental contemplation" in the sense that being on the lookout for whales provides him with a focus or "mantra" for meditation. As Howard Vincent expresses it, "Whaling is the tonic chord to which we turn again and again, finally concentrating on one particular whale."[23] In my understanding of transcendental meditation, there is no contradiction between contemplation and what Kaul terms "sustained action." Contemplation or meditation is a prelude to action, not a retreat from it. The world of action serves to deepen the experience of meditation. In this sense, Ishmael's "pursuit" of the whale is as much metaphysical as it is physical. As Feidelson writes, "He who would follow Ishmael must exert the symbolic imagination, for Ishmael's 'pursuit' of the whale is the evolution of an image. Although the meanings that develop are disquieting, and the whole process tends to become a 'fiery hunt,' he has no other approach."[24] Ishmael's ability to "evolve his image," in Feidelson's words, increases as a result of his time on the masthead. His "meditations" on the whale increase Melville's powers as a symbolist.

But meditation in whatever form produces only moments of transcendence; beneath the masthead exist the "Descartian" vortices, the sharks beneath the surface calm of the sea. If, as Ishmael describes his experience amidst the "grand armada of whales," "amid the tornadoed Atlantic of my being, do I myself still for ever centrally disport in mute calm; and while ponderous planets of unwaning woe revolve round me, deep down and deep inland there I still bathe me in eternal mildness of joy" (p. 326). Amid the "eternal mildness," equally, there lurks the "tornadoed Atlantic of my being." Such is Pip's experience, which Ishmael mentions "is common in that fishery; and in the sequel of the narrative, it will then be seen what like abandonment befell myself" (p. 347):

> The intense concentration of self in the middle of such a heartless immensity, my God! who can tell it? . . . The sea had jeeringly kept his finite body up, but drowned the infinite of his soul. Not drowned entirely, though. Rather carried down alive to wondrous depths, where strange shapes of the unwarped primal world glided to and fro before his passive eyes. . . . He saw God's foot upon the treadle of the loom, and spoke it; and therefore his shipmates called him mad. So man's insanity is heaven's sense. (p. 347)

This loom is the ocean floor in Ishmael's "Vishnoo" analogy; it is the "unwarped primal world;" and it is such a powerful experience that it is, in Wordsworth's phrase, "all gratulant if rightly understood." If imperfectly understood or unknown, those initial "loomings" that prelude manifestation become twisted into the loomings of purposelessness, lack of reference, lunacy; "and therefore his shipmates called him mad. . . ."[25]

In the early chapters of the novel, then, Melville establishes Ishmael's subjective search. He suggests that understanding the unknown, "landlessness," provides the object of his quest, that whaling provides his means, and that Ishmael's fascination with markings expresses his attempt to transcend an inner spiritual dissatisfaction. With the appearance of Ahab, Ishmael's miscellaneous "loomings" find their fullest focus, and Ahab's own quest for Moby Dick becomes Ishmael's adoptive search.

III

Ishmael enters into a consideration of Ahab's significance by examining his physical marks in the same process that has initiated his various speculations from the opening of the narrative. When

Ahab first appears on the deck of the *Pequod* Ishmael states, "reality outran apprehension." Even more scarred than Ishmael had imagined, Ahab's brand literally and completely marks him, as extensive tattooing and hieroglyphs mark Queequeg and the white whale. The visual effect of the scars recalls Hawthorne's treatment of physical marks. "Threading its way out from among his grey hairs, and continuing right down one side of his tawny scorched face and neck, till it disappeared in his clothing, you saw a slender rod-like mark, lividly whitish. . . . Whether that mark was born with him, or whether it was the scar left by some desperate wound, no one could certainly say" (p. 110). The superstition circulates among the crew that "if ever Captain Ahab should be tranquilly laid out—which might hardly come to pass . . .—then, whoever should do that last office for the dead, would find a birthmark on him from crown to sole" (p. 110). Contrary to expectation, it is not the leg itself that Ishmael first notices:

> So powerfully did the whole grim aspect of Ahab affect me, and the livid brand which streaked it, that for the first few moments I hardly noted that not a little of this overbearing grimness was owing to the barbaric white leg upon which he partly stood. . . .
> I was struck with the singular posture he maintained. (p. 110)

And Ishmael concludes, "after that morning, he was every day visible to the crew" (p. 111).

Ahab's visibility has greater significance for Ishmael than for the rest of the sailors, however, and the second major section of the novel, beginning particularly with chapter 28, "Ahab," meditates on this significance.[26] Ishmael attempts, particularly in the chapters "Moby Dick" and "The Whiteness of the Whale," the metaphysical interpretation of markings, of legends; but his metaphysical speculation at this point in the narrative takes the form of his narrative concentration on Ahab, and the order and unity of the section provide a blueprint for both Ishmael's interpretation of Ahab and the reader's interpretation of Ishmael.

The unity of the second major narrative section is established in two ways. First, this is the only section in the novel where Ahab and Ishmael both function together in presence aboard the ship. After chapter 42, "The Whiteness of the Whale," Ishmael as character does not appear again until the end of the novel, with a couple of brief exceptions, and Ahab does not make an extended appearance again until chapter 99, "The Doubloon." Second, although the events within the section do not all take place during the same day, Melville nevertheless achieves temporal unity in the progression from early morning when Ahab first appears on deck, to "The Cabin

Table" (chap. 34) and "The Mast-Head" stillness—"it is noon" (p. 130), to Ahab's solitary watch at "Sunset," to the "First Night-Watch," and to "Forecastle.—Midnight," in the chapter just preceding Ishmael's reflections on "Moby Dick" and "Whiteness."

Ishmael the narrator imposes this order, not Ishmael the sailor; and he resolves not only Ahab's retrospective significance but also his own function as a character in the fiction. Ishmael remains literally on board the *Pequod* in the early chapters of this section until the narrator, revealing the internal logic of the work, draws a correspondence between his own metaphysical fears and Ahab's externalized, physical means of dealing with similar fears. Ahab's entrance into the novel makes it possible for Ishmael to step back from dramatic action. He thus becomes an observer of the scene he narrates, as the middle chapter of the section, "The Mast-Head," indicates.

I have discussed Ishmael's description of the meditative experience the lookout evokes. In the context of "The Mast-Head," it is clear that Ishmael's view operates at some physical remove—"a hundred feet above the silent decks" (p. 136). Throughout the rest of the novel, as omniscient narrator, he retains his position at the mast, able to observe without actually being part of the scene. The microcosmic contrast Melville sets up here between the action below on deck and the drama of Ishmael's metaphysical warfare recalls White-Jacket's moments of introspection. For like White-Jacket, Ishmael, too, experiences the world in a man-of-war; he is such a world, such a man in conflict, and thus the masthead is not a "crow's nest," as much as he might like it to be. (The crow's nest on the Greenland whaler, by contrast, contains a partial enclosure, securely furnished with locker, rifle, and bottle [p. 137].)

In the drama that follows, Ahab becomes an understudy for the Ishmael who remains on the narrative mast. Ishmael's fascination with Ahab seems initiated by the brand Ahab wears; but in fact, Ishmael further "marks" Ahab's meaning because of the similarities, as well as the differences, in their pursuits. Ishmael's narrative treatment of Ahab is not unlike Hawthorne's narrator's treatment of Chillingworth. For Chillingworth, and for the storyteller who would be an interpreter of signs, knowledge may lead to (self) possession.

As Captain Peleg expresses it earlier in the novel, "'stricken, blasted, if he be, Ahab has his humanities!'" (p. 77). And Ishmael apostrophizes him: "Oh, Ahab! what shall be grand in thee, it must needs be plucked at from the skies, and dived for in the deep, and featured in the unbodied air!" (p. 130). Ahab's mystery hides something "grand" for Ishmael, and his narrative exploration of Ahab, "diving deep" into the captain's grimness, is akin to searching for "any as yet undiscoverable prime thing in me." Ahab has his own meditative tendencies, is engaged in his own ontological pursuit: "'Hark ye yet again,—the little lower layer. All visible objects, man, are but as pasteboard masks. But in each event—in the living act, the undoubted deed—there, some unknown but still reasoning thing puts forth the mouldings of its features from behind the unreasoning mask'" (p. 144). His desire to "strike through the mask," to penetrate "that inscrutable thing," is akin to Ishmael's need to experience the unknown, to see beneath the literal surface. Much later in the novel, Ahab again shows his direct metaphysical fraternity with Ishmael's concerns when he states, "O Nature, and O soul of man! how far beyond all utterance are your linked analogies! not the smallest atom stirs or lives in matter, but has its cunning duplicate in mind" (p. 264). But the philosophical contrast is as striking as the similarities; like Ahab, Ishmael views the "linked analogies" but unlike Ahab, who vows, "'and be the white whale agent, or be the white whale principal, I will wreak that hate upon him'" (p. 144), he does not attribute malice to the inscrutable. Yet Ishmael is reticent to reveal any man's weaknesss of character: "for it is a thing most sorrowful, nay shocking, to expose the fall of valor in the soul . . . man, in the ideal, is so noble and so sparkling, such a grand and glowing creature, that over any ignominious blemish in him all his fellows should run to throw their costliest robes" (p. 104). If Ahab, like Chillingworth, is demonically maddened, Ishmael, unlike Hawthorne's narrator, does not condemn him for it. Ahab becomes a focus for Ishmael's own pursuit in spite of his madness, not because of it.[27]

Ishmael explicitly claims his fraternity with Ahab in the opening lines of "Moby Dick":

> I, Ishmael, was one of that crew; my shouts had gone up with the rest; my oath had been welded with theirs; and stronger I shouted, and more did I hammer and clinch my oath, because of the dread in my soul. A wild, mystical, sympathetical feeling was in me; Ahab's quenchless feud seemed mine. (p. 155)

Ishmael initially aligns his sympathies with Ahab in part because he also has "marked" Moby Dick—the "snowhill in the air." Like Ahab, Ishmael attributes a fundamental malice to the whale, an "unexampled, intelligent malignity," but his imagination is "struck" by the whale's marked physical characteristics and legendary intelligence:

But even stripped of these supernatural surmisings, there was enough in the earthly make and incontestable character of the monster to strike the imagination with unwonted power. For, it was not so much his uncommon bulk that so much distinguished him from other sperm whales, but, as was elsewhere thrown out—a peculiar snow-white wrinkled forehead, and a high, pyramidical white hump. These were his prominent features; the tokens whereby, even in the limitless, uncharted seas, he revealed his identity, at a long distance, to those who knew him. (p. 159)

Similarly, the physical encounter, the malignant "assault," initiated Ahab's obsession. Since the moment of that encounter, "Ahab had cherished a wild vindictiveness against the whale, all the more fell for that in his frantic morbidness he at last came to identify with him, not only all his bodily woes, but all his intellectual and spiritual exasperations" (p. 160). Ishmael's spiritual "thirst" manifests itself, in Ahab, as a "quenchless" blood thirst. "Ahab and anguish lay stretched together in one hammock . . . then it was, that his torn body and gashed soul bled into one another; and so interfusing, made him mad" (p. 160). It was not just the physical encounter with the whale but the deepening influence of physical pain, and the gradual "interfusing" of mental and physical anguish, that leads to Ahab's madness—not an ordinary madness, like Ishmael's spleen, but a demoniac madness, "'I am madness maddened! That wild madness that's only calm to comprehend itself!'" (p. 147). Ahab's spiritual anguish turns to physical pain, and his metaphysical quest into a real hunt.

But for Ishmael, Moby Dick's physical markings and Ahab's physical hunt lead to metaphysical speculation, and in the final chapter of the section, he considers the problem of interpreting the whale's "whiteness." Further, he establishes a division between Ahab's hunt and his own pursuit: "What the white whale was to Ahab, has been hinted; what, at times, he was to me, as yet remains unsaid" (p. 163). For Ishmael, the whale is one more vehicle; it is means, not end. For Ahab, Moby Dick remains the goal of the quest. "The Whiteness of the Whale" results from Ishmael's careful plotting, first of his choice of whaling, of the *Pequod*, and then of Ahab and Moby Dick, as his particular focus for narrative quest, and from establishing Ahab as the character within the narrative who will continue the physical pursuit while Ishmael becomes the inconspicuous meditative whaleman content to follow the chase at some distance and to engage in his own metaphysical speculations as accompaniment and counterpoint to the dramatic action taking place below him on deck. The narrator essentially frees himself from participation in the action and achieves, in "Whiteness," his "deepest dive" into interpretive meditation.

"Whiteness" marks the successful achievement of one narrative problem, and thus, after the "First Lowering" into dramatic action following the expository chapter, Ahab does not again appear in the novel until much later. But it also develops a new narrative concern that Ishmael introduced in chapter 32, "Cetology," and that emerges as an extension of both Ishmael's Platonism and his achievement of narrative distance at the masthead. Ishmael's style in "Whiteness" is logical exposition, and he develops his argument by an accumulation of references to whiteness that contrast "whatever is sweet, and honorable, and sublime" with that "elusive something in the innermost idea of this hue, which strikes more of panic to the soul than that redness which affrights in blood" (p. 164). Yet "aside from those more obvious considerations touching Moby Dick, which could not but occasionally awaken in any man's soul some alarm, there was another thought, or rather vague, nameless horror concerning him, which at times by its intensity completely overpowered all the rest; and yet so mystical and well nigh ineffable was it, that I almost despair of putting it in a comprehensible form. It was the whiteness of the whale that above all things appalled me. But how can I hope to explain myself here; and yet, in some dim, random way, explain myself I must, else all these chapters might be naught" (p. 163).

The "despair" that Ishmael expresses in this passage is occasioned by the ineffability he faces, by the difficulty of explaining the whale's "mystical" horror in a "comprehensible form." Yet if he does not succeed in "explaining" himself, "all these chapters might be naught." He has replaced his initial pursuit of the "snowhill in the air" by his search for a way to "explain myself"; Ahab's whale hunt becomes the focus of his story, but he must also find a way to tell that story, must create a comprehensible form for the overpowering intensity that "whitens" him, appalls him. By telling the story, Ishmael may "share" it as well as find a container—hence a finite limitation—for the internal chaos that led him to the sea in the first place. In "Cetology," he stated, "the classification of the constituents of a chaos, nothing less is here essayed" (p. 117). Thus Ishmael's pursuit, for all its metaphysical semblance, is akin to Ahab's physical hunt: if he can make a convincing correspondence between cosmos and microcosmos, he will succeed in externalizing his own demon—the grimness about his mouth, his soul's "drizzly November." Art, for Ishmael, becomes a constructive scapegoat, as well as a vehicle for self-knowledge and spiritual transcendence.

IV

In "Whiteness," he recognizes the goal of his achievement but he recognizes also that he must bridge the elements of his dialectical vision in order to reach that goal. The symbolism by which man accounts for whiteness enables him to view himself, to make objects out of his own subjective perception of the world. But Ishmael is dissatisfied with all symbolizing that emerges from mood making and wants to understand that deepest perception of whiteness, by which it "calls up a peculiar apparition to the soul." To account for this apparition is, "without dissent," necessary for the man of sense, in order to retain his sense and avoid "madness maddened"; and yet, to directly analyze it, "would seem impossible" (p. 166).

Ishmael continues, "Let us try. But in a matter like this, subtlety appeals to subtlety, and without imagination no man can follow another into these halls. And though, doubtless, some at least of the imaginative impressions about to be presented may have been shared by most men, yet few perhaps were entirely conscious of them at the time, and therefore may not be able to recall them now" (p. 167). The logic he would use, in an attempt to achieve that "fixed point," is the logic of imagination, the logic of analogy; and he asserts (recalling his opening claims in "Loomings" that linked every man, whether or not he realizes it, to the sea) that there are levels of experience that may not have been cognized at the conscious level, but that nevertheless remain "imaginative impressions" that may be appealed to by the subliminal logic Ishmael proposes to use. The presentational style of the chapter begins at this point to assume the characteristics of a Platonic dialogue, Ishmael setting forth points that need to be dealt with, backing off in defense, agreeing, disagreeing, questioning; and in all, attempting the objective view of his subject that will lead him to the construction of a formal bridge to ease the dialectical opposition he described as "the one warm spark at the heart of an arctic crystal," and that he begins to clarify in "Whiteness" and succeeding chapters.

After Ishmael's introspections on whiteness, the direction of the narrative moves outwards. In the portion of the novel that "Whiteness" concludes, the narrator's attention seems to have acquired a new focus, Ahab; and although there is a narrative transition here, after which Ahab becomes a tangential concern until the final section, the first question the narrator addresses after "Whiteness" concerns Ahab's management of time before he can hope to find Moby Dick. He writes, "the premature hour of the *Pequod's* sailing had, perhaps, been covertly selected by Ahab, with a view to this very complexion of things. Because, an interval of three hundred and sixty-five days and nights was before him; an interval which, instead of impatiently enduring ashore, he would spend in a miscellaneous hunt" (p. 174). In chapter 46, "Surmises," he considers Ahab's reasons for continuing to hunt other whales besides Moby Dick. It may be, he reasons, that Ahab was "by nature and long habituation far too wedded to a fiery whaleman's ways, altogether to abandon the collateral prosecution of the voyage" (p. 182). He rejects the possibility that Ahab's monomania may have extended to all sperm whales and concludes,

> the subtle insanity of Ahab respecting Moby Dick was noways more significantly manifested than in his superlative sense and shrewdness in foreseeing that, for the present, the hunt should in some way be stripped of that strange imaginative impiousness which naturally invested it; that the full terror of the voyage must be kept withdrawn into the obscure background (for few men's courage is proof against protracted meditation unrelieved by action); that when they stood their long night watches, his officers and men must have some nearer things to think of than Moby Dick. (p. 183)

Ahab realizes that the "final and romantic object," Moby Dick, will not sustain the men throughout the long search, without some "hopes of cash—aye, cash" (p. 184).

The problem Ahab confronts in these chapters is also Ishmael's narrative problem. In the rest of the novel, like Ahab, Ishmael faces the necessity of sustained effort. The "full terror" of the novel, as well as the hunt, must be withdrawn into the background. The narrative parenthesis expresses the significance of introspective tension—"for few men's courage is proof against protracted meditation unrelieved by action." In spite of moments of unity on the masthead, or of extended metaphysical speculation ("Whiteness"), Ishmael understands that prolonged exposure to the elements of nature and of soul may test or break the courage of a strong man. Thus, Pip's excessive concentration of "self" in the middle of the sea clouds his sanity. However surely Ishmael's inner desire continually leads him to return to masthead meditation, his moments of introspection are eased and his capacity renewed in dramatic action. This is the necessary balance he phrases between "meditation and action." The opening moment—"Call me Ishmael"—and the Epilogue collapse the novel into a nucleus. Ishmael arrives at the point in consciousness at which he can state, "Call me Ishmael," by having moved *through* his own concentration of self in the middle of the sea, in the Epilogue. Yet in order to move from opening to ending moments meaningfully in the novel, Ishmael must expand the full cumulative manifestation of deepening awareness; and thus he eases the narrative exposition and masthead reverie by the explicitly dramatic scenes.

The dramatic action not only eases and renews the meditative facility but it also prepares for new insight; it actually creates the physical situation that then may be transcended in meditation. In the broad scheme of the novel, neither the narrator nor the reader is sufficiently prepared to realize the eventual significance of Ahab's encounter with Moby Dick in these yet early moments of the narrative. At the same time, action serves as a necessary prelude to the accumulation of significance, realized and articulated in the introspective moments. Thus, Ahab instructs his men to keep an eye out for whales; and thus, Ishmael comes down from the masthead to participate in the first lowering and enacts his mortal fears by drafting his will. The narration of events in this first lowering pushes ther dramatic action further; it also creates new opportunities for the introspective narrator.[28]

This process—the alternation of introspection and action, inward and outward focus—becomes firmly established throughout the third large narrative section of the novel, which I mark as beginning after "Whiteness," and continuing for more than half the novel's length until another turn occurs roughly between the chapters "The Doubloon" (chap. 99) and "Ahab's Leg" (chap. 106). One clear example of the narrative progression of meditation and action is indicated by the sequence of chapters beginning with "Stubb Kills a Whale" (chap. 61), dramatic action that necessitates explanation in "The Dart" and "The Crotch" (chaps. 62 and 63); these chapters are then followed by more action, in "Stubb's Supper" (64), which necessitates further exposition, "The Whale as a Dish" (65). The introspective extension of the cetological exposition may lead to Ishmael's comic view, as in "The Shark Massacre" (66); or to his metaphysical speculations concerning the treachery hidden beneath life's "loveliest tints of azure," in "Brit" (chap. 58), "Squid" (59), "The Grand Armada" (87), and "The Castaway" (93). The reader must have "nearer things to think of" than Ahab's pursuit, whereas Ishmael tries to overcome the limitations of his own vision—"all this to explain, would be to dive deeper than Ishmael can go"—and like Ahab, he contents himself for the duration with the discrete insights that result from miscellaneous metaphysical meditation and that he expresses as objective exposition.

Stylistically, the formal shifts into dramatic dialogue indicate the duality Ishmael balances. The most extensive stylistic shift occurs just prior to "Moby Dick" and "Whiteness," in the chapter "Forecastle.—Midnight," in which the narrator limits his exposition to brief and parenthetical stage directions. The dramatic presentation emphasizes the absence of a narrator (Ishmael, by this chapter, has ascended the mast), maintaining the contrast between meditation and action, although there are other points to the chapter—few sailors speak or sing more than once, and by far the majority of voices belong to Asian or island sailors, literally emphasizing a statement Ishmael made earlier in the novel, that "the native American liberally provides the brains, the rest of the world as generously supplying the muscles" (p. 108) of the whaling industry. The *Pequod's* deck microcosmically contains representatives from "the rest of the world." Ishmael's metaphysical quest has elements of nationality, for he also discovers, by contrast, his "American" identity. His "diving" into meditation becomes, itself, symbolic activity; by going whaling, he dives also into the past, choosing to disembark from Nantucket, "the place where the first dead American whale was stranded" (p. 17)—suggesting that he must imaginatively travel back in time in order to understand his present historical situation. And he tells the reader to test for himself the truth of his assertion that "meditation and water are wedded forever"— "Should you ever be athirst in the great American desert" (p. 13), he claims, you will invariably be drawn to water if there is any to be found.

The dialectical movement of the novel also explains the temporal inconsistency of "The Town-Ho's Story" (chap. 54) and "A Bower in the Arsacides" (chap. 102). Alan Cheuse suggests that Ishmael's relation of Steelkilt's story to the Spanish dons in Lima becomes one occasion during which he "practices" story telling. The "darker thread" of the story he tells there is the threat of mutiny that, owing to the "strange delicacy" of the sailors on board the *Pequod* who heard the full story of Steelkilt and Radney, but who did not circulate it among the rest of the crew, "never reached the ears of Captain Ahab or his mates" (p. 208). Ishmael realizes that the sailors did not tell the full story because they did not know "how," and Ishmael learns to do so in Lima, sometime after the *Rachel* picks him up but sometime before he begins the narration of *Moby-Dick*, because he is forced to define his terms. "'Lakeman!—Buffalo! Pray, what is a Lakeman, and where is Buffalo?' said Don Sebastian, rising in his swinging mat of grass" (p. 209). "'Canallers!' cried Don Pedro. 'We have seen many whale-ships in our harbors, but never heard of your Canallers. Pardon: who and what are they?'" (p. 214). Cheuse interprets these questions as "the imperative directed to the American narrator to define his terms,"[29] and suggests that "The *Town-Ho's Story*" records that intermediate stage in Ishmael's evolution as a storyteller when he remains the pre-epic narrator.

> "Moby Dick!" cried Don Sebastian; "St. Dominic! Sir sailor, but do whales have christenings? Whom call you Moby Dick?"
> "A very white, and famous, and most deadly immortal monster, Don;—but that would be too long a story." (p. 221)[30]

Similarly, the "Bower in the Arsacides" records Ishmael's invitation "years ago" from the (fictional) lord of Tranque to spend holidays, and to crawl inside the skeleton of the stranded sperm whale that the Arsacideans had deified. The measurements he makes are hasty (the priests object to his measuring their god) and he has them tattooed on his right arm, but "there are skeleton authorities you can refer to, to test my accuracy" (p. 375).

The accuracy and the authority with which Ishmael here and elsewhere invests his metaphysical correspondences reflect his attempt, as he states in "The Affidavit" (chap. 45), "to take away any incredulity which a profound ignorance of the entire subject may induce in some minds" (p. 175). "For this is one of those disheartening instances where truth requires full as much bolstering as error. So ignorant are most landsmen of some of the plainest and most palpable wonders of the world, that without some hints touching the plain facts, historical and otherwise, of the fishery, they might scout at Moby Dick as a monstrous fable, or still worse and more detestable, a hideous and intolerable allegory" (p. 177). "Fable" becomes one element in Ishmael's dialectic that, like theology, no longer sustains; he wants to construct a fabulous history that will assess and extend "plain facts, historical and otherwise," without resorting to the mechanics of allegory. Telling a believable story about the white whale will heal the schism between science and myth, and enable Ishmael to locate, in his authority as teller, his own myth of origins, the "warm spark," and the "prime thing."

The novel becomes, therefore, a schoolroom, and the narrator's stance professorial. Chapter 55 opens, "I shall ere long paint to you as well as one can without canvas, something like the true form of the whale as he actually appears to the eye of the whaleman" (p. 224). But in strict academic fashion, he first takes it upon himself to exhaust the "Monstrous Pictures of Whales" that prove false portraits, to credit the "Less Erroneous Pictures of Whales, and the True Pictures of Whaling Scenes," and to give an account of whales in other media, "in Paint; in Teeth; in Wood; in Sheet-Iron; in Stone; in Mountains; in Stars" (chap. 55, 56, 57). "But these manifold mistakes in depicting the whale are not so very surprising after all. Consider! Most of the scientific drawings have been taken from the stranded fish; and these are about as correct as a drawing of a wrecked ship, with broken back, would correctly represent the noble animal itself in all its undashed pride of hull and spars. . . . The living whale, in his full majesty and significance, is only to be seen at sea in unfathomable waters" (p. 227). In addition, the skeleton of a whale provides very little clue to the appearance of his true form. He concludes, "the great Leviathan is that one creature in the world which must remain unpainted to the last" (p. 228). Precision is impossible in either a purely scientific or a purely imaginative portrayal of the whale. Only the subjective experience of "going a-whaling" will yield "a tolerable idea of his living contour," but the risks involved in such a means of gaining knowledge about the subject are fundamental—"you run no small risk of being eternally stove and sunk by him" (p. 228). In all, he warns the casual student away.

In the following chapter, "Brit," Ishmael suggests that the difficulties in attempting a portrait of the whale that will be both objectively and subjectively valid is the historian's analogue to the dangers the sailor faces in leaving land behind.

> Consider all this; and then turn to this green, gentle, and most docile earth; consider them both, the sea and the land; and do you not find a strange analogy to something in yourself? For as this appalling ocean surrounds the verdant land, so in the soul of man there lies one insular Tahiti, full of peace and joy, but encompassed by all the horrors of the half known life. God keep thee! Push not off from that isle, thou canst never return! (p. 236)

In emphasizing the dangers for the real and the ideal adventurer, the passage contains its own humor. Just as Ishmael's physical concerns push him to desire that same precise knowledge of the whale he warns his readers against, so his metaphysics requires his theological "landlessness"; but the tone of mock danger that the passage reveals suggests a contrast between the physical and metaphysical dangers of Ahab's, contrasted with Ishmael's, quest; there are moments when even Ishmael cannot quite believe that the soul's dangers are as great as the body's, but he has chosen the former "perils" and must convince himself they are real. Ishmael is not alone in his attempt at self-conviction; and his exploration of "cetology" externalizes the problems of the scientific researcher who wishes to add something concrete to the body of knowledge. Just as Starbuck and Stubb represent the Janus faces of subjective perspective, a howl and a laugh,[31] so there are heroic and mock-heroic approaches to objective knowledge and the objective portrayal of imaginative experience.

Ishmael's chief concern, throughout the third expository section, might be phrased as the wisdom of logic compared and contrasted with the teachings of analogy. What lies at the essence of subjective knowledge that impels its objective manifestation? Why is it not in itself sufficient? And, conversely, what are the values as well as the limitations of empirical means of gaining knowledge? The emphasis on "cetology" pushes toward objectivity by using a scientific term to focus on knowledge that, in spite of science, can only be gained by "going a-whaling yourself." But the novelty of the term, in spite of the technical knowledge Melville does in fact reveal, creates a duality. "Cetology" itself is one vast analogy.

Ishmael plays philosophically with this duality after Stubb captures his sperm whale by suspending his explanation of cutting-in and trying-out while Stubb and Flask kill a right whale. He then sets up the "two great whales, laying their heads together" on opposing sides of the ship, and says, "let us join them, and lay together our own. . . . To the Nantucketer, they present the two extremes of all the known varieties of the whale. As the external difference between them is mainly observable in their heads; and as a head of each is this moment hanging from the *Pequod's* side; and as we may freely go from one to the other, by merely stepping across the deck:—where, I should like to know, will you obtain a better chance to study practical cetology than here?" (p. 278). "The Sperm Whale's Head—Contrasted View" (chap. 74) and "The Right Whale's Head—Contrasted View" (chap. 75) set up an artificial balance for the moment of exposition, during which the narrator suggests that the sperm whale's head represents Kant and the right whale's, Locke. The philosophical contrast between subjective versus objective means of gaining knowledge varies the problem of duality, but the narrator rejects the classification itself as an oversimplification that slows his pursuit—"throw all these thunderheads overboard, and then you will float light and right" (p. 277).[32]

He continues his analogical method, cites the whale's visual apparatus as evidence of his comprehensive and subtle mental faculties, then interprets its superiority to man's. Concerning human powers of perception, "so long as a man's eyes are open in the light, the act of seeing is involuntary; that is, he cannot then help mechanically seeing whatever objects are before him" (p. 279). However, the act of seeing may not be equated with the art of focusing; and from experience we know that it is impossible to focus on two separate points at the same instant. "But if you now come to separate these two objects, and surround each by a circle of profound darkness; then, in order to see one of them, in such a manner as to bring your mind to bear on it, the other will be utterly excluded from your contemporary consciousness" (pp. 279–80). In the whale, he theorizes, since each eye possesses its own range of visual perception, without possibility of focus, both "must simultaneously act."

This analysis of the position of the whale's eyes corresponds to the physical description of the scene on board the *Pequod* as well as to Ishmael's philosophical duality. For, as Ishmael implicitly compares the two, the *Pequod* itself becomes a massive head with two fronts, each whale head's "contrasted view" literally suggesting the appearance of each eye on one whale. Thus, he momentarily considers the superiority of the whale's vision and suggests, in effect, that all of man's "intellectual and spiritual exasperations" result from his inability to focus on more than one point at any one instant. This results in a continual running back and forth across the deck: neither man's attempt to reconcile duality, nor his ability to accept it, can match the whale's, whose visual powers support "simultaneous perception."

In a logical deck crossing, he then considers the other side of his contrast, noting in what respect man's visual scope permits his ascendancy over the whale's limited vision. "Man may, in effect, be said to look out on the world from a sentry-box with two joined sashes for his window. But with the whale, these two sashes are separately inserted, making two distinct windows, but sadly impairing the view" (p. 279). Man's scope compensates for the whale's ability to focus; the whale may simultaneously hold opposing views, but man may consider the whole question, even though he must resolve it to a single view. The *Pequod*, whale heads attached, embodies philosophy, where holding opposing views of the world may lend new windows, but result in an overall impaired view. It also provides an analogue for the limitations of whaling, the limitations of Ishmael's chosen focus. The whale hunters on deck cannot appreciate the metaphysical implications of their struggles; in contrast, the man on the mast achieves the elevation requisite to the synthesis of distanced scope, but like Hawthorne's narrator, misses the physical combat.

After he has cut the right whale's head loose, Ishmael returns to an investigation of the sperm whale's head and his literal description of the scene. He compares the whale's "case," where the sperm oil is contained, with the "great Heidelberg Tun," and states, "I know not with what fine and costly material the Heidelberg Tun was coated within, but in superlative richness that coating could not possibly have compared with the silken pearl-colored membrane, like the lining of a fine pelisse, forming the inner surface of the Sperm Whale's case" (p. 287). This Heidelberg Tun of the whale is his "sanctuary," and its contents are his primary source of value. Explicitly in this chapter, Melville's cetology becomes an analogy for sperm oil; in digging out his extensive whale lore, he provides a literary experience of boiling for spermaceti. The "sanctuary," where the oil may be extracted by the bucketful, also provides the sperm whale with his physical power—it is his "battering ram" as well as the clue to his buoyancy. Without the oil, the head sinks "like lead."

As the narrator's detailed physical investigation of the whale proceeds, he continues to stress the unsurpassable difficulties of his task. In the chapter, "The Tail," he writes, "The more I consider this mighty tail, the more do I deplore my inability to express it. . . . Dissect him how I may, then, I but go skin deep; I know him not, and never will" (pp. 317–18). Before he rejects empirical methods as singly adequate means of gaining knowledge, he tests them further in the last chapters of cetology. Up to this point, he states, he has chiefly "dwelt on the marvels of [the whale's] outer aspect" but now wants to "unbutton him still further":

> I confess, that since Jonah, few whalemen have penetrated very far beneath the skin of the adult whale; nevertheless, I have been blessed with an opportunity to dissect him in miniature. In a ship I belonged to, a small cub Sperm Whale was once bodily hoisted to the deck. . . . Think you I let that chance go, without using my boat-hatchet and jack-knife, and breaking the seal and reading all the contents of that young cub?

His conclusion after this attempt repeats his earlier discovery:

> How vain and foolish, then, thought I, for timid untravelled man to try to comprehend aright this wondrous whale, by merely poring over his dead attenuated skeleton, stretched in this peaceful wood. No. Only in the heart of quickest perils; only when within the eddyings of his angry flukes; only on the profound unbounded sea, can the fully invested whale be truly and livingly found out. (p. 378)

He tires of his academics, and in disposing of the whale's spine, talks about the vertebrae as billiard balls and marbles: "Thus we see how that the spine of even the hugest of living things tapers off at last into simple child's play" (p. 378).

While his objective inquiries have occupied his narrative attention, the spiritual claims he made, early, for his choice of a sea voyage and his pursuit of the great "snow hill in the air" have all but disappeared from his tapering narrative. In his final attempt at cetological rendering, the chapter, "The Fossil Whale," he invents some humorous geological terms for describing the "mighty Leviathan skeletons," but the humor undercuts any further value Ishmael might attribute to science. "I am horror-struck at this antemosaic, unsourced existence of the unspeakable terrors of the whale, which, having been before all time, must needs exist after all humane ages are over" (p. 380). In addition to "antemosaic" (before Moses?) he invents the Leviathan's "pre-adamite traces" (before Adam?) and describes his "osseous post-diluvian reality" (p. 381). Each of these terms makes perfect sense in its analogical context; and as geological wordplays, they explicitly record the narrator's triumph over logic, if this exaltation has not already been demonstrated earlier in the chapter:

> Friends, hold my arms! For in the mere act of penning my thoughts of this Leviathan, they weary me, and make me faint with their outreaching comprehensiveness of sweep, as if to include the whole circle of the sciences, and all the generations of whales, and men, and mastodons, past, present, and to come, with all the revolving panoramas of empire on earth, and throughout the whole universe, not excluding its suburbs. Such, and so magnifying, is the virtue of a large and liberal theme! We expand to its bulk. To produce a mighty book, you must choose a mighty theme. No great and enduring volume can ever be written on the flea, though many there be who have tried it. (p. 379)

The oppositions in Ishmael's dialectic may be extensively summarized as follows: "Extracts" and "Loomings"; the Ishmael of the novel and the Ishmael of narration; fact and fable in "The Town-Ho's Story"; objective versus subjective means of attaining Eastern enlightenment (the whale as the incarnation of Vishnu); science ("cetology") and poetry (the novel); logic and analogy; realism and romanticism; Aristotle and Plato; Locke and Kant; the right whale and the sperm whale; Ahab and Ishmael; the physical and the metaphysical; visibility and vision; theology and democracy; and so forth.[33] The coexistence of opposites forms the essential narrative duality of *Moby-Dick*, as we move back and forth between "cetology" and the pursuit of whales. One element is atomistic, when Ishmael explores physical details to their ultimate significance, often ending in absurdities that amuse even himself; the alternate rhythm attempts universality, when he tries to create metaphysical correspondences that will establish overriding unity. The physical seems always to be the initial concern, but as vehicle, and as some tangible starting place. The transcendental method he explored earlier, in his Emersonian analysis of his masthead reveries, becomes his choice of narrative method in an attempt to resolve these dialectical oppositions. Analyzing and interpreting the white whale, because he symbolizes so many essences at the same time as he is physically massive and complex, provides the novel's skeleton. In himself, the whale represents both visible embodiment and the "heartless voids and immensities of the universe" (p. 169). To capture the first is, in some sense, to contain the latter. "Wonder ye then at the fiery hunt?"[34]

In spite of the skill with which he ends by showing the comprehensive ascendancy of analogy over cetology, however, he has not yet achieved the portrait of Moby Dick that served to motivate his initial sailing and became the metaphor for his spiritual quest. He poses a final inquiry, "whether owing to the almost omniscient look-outs at the mast-heads of the whale-ships . . . ; and the thousand harpoons and lances darted along all continental coasts; the moot point is, whether Leviathan can long endure so wide a chase, and so remorseless a havoc; whether he must not at last be exterminated from the waters, and the last whale, like the last man, smoke his last pipe, and then himself evaporate in the final puff" (p. 383). In this passage the whale hunt is fully reinvested with the symbolism of Ishmael's quest for vision and concomitant self-consciousness. Like the narrator of the novel, the lookouts at the mastheads of whale ships have become "almost omniscient" in their visual powers, and Ishmael wonders whether or not, by the very remorselessness of the chase, man may soon achieve a Leviathanic apocalypse, in which not only the last whale but also the last man may "evaporate in the final puff." But he argues in favor of the whale's immortality—and his own: "Wherefore, for all these things, we account the whale immortal in his species, however perishable in his individuality" (p. 384).

The irony of the increased omniscience of the narrator becomes the clue to his mortality, for the "last man" is only alive to the extent that he is a quester, a whale hunter. Thus, committed to the hunt yet desiring the transcendence that might accompany achieving the quest, Ishmael is caught up in the self-consciousness that accompanies his increasing vision. As he concluded in "Stowing Down and Clearing Up" (chap. 98),

> many is the time the poor fellows, just buttoning the necks of their clean frocks, are startled by the cry of "There she blows!" and away they fly to fight another whale, and go through the whole weary thing again. Oh! my friends, but this is man-killing! Yet this is life. For hardly have we mortals by long toilings extracted from this world's vast bulk its small but valuable sperm; and then, with weary patience, cleansed ourselves from its defilements, and learned to live

here in clean tabernacles of the soul; hardly is this done, when—
There she blows!—the ghost is spouted up, and away we sail to fight
some other world, and go through young life's old routine again.
(p. 358)

The theme is more conclusively phrased in a later chapter, "The
Gilder," but its placement here at the end of "Clearing Up" both
prepares for the "spouting up" of Ahab that immediately follows in
"The Doubloon," as an element of the narrative that has been sub-
merged but not resolved, and characterizes the marking or sounding
out for whales as the continuing epistemological modus vivendi for
achieving, if "hardly" or momentarily, "clean tabernacles of the
soul."

V

The mark that signals the presence of a whale—"There she
blows!," and that for Ishmael corresponds to his visionary quest, has
its most significant manifestation in the last section of *Moby-Dick*,
in Ahab's characterization and chase. In the opening sentence of
"The Doubloon," Ishmael states, "in the multiplicity of other things
requiring narration it has not been added how that sometimes . . .
when most plunged in his mood, he [Ahab] was wont to pause in
turn at each spot, and stand there strangely eyeing the particular
object before him" (p. 358). Ahab's own epistemological method is to
focus and by means of focus, to attempt metaphoric scope. "But one
morning, turning to pass the doubloon, he seemed to be newly at-
tracted by the strange figures and inscriptions stamped on it, as
though now for the first time beginning to interpret for himself in
some monomaniac way whatever significance might lurk in them"
(p. 358). The doubloon is the white whale's talisman, the sun's
medal, the globe's circumference, the sign of the zodiac, and for
Ahab, "'this round globe is but the image of the rounder globe,
which, like a magician's glass, to each and every man in turn but
mirrors back his own mysterious self. Great pains, small gains for
those who ask the world to solve them; it cannot solve itself'" (p.
359). The doubloon's zodiac, for Stubb, "is the life of man in one
round chapter" (p. 361), and for another sailor, "whoever raises a
certain whale, this round thing belongs to him." The old Manxman
says, "'If the White Whale be raised, it must be in a month and a
day, when the sun stands in one of these signs. I've studied signs,
and know their marks'" (p. 362). And Pip concludes the chapter,
"'Here's the ship's navel, this doubloon here, and they are all on fire
to unscrew it. . . . Ha, ha! old Ahab! the White Whale; he'll nail ye!'"
(p. 408). The doubloon, as the symbol of the white whale, suggests

the source of the self's mystery; it mirrors the interpreter's own birth. For the one who wins it, or nails it, "the life of man" "belongs to him."

The chapter marks the beginning of Ishmael's final attempt to come to terms wth both the metaphysical origins of his narrative and the analogical search of the cetological chapters by dramatizing Ahab's own monomaniac pursuit of the white whale. Ishmael allows his cetology to taper off for several chapters, so that even after "Doubloon" and "Leg and Arm" Ishmael must still dispose of the whale's skeleton and the fossil whale before taking up, to the end, the chase. But the concentration of the narrator's focus from "Ahab's Leg" (chap. 106) to the Epilogue reintegrates the separation between Ishmael and Ahab, and reveals Ishmael's own place in Ahab's tragedy.

It is tempting to equate Ahab's view of tragedy with Ishmael's, and equally so to look away from *Moby-Dick* in its last chapters—to Shakespeare—for a clue to the novel's meaning. In his essay on *King Lear*, Stanley Cavell equates the blindness of madness with the "avoidance of love." Melville's own recognition of the link between the two is unmistakable, as Ahab ignores Starbuck's appeal to return home: "'This whole act's immutably decreed. 'Twas rehearsed by thee and me a billion years before this ocean rolled. Fool! I am the Fates' lieutenant; I act under orders'" (p. 459). What Cavell says about Lear applies directly to Ahab; it is only necessary to read one for the other in the following quotation from Cavell's essay:

> To overcome knowing is a task Lear shares with Othello and Macbeth and Hamlet, one crazed by knowledge he can neither test nor reject, one haunted by knowledge whose authority he cannot impeach, one cursed by knowledge he cannot share. Lear abdicates sanity for the usual reason: it is his way not to know what he knows, or to know only what he knows. At the end, recovered to the world, he still cannot give up knowledge, the knowledge that he is captured, lost, receiving just punishment, and so he does again the thing for which he will now irrecoverably be punished. It is the thing we do not know that can save us.[35]

In Cavell's terms, we might say that both Ahab and Ishmael want to "overcome knowing." Ahab tries to do so by making the whale the vehicle for all that he knows, then trying to destroy it.[36] For Ishmael, it is precisely to the thing he does not know that he looks for salvation—"in landlessness alone resides the highest truth." Ishmael accepts what he does not know and then investigates alternative means of dealing with it. He recognizes the split between physical and metaphysical, tries to isolate objective means from subjective means of gaining knowledge, and ends on the masthead, where his meditative and introspective moments of transcendence move him effortlessly from objective to subjective realms and he "loses himself" in the transcendental state. The physical becomes a vehicle for Ishmael to "overcome knowledge" by understanding both the whale and Ahab's need to hunt it; by transcending it, not by destroying it.

If the Shakespearean materials in the last section guide our interpretation of Ahab's tragedy, the use of the dramatic form in general clarifies even more Ishmael's relationship to that tragedy. The rapid scene shifts and numerous soliloquies, the parenthetical stage directions, and the carpenter, on his "one grand stage" (p. 387) a kind of puppeteer, fitting Ahab with leather, hinge, and leg, all serve as constant technical reminders that the narrator of the drama remains behind the scenes, as it were, still metaphysically removed to the masthead. Drama, for Ishmael, remains a means of presenting subjective experience objectively, and thus of transcending the dichotomy between the two. Ahab's tragedy as the crew play it on the boards of the *Pequod's* deck dramatically reenacts narrative paradigms Ishmael himself acted out in his pre-omniscient state of consciousness prior to the *Pequod's* sailing and his own achievement of masthead distance.

Ahab's relationship to Starbuck, as a type of Ishmael's relationship to Queequeg, becomes one of the most curious of these dramatic reenactments, beyond Ahab's obvious externalization of Ishmael's spiritual pursuit into a whale hunt. Ahab tells Starbuck, the second day of the chase, "'Starbuck, of late I've felt strangely moved to thee; ever since that hour we both saw—thou know'st what, in one another's eyes'" (p. 459). Starbuck alone witnesses the profundity of Ahab's isolation:

> From beneath his slouched hat Ahab dropped a tear into the sea; nor did all the Pacific contain such wealth as that one wee drop.
>
> Starbuck saw the old man; saw him, how he heavily leaned over the side; and he seemed to hear in his own true heart the measureless sobbing that stole out of the centre of the serenity around. Careful not to touch him, or be noticed by him, he yet drew near to him, and stood there. (p. 443)

In this passage, Starbuck creates for himself the privilege of creeping past Ahab yet at the same time locates his own "centre" in his captain's. The last sentence of the passage emphasizes the physical proximity of the two men, yet the concomitant lack of physical contact—"Careful not to touch him . . . he yet drew near to him." In this unique moment, Ahab's hatred does not defend him against the advances of love, and briefly he seems to allow Starbuck's nostalgia for his wife and boy a place in his own perspective. The moment is accompanied by, perhaps evoked by, Starbuck's apostrophe to Ahab, "'Oh, my Captain! my Captain! noble soul! grand old heart, after all! . . . this instant let me alter the course!'" But the moment passes, and "Ahab's glance was averted; like a blighted fruit tree he shook, and cast his last, cindered apple to the soil" (p. 444). He calls on his own lack of free will to turn anything to good:

> "Aye, toil how we may, we all sleep at last on the field. Sleep? Aye, and rust amid greenness; as last year's scythes flung down, and left in the half-cut swaths—Starbuck!"
> But blanched to a corpse's hue with despair, the mate had stolen away. (p. 445)

The atmosphere of this sequence in "The Symphony" (chap. 132) reminds the narrator of a wedding. He describes the clearness of the day: "Aloft, like a royal czar and king, the sun seemed giving this gentle air to this bold and rolling sea; even as bride to groom" (p. 442). Ahab reminisces about his "young girl-wife I wedded past fifty," and Starbuck has his own vision—"'Tis my Mary, my Mary herself! . . . See, see! the boy's face from the window!'" (p. 444). At the same time, Ahab and Starbuck realize an intimacy paralleled in the novel only by Ishmael and Queequeg, in bed together in Nantucket, as if "in our hearts' honeymoon" (p. 54); as Ahab states, "'I see my wife and my child in thine eye.'"

In this context, it is also significant to note that in one of the few brief appearances of Ishmael in the narrative after the chapter "Whiteness," he finds himself tied to Queequeg by the monkey-rope, as Queequeg climbs on a sperm whale's back. Ishmael's own welfare depends on Queequeg's ability to retain his balance—"we too, for the time, were wedded"—and he states, "So strongly and metaphysically did I conceive of my situation then, that while earnestly watching his motions, I seemed distinctly to perceive that my own individuality was now merged in a joint stock company of two: that my free will had received a mortal wound; and that another's mistake or misfortune might plunge innocent me into unmerited disaster and death . . . still further pondering, I say, I saw that this situation of mine was the precise situation of every mortal that breathes; only, in most cases, he, one way or other, has this Siamese connexion with a plurality of other mortals" (p. 271).

The paradigm the wedding references suggest, in which Ahab and Starbuck reenact the intimacy of Ishmael and Queequeg, sets up Ishmael as a second fictional center, a counterpoint to Ahab in the last section but separate from him, and in spite of his detached stance as narrator. In effect, within the narrative, Starbuck acts out an integration between Ishmael and Ahab that cannot be dramatically enacted by the narrator of *Moby-Dick*. The moment of Starbuck's apostrophe to Ahab echoes Ishmael's own moment in the chapter "The Specksynder," which I cited earlier—"Oh, Ahab! what shall be grand in thee, it must needs be plucked at from the skies, and dived for in the deep, and featured in the unbodied air!" (p. 130). But the kind of intimacy the narrator externalizes into a physical closeness between Ahab and Starbuck is not even possible between Ishmael and Ahab, quite simply because, in order to achieve narrative omniscience, Ishmael forfeits his dramatic role as sailor and "Ahab" becomes his aesthetic creation. It is part of the narrative triumph in the last chapters of the novel, the fictional stowing down and clearing up, that Ishmael, by means of his own projected resemblance to Starbuck, gains such "proximity" to Ahab, yet without sacrificing his masthead distance. Throughout the narration of the chase, Ishmael speaks of the whalers in the third person—"The hand of Fate had snatched all their souls. . . . They were one man, not thirty" (p. 454). And he does not become part of it until the third day, when, as he states in the Epilogue, "I was he whom the Fates ordained to take the place of Ahab's bowsman, when that bowsman assumed the vacant post; the same, who, when on the last day the three men were tossed from out the rocking boat, was dropped astern" (p. 470). The narrator's proximity to Ahab becomes a technical device by which Melville demonstrates the similarities between Ishmael's quest and Ahab's, even to the end of the novel; but a vision of these similarities is available only to Ishmael and the reader, not to Ahab. Ahab sees Starbuck, with his limited vision; but Ishmael is never visible to him. The meaning of Ahab's tragedy, throughout, is accessible to Ishmael, but not to Ahab himself.

In the closing chapters Pip, like Starbuck, strengthens the integration of Ishmael and Ahab and demonstrates Ahab's blindness. I have already quoted Ishmael's fraternity with Pip; in "The Castaway," he describes Pip's isolation in the sea and asserts "what like abandonment befell myself." Ahab's madness occasions his own intimacy with Pip; he finds comfort in Pip's insanity in an echo of Edgar and Lear on the heath: "'Here, boy; Ahab's cabin shall be Pip's home henceforth, while Ahab lives. Thou touchest my inmost centre, boy; thou art tied to me by cords woven of my heart-strings'" (p. 428). And he states a few pages later, "'There is that in thee, poor lad, which I feel too curing to my malady. Like cures like; and for this hunt, my malady becomes my most desired health'" (p. 436). Ahab uses Pip's madness and "maddens" it, thereby disregarding the heightened perception that led to Pip's apparent insanity. Only Ishmael interprets Pip's "wretched laugh" as a mockery of the "black tragedy of the melancholy ship" (p. 405), not an indication of maddened vision. And Ishmael watches the transcendental vision Queequeg experiences when he thinks he is about to die: "like circles on the water, which, as they grow fainter, expand; so his eyes seemed rounding and rounding, like the rings of Eternity" (p. 395). Pip and Queequeg have momentarily transcended the boundaries of death; but only Ishmael is capable of interpreting these experiences in this way. Ahab hastens his own tragedy when he rejects Pip's vision. But even though he is conscious of doing so—"like cures like"—the closest Ahab comes to enlightenment is death.

VI

An obvious critical question arises in dealing with *Moby-Dick:* why is the novel so long and the chase so brief? This narrative problem finds its solution in Ishmael's "intense concentration of self" in the momentary Epilogue. The Epilogue records the combined physical intensity and the transcendental state of consciousness Ishmael experiences, briefly, as he floats on the sea with Queequeg's coffin as a life buoy. The full significance of this moment depends on all the "miscellaneous hunt" that precedes; but it manifests none of it. In the final episode, the mammoth construction of the novel disappears, dissolves into the lyric Epilogue, "and the great shroud of the sea rolled on as it rolled five thousand years ago" (p. 469). In the last moment, Ishmael floats "on the margin" of the scene, yet "in full sight of it." The closing vortex he describes is his intense vision of the "heartless void," and yet, though caught up in the revolving suction, when he gains the center, "the black bubble upward burst," and he is liberated. He has transcended the physical where he is still an orphan and floats unharmed, floats on the waves of unity with the universe that follow the transcendent moment.

Ishmael's suspension in the sea lasts for a day. He floats on a coffin—thus experiencing a symbolic triumph over death that Ahab had implicitly predicted in his final monomaniac curse but does not himself achieve: "'*Thus,* I give up the spear!'" (p. 468). If Ahab attributes to himself, like Dimmesdale, the fate of crucifixion, the narrative, by closely integrating Ahab and Ishmael in the last section, predicts Ishmael's resurrection. The "coffins" Fedallah had ascribed to Ahab's fate are nowhere to be found in the last scene; Ishmael floats on the coffin Queequeg made. Marius Bewley calls this "resurrection" Ishmael's return to life, "cured of that spiritual malady from which we see him suffering in the first chapter of the book."[37]

And yet, in spite of this "resurrection," in spite of the momentary sanctuary Ishmael finds, the real tragedy of *Moby-Dick* obtrudes in the Epilogue. The novel's "solution" to the dialectical opposition that motivates quest—the separation of Ahab and Ishmael—finds its limits. Ishmael's moment is but temporary. "On the second day, a sail drew near, nearer, and picked me up at last. It was the devious-cruising *Rachel,* that in her retracing search after her missing children, only found another orphan" (p. 470). The *Rachel* is errant; and it catches up Ishmael, once again, in its miscellaneous wanderings. The *Rachel* does not find what she is looking for, but "only" finds Ishmael. And Ishmael's moment of metaphysical integration— when "the savage sea-hawks sailed with sheathed beaks"—can only serve to heighten his sense of isolation when he returns, as he must, to the physical. He qualifies his transcendence by his reference to Ixion's wheel. Will Ishmael, like Ixion, be forever chained to the physical vehicle that can only be momentarily transcended if at all? Ishmael floats "on the margin" of Ahab's tragedy, with this relationship to it: Ishmael's tragedy is not the lack but the impermanence of vision; not the promise of death, but the return to viewing.[38]

If there exists any clearer picture of Ishmael's attempt and the final qualifications inherent in his success, it may be found in "The Gilder" (chap. 114) whose title seems to refer back to the doubloon and to interpret (to "gloss' or gild) the novel in its golden light. In this chapter, Ishmael describes first the "times of dreamy quietude, when beholding the tranquil beauty and brilliancy of the ocean's skin, one forgets the tiger heart that pants beneath it" (p. 405). "All this mixes with your most mystic mood; so that fact and fancy, half-way meeting, interpenetrate, and form one seamless whole" (p. 406). Ishmael substitutes this seamless interpretation of "fact and fancy" for theology; he attempts to resolve duality; and he expresses the novel's transcendental rhythms—balancing analogy and cetology, meditation and dramatic action, retrospection and narrative re-creation. But such scenes, however "soothing," are also temporary.

> Would to God these blessed calms would last. But the mingled, mingling threads of life are woven by warp and woof: calms crossed by storms, a storm for every calm. There is no steady unretracing progress in this life; we do not advance through fixed gradations, and at the last one pause:—through infancy's unconscious spell, boyhood's thoughtless faith, adolescence' doubt (the common doom), then skepticism, then disbelief, resting at last in manhood's pondering repose of If. But once gone through, we trace the round again; and are infants,

boys, and men, and Ifs eternally. Where lies the final harbor, whence we unmoor no more? In what rapt ether sails the world, of which the weariest will never weary? Where is the foundling's father hidden? Our souls are like those orphans whose unwedded mothers die in bearing them: the secret of our paternity lies in their grave, and we must there to learn it. (p. 406)

With the sinking of the *Pequod,* the metaphysical distance between Ishmael the sailor and Ishmael the narrator collapses. The moment of transcendence is temporary—time-bound; but in the ordering of time in the novel, Ishmael at the last steps forth to begin again the telling; "Call me Ishmael." The warp and woof of the transcendental method returns Ishmael to the miscellaneous search for a focus that opens the novel, to the lunacy of loomings; and *Moby-Dick* ends by qualifying its own philosophical and methodological assumptions.

Watters states that "for Melville, the more nearly omniscient the observer, the more true and valuable his interpretation."[39] *Moby-Dick* demonstrates the fusion of the interpretative act and the attainment of omniscience. Because Ishmael marks a focus for his interpretations of the cosmos in the microcosmos (the analogies he draws by means of cetology), he dives deeper into understanding each time he engages in the introspection of his masthead meditations. The omniscience he achieves, removed from the deck of the *Pequod,* serves to further his ability to engage in the interpretation of cetology and to create the analogies that transcend the limitations of knowledge of the physical world.

Ishmael's epistemology is so compelling that one feels tempted to ask whether the very act of marking may not reflect the way we learn about the world. The "Extracts," with their suggestion that some sub-sub librarian has gone through and "marked" all the books that exist for references to the whale, imply that the reader's interpretation of the novel involves an analogous process—of underlining or marking. The reader's own "extracts" from the novel become our "reading" of the text in the same way that Ishmael's cetology becomes Melville's "reading" of the world. Ishmael "floats on the margin" like a living marker of (our) life's text. We mark what we find significant in what we read in an attempt to underline or emphasize it.[40]

Melville's own "marginal" notes become integral parts of the text in the chapters on cetology.[41] Melville implies that knowledge transcends method. In *Moby-Dick,* manifest and nonmanifest, like "fact and fancy," become "intertwined." Yet in floating "on the margin" of the scene, Ishmael is preparing to deal once again with landed concerns. The reader can anticipate Ishmael's return to the world of metaphysical "hypos" as the integration of visionary and vision breaks down and Ishmael recognizes the need for further questing.

In the novel that follows *Moby-Dick*, Pierre once again becomes the "dreamer of the avenging dream." Like Ahab, Pierre possesses the "dark, mad mystery in some human hearts, which, sometimes, during the tyranny of a usurper mood, leads them to be all eagerness to cast off the most intense beloved bond, as a hindrance to the attainment of whatever transcendental object that usurper mood so tyrannically suggests. . . . Weary with the invariable earth, the restless sailor breaks from every enfolding arm, and puts to sea in height of tempest that blows off shore."[42] When man pursues the transcendental object without regard for the bonds of human relationship, his heart turns to stone and his attempt to resolve ambiguities results in violence. In the limitations of Ishmael's visionary transcendence and the despair that leads Pierre to suicide, Melville anticipates the return, in Faulkner, to a fictional community that regards social exclusion as religious ritual, and for which the catharsis of violence replaces spiritual peace. In Faulkner's studies of marked or "marginal" men, sociology becomes just one manifestation of the truths Melville reveals in his cetological, analogical "reading" of the world.

Notes

1. Charles Feidelson, *Symbolism and American Literature* (Chicago: University of Chicago Press, 1953), p. 184.

2. Ibid., p. 179.

3. This is Harry Levin's term. See *The Power of Blackness: Hawthorne, Poe, Melville* (New York: Knopf, 1958).

4. Marius Bewley, *The Eccentric Design: Form in the Classic Ameican Novel* (New York: Columbia University Press, 1957), p. 207.

5. Herman Melville, *Moby-Dick,* ed. Harrison Hayford and Hershel Parker (New York: Norton, 1967), p. 12. All further references to this work in this chapter appear in the text.

6. Ralph Waldo Emerson, *The Complete Works of Ralph Waldo Emerson,* The Concord Edition, 12 vols. (Cambridge, Mass.: Harvard University Press, 1903), 1:332–33.

7. Herman Melville, *White-Jacket*, MLA text, ed. Harrison Hayford, Hershel Parker, and G. Thomas Tanselle (Evanston, Ill.: Northwestern University Press, 1970), p. 226.

8. Harry Henderson's discussion of *White-Jacket* is interesting in this context. He writes, "*White-Jacket,* as a novel of protest, not only strikes out for the abolition of flogging, but penetrates beyond an attack on a single evil to get to the roots of a multiform contradiction between democratic professions and practices of tyranny and privilege." In *Moby-Dick, "*Melville was able to shift the locus of revolt from the social plane [of *White-Jacket*] to the metaphysical. . . . [*Moby-Dick*] is the unique example, among [Melville's] many formulations of the dilemma of progressive revolt, of a work

in which the social and metaphysical levels of his drama of ideas do not threaten to drown each other out . . ." (*Versions of the Past: The Historical Imagination in American Fiction* [New York: Oxford University Press, 1974], pp. 134–35).

9. As Ishmael observes, "By some tacit consent, throughout the voyage little or no allusion was made to it, especially by the mates" (p. 109). They do, however, interpret the doubloon's meanings. The doubloon is a symbol, whereas Ahab's leg is a stigma.

10. *White-Jacket,* pp. 120–21.

11. Ibid., p. 76.

12. Ibid., p. 394.

13. As critics have frequently noted, "loomings" also anticipates "God's foot upon the treadle of the loom" which Pip sees (p. 347) and the metaphor of weaving, which Melville uses throughout (for example, in the phase "one seamless whole" [p. 406]).

14. This is Newton Arvin's interpretation of the novel. See his critical biography, *Herman Melville* (New York: Viking, 1950).

15. Feidelson, p. 28.

16. As A. N. Kaul remarks, "whale fishing in itself has no ultimate significance. It is a vehicle for the fulfillment of man's moral, social and metaphysical destiny (*The American Vision: Actual and Ideal Society in Nineteenth-Century Fiction* [New Haven: Yale University Press, 1963], pp. 265–66). Marking becomes Ishmael's method and whaling is his focus.

17. In his excellent study of Melville's sources, Howard Vincent is unfortunately unable to provide the reader with a definitive source for Melville's interest in and/or information about Indian religion and oriental mythology in general. See *The Trying-Out of Moby-Dick* (Carbondale, Ill.; Southern Illinois University Press, 1965), pp. 277–80, for an incomplete discussion of the subject.

18. See Maharishi Mahesh Yogi (trans.), *On the Bhagavad-Gita: A New Translation and Commentary* (Baltimore: Penguin, 1969), preface.

19. Ibid., p. 128.

20. For a detailed discussion of Moby Dick as Vishnu, see chapter 11 of James Baird's *Ishmael: A Study of the Symbolic Mode in Primitivism* (Baltimore: Johns Hopkins University Press, 1956).

21. The analogue of ocean diving is used by Maharishi in his commentary on the *Bhagavad-Gita* to describe the process of meditation. He states, "Part of the training for one who wishes to become a good swimmer is the art of diving. When one is able to maintain oneself successfully in deep water, then swimming on the surface becomes easy. All action is the result of the play of the conscious mind. If the mind is strong, then action is also strong and successful. The conscious mind becomes powerful when the deeper levels of the ocean of mind are activated during the process of transcendental meditation, which leads the attention from the surface of the conscious mind to the transcendental field of Being. The process of diving within is the way to become established in Yoga" (p. 136). Maharishi's technique of settling down the mind and leading it to the transcendental field is accompanied by a vehicle of sound, which Maharishi prescribes as that particular sound most harmonious for the individual. See chapter 1 for a more detailed description of transcendental meditation.

22. Kaul, p. 266.

23. Vincent, p. 122.

24. Fieldelson, p. 31.

25. Vincent interprets these passages differently. He suggests, "The paragraphs descriptive of the dreamer in the masthead may well bear the weight of another interpretation: that they here constitute an implicit satire of the unitarian point of view, especially as manifest in the Transcendental philosophy of the Over-Soul" (p. 151).

26. Actually there is a narrative transition at work for several chapters, during which the *Pequod* leaves shore behind; Peleg and Bildad depart; "Postscript" suggests that a major break has been achieved; and some introductory chapters describe the names and positions of the mates aboard ship.

There have been other attempts to split the novel into sections for purposes of critical exposition, for example Newton Arvin's fourfold design in *Herman Melville* (New York: Viking Press, 1950). Arvin describes the four basic "movements" of the narrative as follows: "All the introductory chapters, up to the sailing of the *Pequod*" form the first; "A second unmistakable wave is the one that comes to its crest in the scene on the quarter-deck, when Ahab nails the doubloon to the mainmast. The whole central portion of the book, from the sunset scene in Ahab's cabin to the encounter with the bitterly misnamed craft, the *Delight,* forms a third movement. . . . The fourth movement naturally begins with 'The Symphony' and comes to a close with the catastrophe itself—the Epilogue forming a kind of musical coda . . ." (pp. 157–58). Although Arvin's demarcations emphasize some of the narrative high points, they do not reveal the design of Ishmael's metaphysical search as the organizing principle of the narrative.

27. Another way to express the contrast between Ahab and Ishmael is to see Ahab's quest as flawed in the same way that the Puritan meditation is doomed to failure. Kaul calls Ahab's "total egocentricity: the recurring fatal flaw in the literature of a culture where Calvinistic self-absorption had finally issued into action as the unfettered activity of isolated and self-sufficient individuals" (p. 268). In Ishmael's quest, Puritanism "issues into action" as epistemology; in Ahab's quest, monomania replaces inner scrutiny. Thus, as Charles H. Cook, Jr., writes, "Aware of the human temptation to project simple, personal meanings upon things which are formless or incomprehensible, Melville may be giving us the tragedy of a man who yields his whole soul to this temptation, who inflates his own private hurt into the hurt of all mankind, and who allegorizes the inflictor of this hurt as the dwelling place of all evil. Is Ahab an example of that deadly brand of reformer whose obsession with one evil blinds him to the enigmatic ambiguity of the moral world?" ("Ahab's 'Intolerable Allegory,'" *Boston University Studies in English,* 1 [1955–56], p. 45). Ahab resembles that particular "brand of reformer" in *The Scarlet Letter* whom Hawthorne gives us in the personages of the Puritan magistrates. Is Ahab "the creator of a hideous and intolerable allegory?" Cook asks (p. 45), implying that allegory represents the failure of the Puritan imagination to comprehend ambiguity. Such is the nature of the "flaw" Kaul refers to that, without it, Ishmael is able to transcend the limitations of Ahab's perception of the world.

28. Vincent suggests that the same process explains Ishmael's shift to cetology: "In order to build to the first great climax of the book—the doubloon scene at the mainmast—Melville must momentarily change pace, descend to a *pianissimo.* Nothing is more fatiguing, either in art or in life, than unrelieved tension. . . . Melville later acknowledges this, obliquely, when he mentions Ahab's recognition that although his men consent to pursue the White Whale with him, nevertheless they must be allowed diversion, for instance, to hunt for other whales along the way" (p. 122).

29. In a lecture on American narrative, Bennington College, Spring 1973.

30. There are several excellent discussions of the relationship between "The *Town-Ho*'s Story" and the novel. See for example Warner Berthoff, *The Example of Melville* (Princeton: Princeton University Press, 1962), pp. 133–38. According to Berthoff, "The *Town-Ho*'s Story" was published a month before *Moby-Dick* (Vincent confirms this) and attests to Melville's originality within the then-popular mode of the picturesque anecdote (p. 137). Don Geiger, in "Melville's Black God: Contrary Evidence in 'The *Town-Ho*'s Story,'" in *Discussions of Moby-Dick,* ed. Milton R. Stern (Boston: D. C. Heath, 1960), pp. 93–97, argues that Melville portrays a "special, Calvinist version of Christian justice, more marked by wrath and punishment than by love" in both the tale and the novel. Sherman Paul's analysis is possibly the best of all. He states, in "Melville's 'The *Town-Ho*'s Story,'" (*American Literature* 21 [1949]: 212–22. Copyright 1949 by Duke University Press. Reprinted in Stern, pp. 87–92.All page references are to the reprint edition.). "'The *Town Ho*'s Story' offers an alternative and variant meaning of the significance of the white whale. It is a tragic but not an unwarrantably pessimistic tale that inspires an awe of, but not an aversion to the whale; it marks the beginning of that feeling of attraction for the whale which Melville nurses carefully in the seven remaining [encounters with whaling ships] and without which the dramatic focus on Ahab's monomania would be diminished. Furthermore, the themes and characters of the story, and its symbolic techniques, make it Melville's 'Ethan Brand,' the kind of short story whose significance of which . . . penetrates the main body of an author's work" (p. 87). Paul further states, commenting on the larger significance of the tale, that the "apparent failure in the basis of American democracy has its counterpart in the mutiny that takes place on the *Town-Ho.* The ship-as-society or world-in-itself is a recurrent symbol in Melville's work and in 'The *Town-Ho*'s Story' becomes a stage on which is acted one possible failure in human institutions. . . . [T]he evil . . . brings on a mutiny by enlarging the sense of separation that had taken place between

Steelkilt and Radney, or, symbolically, between those who rule and those who obey. Melville suggests that all would have been well if Radney had only recognized that portion of the right of manhood in Steelkilt which was due even a slave . . ." (p. 92).

31. See the chapters "Dusk" and "First Night-Watch."

32. For one full discussion of the philosophical polarities Kant and Locke represent for Ishmael, see Robert Zoellner, *The Salt-Sea Mastodon: A Reading of Moby-Dick* (Berkeley: University of California Press, 1973), chapter one, "Kant and Locke: The Protometaphorical Substrate." (Zoellner's usefulness is limited, however, by his insistence on using jargon, often at the expense of clarity.)

33. As Feidelson states: "It is quite possible to take poetry as the norm and to regard logical statement as the fantasy. . . . The literary symbolist is inclined to consider poetry as *peculiarly* symbolic, in that poetry (and, by extension, all literature) holds to the creative speech from which logic tends to depart. From this point of view, the symbolic status of literature constitutes a positive victory over logic, the reinstatement of 'concrete fact' in the face of abstract fiction" (p. 55).

34. R. E. Watters supports this view. He states, in "The Meanings of the White Whale," in Stern, pp. 77–86: "This necessity to learn and include everything in order to comprehend the essential principle is the true artistic justification of Ishmael's compiling the mass of whaling details given in *Moby-Dick*. He is attempting to see the whale not partially, as a personified malignancy, a natural peril, a challenge, or a monetary value, but omnisciently, as a possibly intelligible microcosm in a possibly intelligible cosmos. The meaning of the white whale, for Ishmael, seems to be either the totality or essential of all meanings—in a word, attainable only by omniscience" (p. 83).

35. Stanley Cavell, "The Avoidance of Love: A Reading of *King Lear,*" chapter 10 in *Must We Mean What We Say?* (New York: Scribner's, 1969), p. 325.

36. Feidelson terms this Ahab's "refusal to remain in suspense" (p. 33).

37. Bewley, p. 209.

38. Feidelson states: "Ishmael's status remains provisional. He accepts ambiguity and indefiniteness—he is 'buoyed up by that coffin'—and yet somehow manages to retain his own identity" (p. 33). Ishmael retains his own identity because he cannot permanently transcend physical reality. Feidelson's choice of the word "provisional" is interesting in this context. In the sense that Ishmael, in spite of the vision he achieves, must "return to viewing," must go off, like the *Pequod*'s crew, in search of other whales, he does remain pro- or pre-visional.

39. Watters, p. 78.

40. See Charles Olson's *Call Me Ishmael* (New York: Reynal & Hitchcock, 1947), for a discussion of Melville's own markings in his edition of Shakespeare. The references to Shakespeare in *Moby-Dick* serve as Melville's "interpretation" of Shakespeare's work.

41. Alan Cheuse formulated the expression of this idea.

42. Herman Melville, *Pierre, or The Ambiguities,* MLA text, ed. Harrison Hayford, Hershel Parker, and G. Thomas Tanselle (Evanston, Ill.: Northwestern University Press, 1971), pp. 180–81.

4

Faulkner's "Dry September" and "Red Leaves": Caste and Outcast

With respect to the symmetry of the chapters in this book, a study of "Dry September" and "Red Leaves" may seem out of place.[1] I have chosen to deal with them at length and apart from *Light in August* because they not only illustrate that Melville's "social physics and metaphysics" may be usefully explored in Faulkner, but they also demonstrate in microcosm my concerns throughout. I have read *Moby-Dick* as a metaphysical extension of social concerns in *The Scarlet Letter* and *White-Jacket;* a reading of "Dry September" and "Red Leaves" indicates that, for Faulkner, social exclusion may result from metaphysical isolation. Furthermore, in a social analogue of Ishmael's romantic quest, the marking of scapegoats becomes the community's attempt to substitute social theology for a metaphysical one. Faulkner clearly reveals this process in these two particular stories. Therefore they serve as a model by which Faulkner demonstrates my thesis in this study.

It is important, in considering works that span two centuries of American fiction, to locate those elements of continuity that allow us to interpret them in meaningful ways. In establishing their emphasis on the mark as one of these elements, I do not mean to imply that the novelists in my study arrive at similar conclusions about the nature of American community, but rather that they face similar problems. The conclusions we may point to by interpreting their fictions establish the ways in which the novelists' versions of that community have changed in two centuries. One of Faulkner's significant contributions to American fiction, as I will show in the next two chapters, is the demonstration that many of our "new" social and metaphysical dilemmas in the early twentieth century have their origins, if not their solutions, in our history. For the purposes of my study, only Faulkner among the early twentieth-century novelists provides us with a glimpse of those origins. He does this best of all, most single-mindedly, in the two stories "Dry September" and "Red Leaves," in which he addresses himself particularly to social and metaphysical isolation. What literary critics isolate as "themes" in American fiction Faulkner establishes as real dilemmas that have no easy resolution.

The reaction of the community to marked individuals in Faulkner differs considerably from the reaction of the Boston townspeople to Hawthorne's Hester. In *The Scarlet Letter*, as I have suggested, the theology by which the Puritans try to inform their lives leads to a social paradigm for self-scrutiny in which the community as a body looks "within itself," as it were, for marks of the presence of evil in their midst, and tries to strengthen its own identity by assigning social stigma. In *Moby-Dick*, Ishmael adopts the epistemology of marking but moves beyond the "landed concerns" of the Puritan community. However, Melville indicates that what the Puritans recognized as theology allows the "isolatoe" Ishmael to construct his own myth of analogical relationship to the universe. Ishmael transcends the limitations of theology but retains the meditative process. In Faulkner, as I will indicate in my analysis of these two short stories and *Light in August*, the process of social exclusion, inherited from Hawthorne's Puritans but divorced of its theological proscriptions, continues to provide the American community with a means of affirming its tenuous identity. However, Faulkner's comment on this process shows the extent to which social exclusion, in and of itself, attains the force, if not the tenets, of theology. In Faulkner's studies of fictional community, social violence becomes the group's "meditation" on who they are.

In both "Dry September and "Red Leaves," Faulkner achieves a sociological effect by commenting on a historical situation. In "Dry September," he examines the lynching of Will Mayes in a Jefferson, Mississippi, of the 1920s; the figures William Cash provides validate the historical authenticity of the story, for during this decade, lynching remained a means of dealing with the social eccentric.[2] And Indians like the ones in "Red Leaves" did occupy the northwest corner of Mississippi a decade or two into the nineteenth century and keep black slaves there. However, in "Red Leaves," Faulkner's temporal and chronological accuracy serves only to remind the reader that, by contrast with white slavery, Indian slavery exists historically as an arcane and local crime. Thus Faulkner's fictional world, a century later, comments on white and black caste society in the South. He has placed his Negroes in Indian hogans and dressed his Indians in white men's clothes. The particular historical situation projects the attitudes of Faulkner's own century.[3] The historical authenticity of "Dry September" approaches social satire in "Red Leaves," if we read this story as Faulkner's portrait of his society's own tragedy; the aesthetic distance Faulkner achieves as a result demonstrates the similarities between the body servant's archetypal metaphysical isolation and the social alienation that individual members of American fictional communities experience.

"Red Leaves," like "Dry September," expresses Faulkner's concern with caste and outcast; it also studies metaphysical exclusion, in which ritual becomes social reality. "Red Leaves" thus focuses my interest in this book. The Negro body servant, archetypally marked by the Indians as their scapegoat, yet manages to transcend his social role as lower caste member by translating his social exclusion into metaphysical terms. Although it is *because* he is a servant that he must run the Indians' race, and although he never achieves any other social identity or even any other name than that of "body servant," it is not *as* a servant that he experiences his isolation. His metaphysical experience transcends the limitations of social caste. His social role becomes his personal quest, and Faulkner, in his analysis of the body servant, models for us the intimate relationship between personal and social identities. He shows us that social ritual may become a vehicle for attaining knowledge, both for the Negro and for the Indians in the story, and in his title, as I will indicate, defines metaphor as methodology, emphasizes the logic of analogy, and marks the personal as social.

I

Faulkner does not mark his characters physically, as Melville marks Ahab; socially, as Hawthorne's Boston marks Hester Prynne; or metaphysically, as Ishmael at the beginning of *Moby-Dick* marks himself. Yet each of the major characters in "Dry September" becomes marked, set apart, or outcast—becomes visible in a society that insists on invisibility. By making manifest ambiguities within a white society (the blackness within white) and casting them out by "out-caste-ing" the racial deviant (marked by skin color), the members of the society protect their homogeneity, their aggregate invisibility.

The reader first encounters Minnie Cooper as a marked character, and she becomes the focus of several different impulses of social exclusion. In the narrative present of "Dry September," the men in the barbershop make her the subject of their gossip, the branded object of rumor.[4] The rumor has sexual connotations; and when

McLendon enters the barbershop in section 1, he labels these connotations, calls the rumor "rape." His act is a form of linguistic marking. By labeling, he effectively turns the rumor into fact, into an
unacceptable act in a white male society that views sexuality as its
strongest threat—"'Are you going to sit there and let a black son
rape a white woman on the streets of Jefferson?'"[5]

The motivations that subsequently set off a lynch mob are several
and complex. Strangers and observers become visible when a lynch
mob forms. They experience social pressure to place themselves well
within the ranks of the invisible and, in addition, to collectively
force the fear of sexual encounter between black man and white
woman out of the range of sexual possibilities within the society.[6]
The mob accomplishes this by eliminating the black man; and hence
when rumor becomes fact, it no longer suffices that the black man is
chronically placed outside the white caste—a particular one must be
killed. In "Dry September," as long as the rumor with its sexual
connotations remains rumor, the group speculating in the barbershop may consider Minnie Cooper as a pornographic object. Each
man may mentally "attack, insult, frighten" Minnie. But once the
rumor becomes established fact and speculation becomes "rape,"
then the men experience the frustration of vicarious violation—and
they subordinate the sexual realities of lynching.

In section 2, a flashback from the dry September present, the
narrator describes Minnie's separateness. The significant details in
this description emphasize Minnie's history of sexual ambiguity and
her extreme visibility. Her manner, during her youth, became
"brighter and louder" than her companions'; and she carried her
"bright, haggard look" to parties "like a mask or a flag." This particular phrase suggests the irony of social exclusion. Minnie's
marked behavior both obscures and reveals. During her affair with
the bank cashier, she emphasized her visibility while riding in the
red runabout by wearing "the first motoring bonnet and veil the
town ever saw." Faulkner implies that her exhibitionism indicated
her desire to win social acceptance, but she managed to earn instead
a place in rumor, "relegated into adultery by public opinion." The
ambiguity that characterized Minnie's public behavior carries over
into her private life and the present tense, as she sits on her porch
during middle age in a "lace-trimmed boudoir cap" and translucent
voile dresses.

Section 4, the reader's next view of Minnie, takes place in the
narrative present, and enacts the hidden ambiguities Faulkner
hints at in section 2. Her excitement as she dresses, her trembling as
she walks with her friends towards the movie house, her tingling

lips, her attempt to "hold back the laughing so it would not waste away so fast and so soon," all suggest that becoming the object of rumor has stimulated her senses. She dresses for visibility and anticipates a vision of sorts—the picture show "was like a miniature fairyland with its lighted lobby and colored lithographs of life. . . ." The "silver dream" focuses her longing.

Sexuality and visibility are accompanied by voyeurism. Her friends watch Minnie dress, their eyes "bright . . . with a dark glitter," and the people who watch her enter the movie house muffle their reactions in "undertones of low astonishment." The women who take her home after her collapse are very curious about her. Their initial reactions—"'You must tell us what happened. What he said and did; everything'" becomes "'Do you suppose anything really happened?' [they asked] their eyes darkly aglitter, secret and passionate." What Minnie sees, in accordance with her "furious unreality," as Faulkner describes it in section 2, is "life caught in its terrible and beautiful mutations."

Ironically, the dramatic moment in 4 where these ambiguities manifest themselves also leads to Minnie's moment of integration, in which the eccentric becomes, once again, a social focus. She assumes for a moment, her place in the center of the group as she enters the square with her friends, and "even the young men lounging in the doorway tipped their hats and followed with their eyes the motion of her hips and legs when she passed."

The laugh at the end of the section serves as a dramatic climax, suggests that Minnie's sensual excitement has reached an analogous climax, and stresses the irony of her momentary centrality. Her absurd laugh, which seems to begin as an expression of pleasure and end in echolalia, evades interpretation. The rape rumor that branded Minnie at the beginning of the story serves to grant her perverse satisfaction in 4, but this satisfaction does not exist in reality; her sexual experience partakes of fantasy, resembles the silver dream. Yet the young men have it both ways—they first act, by lynching Mayes, and then indulge in sexual speculation when Minnie walks by.[7]

If Minnie's visibility yields her some measure of satisfaction and security, however, the black man's does not. Will Mayes is the second marked character in the story, and the reasons for his marking and his lynching are only too obvious. In addition to his blackness, which makes him a potential scapegoat, he has tried to integrate himself into his community—he has a job, behaves respectfully and passively. That he should become the lynch mob's choice suggests that attempts at integration, invisibility, and sobriety only make the Negro more of a threat to the men of Jefferson. Mayes does not know his place, in effect, as an outcast, and when McLendon and his followers lynch him, they take care of two problems at once—they ritualistically eliminate their projected fear of the black man as a sexual threat, and they force once again the visible separation of castes; lower caste members are simply not permitted to act like white men.[8]

The third marked character in "Dry September," who becomes the most problematic for the reader, is Hawkshaw. In the first section of the story, he seems to function as an impartial observer, but as his impartiality becomes visible, he becomes socially unacceptable. The men in the barbershop imply that he is a northerner and a "nigger-lover." He tries to hide behind this pose of impartiality, even when he follows McLendon into the street. But the other barbers point out Hawkshaw's conflict, as well as his danger, by swearing "Jees Christ" four times. "'I'd just as lief be Will Mayes as Hawk, if he gets McLendon riled.'" one of the barbers states. Hawkshaw's visibility casts him out, like Mayes, for potential crucifixion.

Hawkshaw's motivation for accompanying McLendon is not perfectly clear. The narrator hints that, although his desire to stop the lynching may be strong, he experiences an equally strong curiosity, a compulsion to witness. Thus, to McLendon, he maintains an agreeable appearance, although the war veteran detects protest in his silence: "'What's the matter, Hawk' . . . 'Nothing.'" That Hawkshaw strikes Mayes with the others may be interpreted as his attempt to strengthen his position with McLendon, but the action may also suggest Hawkshaw's own inner conflict—that even the barber shares some of the white man's fear. But when he protests in the car ("'John,' the barber said") and receives implicit encouragement from Mayes ("'Mr Henry'"), he can no longer retain his invisibility; Mayes places a claim on him, asks him to become an outcast in his defense, and Hawkshaw reacts by jumping out of the car.[9]

At the crucial moment, he refuses to share the black man's visibility, and when he retches into the ditch, reveals a complex of emotions. The narrator states, "Dust puffed about him, and in a thin, vicious crackling of sapless stems he lay choking and retching." On one hand, Hawkshaw has shown himself to be just such a sapless stem; he has been powerless to stop McLendon. On the other hand knowledge of what is going to happen to Mayes becomes physically experiential for Hawkshaw as he just avoids a similar fate.[10] And yet, finally, he also achieves a cathartic reaction to the initial rumor by witnessing the lynching from a particular position of danger. This brings on the physical release, turns his stomach.

Hawkshaw's action leads to a technical question: why does the barber literally drop out of "Dry September" when he jumps out of the car? His subsequent absence produces a lack of mediation for the reader throughout the rest of the story. Yet there seems little place in sections 4 and 5 for the presence of an observer. The highly evocative language of section 4 requires unmediated ambiguity; and the narrator hints in the last sentence of section 5 that greater powers than Hawkshaw observe the community—"The dark world seemed to lie stricken beneath the cold moon and the lidless stars." A partial answer to the technical question might be that, throughout, Faulkner needs to preserve ambiguity for full effect; and the unbalancing force of McLendon, who reduces ambiguity for the men in the barbershop by making rumor fact, requires the balance of Hawkshaw to reestablish this ambiguity. When Hawkshaw himself becomes a marked character, he potentially changes the direction of the narrative. He must cast himself out of the car in order to retain his invisibility of whiteness in a white and black world; and Faulkner must eliminate Hawkshaw from the story in order to prevent his observer from becoming a major focus.

But the influence of Hawkshaw's powers of observation remains *within* the story; the reader's unmediated, immediate response in 4 and 5 replaces the observer in sections 1 and 3. The reader sees with the other observers—the voyeuristic friends who surround Minnie and the wife McLendon thinks has been spying on him. Hawkshaw's perverse release reduces the aesthetic distance; the reader moves uncomfortably close to the story. And Faulkner thus raises other questions: What is the relationship between the seer and the viewer? Where does the fiction writer stand in a work like "Dry September"? Is he observer or voyeur?

Even McLendon becomes a marked character by the end of "Dry September," but unlike the other three, his marking exists only for the reader, not for the townspeople of Jefferson. In his social context, McLendon certainly "stands out" in section 1 by "standing up" for the women and children of Jefferson, by issuing his war call; but his visibility is the only acceptable kind. Since he is the whitest southerner in the town, and the most powerful catalytic agent for eliminating social deviance, the people of Jefferson do not mark him, but grant him invisibility. In section 5, McLendon's wife has waited up for him; she is an impartial observer but he views her as inquisitor, as voyeur, and he shows her violence instead of love. There is public release for the town in "Dry September"—the social deviant is eliminated. But there is no private release for McLendon; the inner ambiguities remain.[11]

II

"Red Leaves" is also a study of the alien, but from a metaphysical perspective as well as a social one. There is no mediating observer in "Red Leaves"; Faulkner employs instead a combination of historical distance and Eastern philosophical detachment, depicts the slaveholders as both Indian and American Indian, and forces aesthetic distance from social reality. Thus, the reader does not respond physically, as he may to sections 4 and 5 of "Dry September." "Red Leaves" compels our intellectual sympathy, our contemplation of the metaphysical significance of social sacrifice rather than our witness to the physical immediacy of lynching.

The ritualistic quality of action in "Red Leaves" contributes to the aesthetic distance. The Indians exclude and kill the nameless Negro body servant only to fulfill the requirements of ritual—they do not physically mark him in any way, no more than they do his fellow Negroes—and in this particular society, where Indian women receive no emphasis, sexual tension between upper and lower castes does not seem to exist. "Red Leaves" is not, then, a study of racism, or an evocation of white man's fear. The Negro is marked out to be put to death because whenever the Man dies, by tradition so must his horse, his dog, and his body servant. Implicit in the ritual is the race.[12] When Doom died, it took the Indians three days to catch his body servant, and although the narrator does not state that these Indians expect the body servant to run, they take no precautions against his doing so, and do not seem particularly surprised when they find him gone. The meaning of the body servant's mark derives not from his caste, but from the ritual he performs, for both himself and the Indians, in his race from and against death.

The first section of "Red Leaves" explicitly fails to explain. The language is decidely vague: I count sixteen relative pronouns, or phrases that function as relative pronouns, that do not *relate* specifically to previous information in the text. For example, the first Indian says, in the second paragraph, "'I know what we will find,'" The second answers "'What we will not find.'" If we look back at the first paragraph of the story, however, which immediately precedes this interchange, we find no explanation for what the pronoun "what" refers to. Another example of this same device occurs a few paragraphs later, when the first Indian states, "'I have said all the time that *this* is not *the good way*,'" and further on, "'I do not like slavery. It is not *the good way*. In the old days there was *the good way*. But not now.'" The second Indian answers, "'You do not remember *the old way* either.'" The phrases *the good way* and *the old way* (my italics) function as relative pronouns; but we do not learn what they refer to, except in terms of what it is *not*. It is *not* slavery, and it is *not* sweating—"'I have listened to them who do. And I have tried *this way*. Man was not made to sweat.'" The confusion here is not just the reader's—the Indians' own ignorance of the legendary "good way" and their inability to describe it any further than with these inadequate phrases create the confusion. This particular linguistic pattern enforces ambiguity, creates an atmosphere of inscrutability.

In addition to the inscrutability, the first section also establishes a pattern of excessive negation, of defining things in terms of the things they are not, conspicuous in the imagery as well as in the dialogues between the two Indians. "There was no sign of life," we learn in the first paragraph. "The lane was vacant, the doors of the cabins empty and quiet; no cooking smoke rose. . . . In the old days there were no quarters, no Negroes."

A third pattern qualifies the process by which the Indians per-·ceive reality and the narrator creates the fictional world—objects are masked, hidden, covered up. For example, the doorsteps at the Negro quarters are "neat with whitewash" and "patinaed." When the two Indians enter the central cabin, the Negroes "seemed to be musing as one upon something remote, inscrutable." The masking ranges from the physical image of the whitewashed slave quarters and the later mud mask with which the body servant covers his face to the connotations of the Indians' "blurred serenity" or their analogy to carved heads "looming out of a mist." The Indians respond inscrutably to their environment; they mask it with ritual and artifact (the red shoes, the gilt bed, and the steamboat); and unable to perceive what it is, they notice only what it is *not*.

The dramatic action in the story focuses on the death and funeral of Issetibbeha and the subsequent race the body servant runs. Because we do not see Issetibbeha in life, but only read about his funeral, and because the man who replaces Issetibbeha, Moketubbe, is almost dead himself, the story becomes an exploration of what life means by examining its conceptual opposite. The body servant is marked out as the person who will actually experience the death, and the Indians invest this ritual with the cumulative meaning of Issetibbeha's life—the body servant must run his (Issetibbeha's) life's race. This interpretation finds support in the comment an Indian makes to the Negro when they catch him, "'You ran well. Do not be ashamed.'" Exploration of the meaning of life becomes, for the marked man, a movement toward experiencing dying, and for

Moketubbe and the Indians, the ritualistic pursuit of the body servant in his race for life.[13]

There is a physical parallel between the race and the death of Issetibbeha as well as the ritualistic one. On the day the Indians find the Negro's blood ("'He has injured himself'"), Issetibbeha begins to smell (section 5). For the first time the fact of Issetibbeha's death becomes more than a concept—it is a tangible physical presence. The end of section 4 clarifies the parallel. The Negro's own understanding of death remains similarly conceptual until the cottonmouth bites him. From that point on, death is inevitable and real to him. The poison provides a tangible reason for his dying and for his "rank smell." The Negro's flight, then, is a symbolic, ritualistic counterpart to Issetibbeha's dying. It enables the Indians to vicariously understand Issetibbeha's death, and, indirectly but more significantly, their own lives by the process of perception that the language of the first section reveals as definition by negation.

The Negro, familiar with the traditional ritual, knows that when Issetibbeha dies, he will be as good as dead also. His vigil in the loft becomes his own death watch. The reader learns that for the body servant, "a fire would signify life," so that when the doctor emerges from the steamboat and lights two sticks, the Negro knows Issetibbeha is still alive.

> "So he is not dead yet," the Negro said into the whispering gloom of the loft, answering himself; he could hear two voices, himself and himself:
> "Who not dead?"
> "You are dead."
> "Yao, I am dead," he said quietly.

The lighting of the clay-daubed sticks only postpones the actual moment of Issetibbeha's death, and of the body servant's own, and it is the conception of his own death that he tries to understand. He knows he is dead also, rather will shortly be, and tries to imagine the moment of dying. "He imagined himself springing out of the bushes, leaping among the drums on his bare, lean, greasy, invisible limbs. But he could not do that, because man leaped past life, into where death was; he dashed into death and did not die, because when death took a man, it took him just this side of the end of living. It was when death overran him from behind, still in life." Man does not choose death, but death takes man, and takes him "just this side of the end of living." This, for the Negro, would be the desirable way to die—to be fully alive until the moment of death, then be "taken," in all the force and immediacy of the word. At the same time, however, he understands that his own death will not happen in this way. The final sentence in the passage is left unfinished. The worst kind of dying, the Negro seems to feel, would be, still alive, to watch death catch up from behind—to experience a state of death in life. He understands that he will die this way—and because he has not experienced it, yet conceptually knows it, he is afraid.

The passage suggests that the body servant's race is symbolic for him as well as for his pursuers—death chases him in the form of the Indians. But his fear makes it real. He finds it strange, after Issetibbeha dies, "that he was still breathing . . . that he still breathed air, still needed air." His life processes, which the breathing represents for him, become exaggeraterd. He has become more conscious than ever of living, in the face of death.

When he allows himself to be bitten by the cottonmouth at the end of section 4, he seems to feel that, since he is doomed to imminent death, the snake can do him no more damage. But it is only after the existential moment, after the snake has bitten him three times and there now exists a physical cause for death, that he comes closer to understanding by experience what has been up to this point in his life only a concept, a ritual.[14] "'Olé, grandfather,' the Negro said. He touched its head and watched it slash him again across his arm and again, with thick, raking, awkward blows. 'It's that I do not wish to die,' he said. Then he said it again—'It's that I do not wish to die'— in a quiet tone, of slow and low amaze, as though it were something that, until the words had said themselves, he found that he had not known, or had not known the depth and extent of his desire." Death, for him, becomes understandable in terms of life—"'It's that I do not wish to die'"—and only after he says the words, articulates the understanding for himself, does he know the "depth and extent of his desire" to live. He has approached an understanding of death by understanding what it means to be alive.

At one point in the Negro's race, he comes face to face with an Indian. "They were both on a footlog across a slough—the Negro gaunt, lean, hard, tireless and desperate; the Indian thick, soft-looking, the apparent embodiment of the ultimate and the supreme reluctance and inertia." In the contrast between Negro and Indian, Faulkner manifests the significance of his story. For the Negro not only acts out Issetibbeha's death for the Indians by running life's "race" with death in sight, but he also illuminates the nature of the Indians' lives. Moketubbe, now the Man, is a paradigm for the Indian slaveholder's condition—death in life—and the Negro's race becomes symbolic of the kind of race Moketubbe also runs.

Part of the ritual involves the necessity for the new Man to lead the hunt in search of the predecessor's body servant. This ritual becomes a pivotal transition from death back into life—it is the act that earns the living Man the right to the dead Man's title. But the Negro experiences death in life, the worst possible form of either living or dying. And in so doing, he describes precisely the nature of the Indians' lives, which the figure of Moketubbe markedly indicates.

We learn that from his birth, Moketubbe has seemed "to exist in a complete and unfathomable lethargy," and that "he might have been dead himself. It was as though he were cased so in flesh that even breathing took place too deep within him to show." As we see elsewhere, none of the Indians likes to sweat or to work; Moketubbe is not an exception—and in his own extreme way, he *embodies*, in all the physical as well as symbolic connotations of the word, what is deathlike about the Indians.

At the end of "Red Leaves," after the Negro has been captured,[15] the Indians wait "patient, grave, decorous, implacable" while the body servant tries to drink.

> Then the water ceased, though still the empty gourd tilted higher and higher, and still his black throat aped the vain motion of his frustrated swallowing. A piece of water-loosened mud carried away from his chest and broke at his muddy feet, and in the empty gourd they could hear his breath: ah-ah-ah.
> "Come," Basket said, taking the gourd from the negro and hanging it back in the well.

The story ends at the moment just before the one in which the Negro will actually die, completely and irrevocably, the moment of utter darkness when death in life will become simply death. This moment comments on Moketubbe; for every time he tries to wear the red shoes, he begins to faint, and when the Indians remove the shoes, "Moketubbe's face would not alter, but only then would his breathing become perceptible, going in and out of his pale lips with a faint ah-ah-ah sound."

In "Red Leaves," marking is the means by which the Indians try to understand the inscrutable; and by which Faulkner explores the experiential meaning of words like "life" and "death." He studies markedness at its farthest remove from the physical—the metaphysical. Even the physical badge that the body servant puts on—his mud mask—becomes a symbolic veil. In the moment just prior to his death, the mask drops off—and just as the story does not view death, neither does it reveal the secrets behind his mask.

Faulkner offers us his title—"red leaves"—as a way of guiding our interpretation of his story, but the title itself requires interpretation. Faulkner himself once stated that the title derives from what he termed the process of "deciduation."[16] In the process of dying, leaves on a deciduous tree become very beautiful. They are reddest and seem to be most alive just prior to the moment in which they fall. The body servant's race against death is analogous to the reddening of the leaves; and like the leaves, in the moment of death, his mask falls off. But Faulkner leaves us with the metaphor. Even at the end of the story, its meaning is masked. Its title both obscures and reveals.

In spite of the atmosphere of detachment in "Red Leaves," the story ultimately achieves an intensity as great if not greater than "Dry September," analogous to the comparable intensity with which *Moby-Dick* succeeds *White-Jacket*. Faulkner's inner view of the marked man, in "Red Leaves," compels the reader's sympathy. By distancing his fiction from social reality, he avoids layering his portrait of slavery with contemporary attitudes. The reader approaches the body servant without the stereotype of racial stigma—the man does not become Faulkner's "Negro character." Thus Faulkner permits the human response. The result lends the reader the mask of the mark: and he achieves a vision of the black servant's visibility.

The thematic explorations of social marking and transcendental vision in "Red Leaves" seem to resemble the concerns of Hawthorne and Melville more than those of modern fiction. Within the fictional worlds of both stories, communities are essentially closed, like Hawthorne's Boston: the road that leads out of town in "Dry September" and the park-like forest surrounding "Red Leaves" both serve to isolate the enclosed fictional environments. Such is particularly the case in "Red Leaves," where the body servant runs blindly, "since there was nowhere for him to go." Even the social deviant, the ritual scapegoat, remains within the closed community, just as Hester Prynne becomes part of the daily life of the Puritan townspeople.

In *Light in August*, the closed community emphasizes Joe Christmas's metaphysical isolation. Joe's murder of Joanna Burden becomes a sociological version of the transcendental method that leads Hawthorne to allegory and Melville to qualify Ishmael's "resurrection" of Ahab's tragedy. It is not until Ralph Ellison, as I will discuss, that the marked man leaves the closure and goes North to find that his stigma is invisibility. *Light in August* continues to underline the isolation of the individual within American community. McLendon and Moketubbe are the representative men of this isolation. And in such a social system, only the scapegoat achieves nobility and truth.

Notes

1. Except for brief comments within larger studies of Faulkner's work, there have been few comprehensive attempts to deal with these stories. This is not to say that no studies exist but rather that, in my view, they are inadequate. Among the dozen articles that have appeared on "Dry September" in recent years, John B. Vickery, "Ritual and Theme in Faulkner's 'Dry September,'" *Arizona Quarterly*, 18 (Spring 1962), and Howard J. Faulkner, "The Stricken World of 'Dry September,'" *Studies in Short Fiction*, 10 (Winter 1973) are the best. Joseph W. Reed, Jr., gives "Dry September" space in his useful book, *Faulkner's Narrative* (New Haven: Yale University Press, 1973), as does Hyatt H. Waggoner, in *William Faulkner: From Jefferson to the World* (Lexington: University of Kentucky Press, 1959). Arthur L. Ford's early essay, "Dust and Dreams: A Study of Faulkner's 'Dry September,'" *College English*, 24 (December 1962), interprets the presence of the dust but does not deal with the story's sociological implications.

Bibliography on "Red Leaves" is even more limited than that available on "Dry September." In his essay "The Descent of the Gods: Faulkner's 'Red Leaves' and the Garden of the South," *Studies in Short Fiction*, 11 (Summer 1974), Gilbert H. Mullen notes: "Given the remarkable calibre of this short story, and the proliferation of Faulkner criticism in the past two decades, it is curious that this story remains unexplicated; to a large extent, this failure is a reflection of the cursory treatment of Faulkner's short fiction in most major studies of his work" (p. 244). In a footnote to this statement, Mullen goes on to specify the limitations of criticism on the story: "The only valid exception to this remark is Michael Millgate, who in *The Achievement of William Faulkner* (New York: Random House, 1965) makes an incisive evaluation of the significance of Faulkner's short fiction. Although he does not explicate 'Red Leaves,' Millgate thinks that the story is one of the best in *These Thirteen*. [Millgate makes the same statement about "Dry September."] In *William Faulkner: A Critical Study* (New York: Vintage, 1962), Irving Howe goes further than Millgate and terms the story one of the three best in contemporary American fiction, but Howe also fails to analyze 'Red Leaves' closely. Far more typical reactions to 'Red Leaves' are expressed by William Van O'Connor, who in *The Tangled Fire of William Faulkner* (Minneapolis: University of Minnesota Press, 1954) is frankly confused by the symbolism of the story; and by Hyatt Howe Waggoner, who . . . doesn't mention the story at all."

Mullen's own essay helps considerably to redress the neglect he cites in the above statements. He fails to credit Charles H. Nilon, *Faulkner and the Negro* (New York: Citadel Press, 1965) for devoting five pages to analysis of the story and does not mention one useful article by Robert W. Funk, "Satire and Existentialism in Faulkner's 'Red Leaves,'" *Mississippi Quarterly*, 25 (Summer 1972).

2. William J. Cash, *The Mind of the South* (New York: Vintage, 1942), p. 307.

3. Robert Funk supports this reading to a point but insists that the story becomes a "universal comment on human mortality" (p. 348). I agree more with Mullen's reading: "For rather than attacking the cultural ethic of the Old South directly, he creates a parable on slavery by casting the Indians in the role of plantation masters, while the blacks, rather than being an economic asset, become useless chattel. In short, he develops a startling conceit in which plantation culture and the institution of slavery that supported it are reduced to decadence and parody" (p. 245).

4. Howard Faulkner suggests that Minnie originated the accusation of rape (p. 48). He states, further: "It is as if in their attempt to destroy another human being, Minnie Cooper and McLendon have succeeded in destroying their own humanity as well" (p. 49). Ralph Haven Wolfe and Edgar F. Daniels, in "Beneath the Dust of 'Dry September,'" *Studies in Short Fiction*, 1 (Winter 1964), suggest, more blatantly, that "Minnie Cooper . . . is surely motivated by something far more specialized than the desire, as Professor Ford says, 'to recapture her past glory'. . . . [W]ith whisky and with her determined association with the young people, she has managed until this moment to hide from herself the increasingly evident truth of her 'dry September.' Like the lynchers, she has reached a crisis fully sexual in its meaning" (pp. 158–59).

However, there is no evidence in the text to support the interpretation that Minnie originated an "accusation" against Will Mayes. Who can trace the origin of a rumor? And Faulkner makes it clear that the men in the barbershop do not even know what they are talking about until McLendon utters the word "rape."

5. "Dry September," in *Collected Stories of William Faulkner* (New York: Random House, 1943), pp. 169–84. The collection includes "Red Leaves," pp. 313–42. In order

to avoid unnecessary notation in the text, I have omitted page references in this chapter only. I have generally specified section numbers instead, and the reader who is familiar with the context of each story should have no difficulty locating particular lines.

6. For a comprehensive discussion of the sociology of lynching, see John Dollard, *Caste and Class in a Southern Town* (Garden City, N.Y.: Doubleday, 1957).

7. Wolfe and Daniels propose a sexually oriented interpretation that moves far beyond my own suggestions here. They argue: "Behind the facade of social indignation lies this immensely powerful sexual preoccupation. The actual lynching . . . is not a community action. . . . [T]he degree of emotional involvement in the affair of the supposed rape is in direct proportion to the degree of the characters' own sexual maladjustment" (p. 158).

This is a tendentious reading of the story that does not consider that the barbershop acts as a microcosm for the community as a whole. The only people in the community who do not have representatives in the barbershop are women and Negroes. As Reed states, "The bond of the barbershop here cements a lynch mob; the community's concern for its inhabitants here only alienates and isolates Minnie. The boundary of the small town, in other stories marking the closeness of familiarity, here turns everything sour, septic, promotes rumor, and makes inevitable the violence of reaction" (p. 51).

It is possible to infer from Wolfe and Daniels's reading sexual motivation on the part of all the main characters. Wolfe and Daniels conclude their essay by stating that "the accusation . . . gives Minnie momentary respite from sexual death, the lynching . . . gives perverted sexual release to McLendon; the fraudulent protest . . . allows the 'virtuous' barber vicarious participation in the lynching" (p. 159). Although this motivation may be one aspect of the forces that build to the lynching, certainly Wolfe and Daniels do not mean to suggest that racial prejudice, what Reed terms "the violence of reaction," and the dry heat itself do not contribute in even more substantial ways to produce tension in the story.

8. Charles Nilon writes, "Will Mayes . . . is any Negro man. Like Hawthorne, and his attitude toward Hester's sin, Faulkner is more interested in examining the causes and results of lynching than he is in the crime itself. For this reason he does not give the details of Will Mayes' death" (p. 44). However, Mayes is not just *any* Negro man. As I point out in the text, he has tried to integrate himself into the community and therefore becomes a likely target of McLendon's wrath. Nilon is correct, I think, when he focuses on the lynching rather than the crime—particularly since, again, the crime originates not in direct accusation but in rumor.

9. Here again Wolfe and Daniels offer a distorted reading of the text. They accuse Hawkshaw of insidiously introducing Mayes's name into the conversation in the first place because he wants him to become the focus of the mob. "Once the name has entered the discussion, he is able to deny Will's guilt and protest against the proceedings to his heart's content, knowing full well that he is merely fanning the flames" (p. 159). If this is the case, McLendon certainly does not know it, and Hawkshaw risks his security in the town at the same time as he betrays his cowardice when he jumps into the ditch, refusing to accompany the mob any further.

10. Howard Faulkner focuses on the symbolism of the moon in "Dry September" and offers this interpretation of Hawkshaw's actions: "Only once in the story does the moon rise above its connection with Jefferson's physical and moral landscape . . ." —when Hawkshaw walks back to town after jumping from the car. Howard Faulkner concludes, "If Hawkshaw has not been able to save Will Mayes, he has at least been able to save himself" (p. 48). This reading partially corrects Wolfe and Daniels's interpretation, but it does not completely exonerate Hawkshaw of moral responsibility.

11. Hyatt Waggoner's interpretation of the story is well stated: "In the largest sense, the story may be seen as a parable of what happens to man in the wasteland where, driven by an intolerable sense of insecurity and isolation, faced by an overwhelming threat, he turns to sadistic violence as a means of asserting his existence. The story develops the insight that sadism and a sense of insecurity are closely linked" (*From Jefferson to the World*, p. 196).

12. For the best naturalistic description of tracking a man in a swamp I have ever read, see William Humphrey's autobiography, *Farther Off From Heaven* (New York: Knopf, 1977), pp. 82–97.

13. Charles Nilon states of the Indians that "it is learned from their conversation that they were powerless to take him against his will: 'But you turned him back?' 'He turned back. We feared for a moment'" (p. 42). In the context of the story the Indian states, "'we could smell something else, which we did not know. That was why we feared. . . .'" In my interpretation of the story, any fear the Indians have other than the fear of death itself is the fear that the body servant will turn back and not complete his race, their ritual.

14. Nilon supports this point. "It is as if his flight from the Indians was merely an abstraction to which his intelligence had not given meaning, for he does not realize that he does not wish to die until the poison bite of the snake has given him an immediate fear of death" (p. 43). Mullen calls this the body servant's "moment of absolute dignity" in which "he manages to hold the horror of death in abeyance" (p. 247).

15. Nilon interprets the story differently at this point. "After he discovers through the snake's bite that he wants to live, he is afraid of dying. The slave gives up flight, not because he has fear of the Indians, but as an acceptance of the inevitable" (p. 42). We see the body servant sitting on a log singing at the end of section 5. Faulkner writes, "His voice was clear, full, with a quality wild and sad. 'Let him have time,' the Indians said, squatting, patient, waiting. He ceased and they approached." The Negro does not give himself up, as Nilon implies, but recognizes that he has been captured by the Indians, who praise him: "'You ran well. Do not be ashamed.'"

16. *Faulkner in the University*, ed. Frederick L. Gwynn and Joseph L. Blotner (Charlottesville: University of Virginia Press, 1959), p. 39.

5

Light in August: **Violence and Excommunity**

From the earliest formation of communities in America, religion served as a principle of exclusion. The elect defined themselves by excommunicating the damned, as in *The Scarlet Letter*. In southern culture and in Faulkner's narratives, Puritanism survived in the form of Calvinist fundamentalism. The community no longer defined itself in strictly religious terms, but its need for definition by exclusion, expressed in "Red Leaves" by the Indians' attempts to define things by what they are not, remained. Melville translates social isolation into a metaphysical quest; Faulkner studies the way in which social exclusion results from metaphysical isolation. The Salem witch trials were over, but they were replaced, in the postwar South, with Negro lynchings.

In the Puritan community, as I have discussed in my reading of *The Scarlet Letter*, the worst social transgression was spiritual. As part of the doctrine of predestination, souls were born either saved or damned; and it was the spiritual task of every good Puritan to engage in "meditation," to search his soul for an indication of his own salvation. But for the arbitrary grace of God, any man would certainly find himself in hell. Jonathan Edwards's famous sermon, "Sinners in the Hands of an Angry God" (1741) reminded the Puritans:

> How dreadful is the state of those that are daily and hourly in danger of this great wrath and infinite misery! But this is the dismal case of every soul in this congregation that has not been born again. . . . If we knew that there was one person, and but one, in the whole congregation, that was to be the subject of this misery, what an awful thing it would be to think of! If we knew who it was, what an awful sight would it be to see such a person! How might all the rest of the congregation lift up a lamentable and bitter cry over him! . . . And it would

be no wonder if some persons, that now sit here, in some seats of this meeting-house, in health, quiet and secure, should be there before to-morrow morning.[1]

The "mark" in the Puritan community referred to a physical manifestation of God's will, reflecting the belief of the early Christians that, as Erving Goffman points out, *stigma* referred to "bodily signs of holy grace that took the form of eruptive blossoms on the skin."[2] However, the judgment concerning the usually ambiguous implications of the bodily signs lay in the province of the observers, not the afflicted individual. Any doubt that the Puritans could not resolve concerning the good or evil nature of the physical mark or moral irregularity led them to interpret the bearer as marked by Satan himself, and each Puritan citizen became the instrument of divine retribution.

The community's desire to reflect divine will in its social rituals was analogous to the individual's continual soul searching. It is not inconceivable that much of the social wrath exercised by Puritan communities was in fact generated by individual frustration; the inability of the individual to absolutely detect inner good, accompanied by his secret reluctance to probe too deeply, must certainly have led him to externalize his soul's search in the process of communal exclusion. Casting out devils was analogous to defining those who are saved: namely, those who successfully participate in the eradication of evil.

Olga Vickery's analysis of the relation between the individual and the community in *Light in August* is enlightening in this context and worth quoting at length:

> no matter how isolated and impenetrable the private world of an individual, he still has a physical and social existence in the public world which makes its demands of him. His comfort, if not his life, depends on his accepting and exemplifying in his own life those stereotypes which represent society's vision of itself and its past. And since withdrawal or rebellion are as much public acts as is affirmation, no-one can escape. Society has myths not only of the hero but also of the antagonist, and it has evolved rituals to deal with each. Collectively, Jefferson is Southern, White, and Elect, qualities which have meaning only within a context which recognizes something or someone as Northern or Black or Damned. This antithesis is periodically affirmed through the sacrifice of a scapegoat who represents, in fact or popular conviction, those qualities which must be rejected if Jefferson is to maintain its self-defined character.[3]

Man creates categories that give an individual social identification. "The sheer weight of generations," Vickery writes, "each in its turn

conforming to and therefore affirming this process of public label-
ling, establishes the labels not only as a matter of tradition but as a
kind of revealed truth."[4]

The antithesis and the process of public labeling that Vickery
describes in Faulkner may also be viewed in Hawthorne, as my
study of *The Scarlet Letter* indicates. By pointing out these concerns,
Vickery implicitly allows us to compare Faulkner's fictional world
with Hawthorne's. Joanna's ancestors originated in Exeter, New
Hampshire, and as Peter Swiggart writes, Calvin Burden "stands
for a tradition of New England Puritanism that is related in both
spirit and doctrinal roots to the more evangelical Presbyterian sects
dominating the American Midwest and Deep South."[5] Historically,
Jefferson, Mississippi, is a direct descendant of Boston and Salem,
Massachusetts.

However, many critics incorrectly interpret the significance of
Calvinism in *Light in August*. They see its heritage in the community's attitudes toward sin and the punishment of sin[6] as what one
critic terms "punitive religious moralism."[7] Therefore for these critics Christmas becomes a "victim" of Calvinism. In light of Vickery's
analysis and my own, *Light in August* demonstrates not the simple
consequences of Puritan moralism but rather the way the Puritans'
habit of mind has determined the quality of community life in
America. Francois Pitavy writes about Christmas: "While rejecting
Calvinism as a religion, he does retain its modes of thought."[8] What
I take Pitavy to mean here is that Christmas "becomes" a
Calvinist—but not a "religious moralist." He does "become" a Puritan, in my analysis, not only because he is the object of the Jefferson
community's "periodic affirmation" of its "self-defined character,"
but also because he "volunteers" to become its sacrificial victim. He
seems to believe in the very antithesis by which Vickery characterizes his community.

In such a world, where an individual's relation to the community
receives the support of dogma, social definition can seem to ease
metaphysical isolation, can provide one cure for the "hypos." In
Light in August, as I will demonstrate in this chapter, Joe Christmas focuses on stigma as surely as Hester Prynne or Arthur Dimmesdale, as Ahab or Ishmael, in his search for an identity. The
stigma he chooses as a vehicle, unlike the scarlet letter, cannot be
removed once he embraces it; and unlike the whale, cannot be de-
stroyed without destroying himself. Yet Christmas discovers, ironically, that he can only achieve social identity by allowing himself to
be discredited. As Cleanth Brooks writes, "Faulkner's story of Joe

Christmas can thus be read as an account of a thoroughly alienated individual, a modern Ishmael who lives in chronic revolt against every kind of community. . . ."[9] It is society's fault that Christmas has no identity of his own; by pursuing discreditability, he forces society to yield him one. The most we can definitively say about Christmas is that he achieves the status of a marked man in Jefferson and that this allows him to transcend his metaphysical isolation. Like the body servant in "Red Leaves," he has no choice but to run his life's race. And like the body servant, he has nowhere to run but into the hands of his pursuers.

I

No character in American fiction emerges as tragically marked as Joe Christmas. Unlike Hester or Dimmesdale, Christmas neither stands accused nor recognizes his accusers. And unlike Ishmael, who defines his condition in metaphysical terms, Christmas cannot even understand his crime. His very name a travesty of redemption and rebirth, the burden of transcending social, moral, and ontological isolation seems to fall to the survivors—Lena, Byron, and Hightower. As Ilse Dusoir Lind interprets Christmas's role in the novel, "Its relation to the remaining narratives may be schematically indicated as follows: the Christmas tragedy, a tale of personal and social violence, poses the problem which the remaining narratives must resolve."[10]

The relationship between the Christmas story and the remaining narratives emphasizes the separation that exists between Christmas's social position and that of the other major characters. Yet although the novel concentrates on Christmas's struggle, we might describe *Light in August* as a spectrum of excommunication, of exclusion from community.[11] Though each is marked and isolated for different reasons, Byron, Lena, Joanna, and Hightower share the security Hester Prynne experienced as a result of her well-defined social position as an outcast. Their isolation has enabled them to achieve social invisibility and a stable anonymity.

Byron Bunch, self-isolated, stands at one extreme. Byron chooses not to participate in the community, keeps his own time on Saturdays, and does not reveal the details of his intensely private life to his fellow workers. "Hightower alone knows where he goes and what he does."[12] Byron pays no price within the community for his anonymity; he occupies the safest position on the spectrum of individual isolates.[13] Unlike Byron's, Lena Grove's physical appearance makes visible the most intimate details of her private life. She senses her own alienation at the same time as she accepts Armstid's aid.

> "It's a strange thing," she says.
> "How folks can look at a strange young gal walking the road in your shape and know that her husband has left her?" (p. 10)

Her pregnancy marks her violation of the community's social and moral code. Armstid knows "exactly" what his wife will say, and thinks, "'But that's the woman of it. Her own self one of the first ones to cut the ground from under a sister woman, she'll walk the public country herself without shame because she knows that folks, menfolks, will take care of her. She don't care nothing about womenfolks. It wasn't any woman that got her into what she don't even call trouble. Yes, sir. You just let one of them get married or get into trouble without being married, and right then and there is where she secedes from the woman race and species and spends the balance of her life trying to get joined up with the man race. That's why they dip snuff and smoke and want to vote'" (p. 12). Lena's transgression is social and her exclusion is social—she is forced to choose between shame and "secession from the woman race."[14]

Joanna and Hightower both hold positions in the community that are considerably less secure than those held by Byron and Lena, yet do not approach the degree of instability nor evoke the level of violence that Christmas's does. Joanna is shunned and ignored because the town's remembrance of her ancestors has survived sixty years: "But it still lingers about her and about the place: something dark and outlandish and threatful, even though she is but a woman and but the descendant of them whom the ancestors of the town had reason (or thought that they had) to hate and dread. But it is there: the descendants of both in their relationship to one another ghosts, with between them the phantom of the old spilled blood and the old horror and anger and fear" (p. 42). But Joanna has achieved an agreement of sorts with the community; she pays for her anonymity with isolation and spinsterdom. Even after her death, she pays, Faulkner suggests—or she would pay if they could make her pay: "They would never forgive her and let her be dead in peace and quiet. Not that. Peace is not that often" (p. 273).[15]

Hightower's offense involved moral transgression—his wife's adultery and suicide—and indirectly the "sacrilege" he preached in church. First the community forces him to resign from the pulpit. "Then the town was sorry with being glad, as people sometimes are sorry for those whom they have at last forced to do as they wanted them to" (p. 64). Later, a rumor circulates that Hightower, himself unfaithful with his Negro cook, was responsible for his wife's infidelity. "And that's all it took; all that was lacking. Byron listened quietly, thinking to himself how people everywhere are about the same, but that it did seem that in a small town, where evil is harder to accomplish, where opportunities for privacy are scarcer, that people can invent more of it in other people's names. Because that was all it required: that idea, that single idle word blown from mind to mind" (p. 66). The rumor leads the Klan to lynch Hightower, and they almost succeed; they leave him tied to a tree, unconscious. Hightower escapes the fate of Christmas—"then all of a sudden the whole thing seemed to blow away, like an evil wind" (p. 67). Both a white man and a minister, Hightower avoids the wrath of the lynch mob, but he is simply and virtually excommunicated—first from his church, then from his community.[16]

It is finally Christmas who poses the severest threat to the group's collective identity. As Frank Baldanza writes, contrasting Lena's "indisguisably pregnant condition" with Christmas's plight, Christmas "could easily disguise his problem" but "chooses not to take advantage of the disguise, and he is also not oblivious to the social disapproval, but purposely stimulates the prejudices of whites and Negroes alike."[17] "Inescapably," therefore, "Joe is forced into the ritual of pursuit and lynching performed almost casually by a society which has been elaborating it for generations."[18] The novel considers Christmas's struggle as an ongoing process, as an unstable, ill-defined, but dynamic and inevitable and even desirable movement towards stigmatization, community exclusion, and concomitant crucifixion. Precisely the reverse of Lind's formulation of the relationship among the several narratives of *Light in August*, the chronology of the novel and the separation the novel creates between present and past indicate that Christmas works out the personal and social struggles of the other major characters.

The novel's past includes the history of Joe's childhood and his relationship with Joanna. The present time of narration includes only the ten days just following the murder of Joanna (the distant view of the burning house introduces the reader to the Christmas story). The novel suspends resolution of the "present" situation, in which Lena is pregnant, Byron alone, and Hightower excommunicated, until Christmas's story can be told. And it does not dramatize the isolation or excommunication that the other characters experience (with the possible exception of Lena). Hightower's confrontation with the Klan, for example, is reported rather than enacted. Only in Christmas's case does Faulkner narrate the drama of social exclusion. Redemption exists in the Christmas story, Faulkner seems to be saying, only as representation; Christmas reenacts the social and metaphysical isolation of every individual cast out from community.

The exposition of Christmas's story does not become dramatic until it is placed within a local context. Christmas commits many acts of violence and murder that are either dramatized (as with McEachern) or reported to us (as with the Northern prostitute Christmas almost kills, p. 212). But Christmas's "past" does not become "present" until, as Faulkner expresses it, "one afternoon the street had become a Mississippi country road" (p. 213). Faulkner explores for the space of a novel Christmas's murder of Joanna rather than his murder of McEachern because the later murder possesses symbolic significance that McEachern's does not.[19] As a judge might say, Christmas committed an unpremeditated crime, an act of passion. But because striking McEachern *is* an isolated, personal act (a family matter), it is an act of violence that society, composed of institutions rather than individuals, absorbs unaffected. Thus, although we may trace Christmas's act of rage to the institutional religious and family pressures that McEachern represents, the fictional society does not, cannot, interpret it this way. Once Christmas enters a community for the first time in his life, his actions acquire potential social significance. Joanna becomes a symbolic victim of social injustice.

Light in August emphasizes a distinction between society and community. Cleanth Brooks writes, "W. H. Auden has provided us with a helpful definition [of community]. It is more than a crowd—a crowd is a group of individuals who come together purely at random. ... A community is also more than a society. A society is a group of individuals related by function. ... [A community] is a group of people held together by common likes and dislikes, loves and hates held in common, shared values. Where there is a loss of shared values, communities may break down into mere societies or even be reduced to mobs."[20] The orphanage in which Christmas lives for his first five years (an institution, not a home), introduces him to society's demands and expectations before he ever learns his place within a family or kin (community) group context. He learns that he is different from the other children (they call him "nigger" and Doc Hines constantly watches him) but at the same time he cannot achieve separation from them. His identity derives from his functional position in the orphanage, and he is therefore not surprised when Doc Hines takes him away by night—it has happened before to other children. When he mutely agrees to accompany McEachern, he trades one institution for another. McEachern would have him devout and obedient, but creates only rebellion in Christmas. As an individual, Christmas has no place in the McEachern household and he constantly tries to achieve separation from it—by cruelty to Mrs. McEachern and disobedience to McEachern.[21] As if he can find out who he is only by achieving this separation, he is a man ever isolated from community but never separated from those institutional forces already set in motion at his birth that marked him out, isolated him, before he could ever have become aware of them. As a result, he cannot escape mirroring the internal conflicts in his social world.[22]

Goffman's sociological model of stigma, as I summarized it briefly in my discussion of Hawthorne,[23] is useful in understanding the conflict of identity in Christmas. Born a discreditable individual, he looks like a white man (Byron calls him "foreign") but is really (or thinks he may be) black. If we compare Christmas's motives before he reaches Jefferson, and specifically those before he murders Joanna, with his motives after he has committed the murder, we find that his basic desire, wherever he goes, is to discredit himself. Until he murders Joanna, the attempt is always either temporary or unsuccessful.

While he travels in the South he uses white prostitutes, then tells them he is a Negro to avoid paying. In the North this ruse does not work. When he meets a woman who does not mind that he is black (in effect, does not respond to him as outside her "caste" when he discredits himself), he almost kills her.

> He was sick after that. He did not know until then that there were white women who would take a man with a black skin. He stayed sick for two years. Sometimes he would remember how he had once tricked or teased white men into calling him a negro in order to fight them, to beat them or be beaten; now he fought the negro who called him white. He was in the north now, in Chicago and then Detroit. He lived with negroes, shunning white people. He ate with them, slept with them, belligerent, unpredictable, uncommunicative. He now lived as man and wife with a woman who resembled an ebony carving. At night he would lie in bed beside her, sleepless, beginning to breathe deep and hard. He would do it deliberately, feeling, even watching, his white chest arch deeper and deeper within his ribcage, trying to breathe into himself the dark odor, the dark and inscrutable thinking and being of negroes, with each suspiration trying to expel from himself the white blood and the white thinking and being. (p. 212)

This passage points out the various ways Christmas attempted to achieve isolation from his fellows, in effect to externalize the inner isolation he felt by separating himself from the society that created him. He had once "tricked or teased" white men into fighting with him—as if even the act of fighting, of finding himself being beaten, earned him more of a place among them than he felt while simply discreditable. For awhile, the name "Negro" is not enough to discredit him, especially in the North—so that he tries to assimilate blackness by living with the woman "who resembled an ebony carving." He wants to make his own situation more visible, to expel from himself "the white blood and the white thinking and being" in order to achieve permanent discredit. But he is not successful. He is forced to fight "the negro who called him white." Later in his life, when he walks through Freedman Town in the hours just prior to the murder, he is also "mistaken" for a white man by some Negro men.

It is not until Christmas enters Jefferson that the nebulous social forces at work in him "on the street which was to run for fifteen years" manifest themselves. As Peter Swiggart writes, "In her inverted religious feeling, in her obsession with the Negro race, and in her sexual masochism, Joanna Burden mirrors the important features of Joe Christmas's destiny."[24] The narrative telescopes from the small town of Jefferson to the Burden house to Joanna's kitchen and finally to Christmas climbing in the window: "a shadow returning without a sound and without locomotion to the allmother of obscurity and darkness" (p. 216). Joanna is the phantom that "looms" on Christmas's horizon. The language here ("returning" and "allmother") suggests that Christmas finds himself in a familiar context, and as he becomes aware of the associations that the kitchen generates, he finds himself led "twentyfive years back down the street" to Mrs. McEachern. "He ate something from an invisible dish, with invisible fingers: invisible food. . . . 'It's peas,' he said aloud. 'For sweet Jesus. Field peas cooked with molasses'" (pp. 216–17).

Joanna Burden carries the "burden" of southern history—the cross of the Negro—and the novel also portrays her as Joe's particular burden. All of the separate conflicts in his early life—women and sex, racial identity and institutional pressures, religion and violence—coalesce in his three years with Joanna. Ilse Dusoir Lind comments, "That Faulkner intends to equate Joanna and Joe as victims of analogous cultural neuroses is suggested in his designation of them as name-twins (Joe and Joanna) and in his care to supply each with a genealogy covering three generations. . . . An astonishing symmetry emerges when the biographical and psychological data contained in the accounts of Joanna and Joe are assembled. The forces which shaped Christmas are identical with those which shaped Joanna."[25] The connection is an obvious one; Faulkner does not need to stylize Joanna in order to make the reader aware of the combination of influences she represents for Joe. There are moments in the narrative when the connection is made—when "invisible food" becomes field peas, for example; or when Christmas keeps his bootlegging a secret from Joanna. "Very likely she would not have objected. But neither would Mrs McEachern have objected to the hidden rope; perhaps he did not tell her for the same reason that he did not tell Mrs McEachern. Thinking of Mrs McEachern and the rope, and of the waitress whom he had never told where the money came from which he gave to her, and now of his present mistress and the whiskey, he could almost believe that it was not to make money that he sold the whiskey but because he was doomed to conceal always something from the women who surrounded him" (p. 247). Mrs. McEachern in particular prefigures Joe's relationship with Joanna, and he throws Joanna's food on the floor just as he did when he was a foster child.

II

The narrative design rather than an actual narrator (conspicuously absent in *Light in August* except as the embodiment of a "force" in the final third), directs the reader's interpretation of Joe Christmas's actions. A summary of the events that take place at the beginning of the novel illustrate Faulkner's exploitation of narrative technique—in particular the flashback—to focus the reader's attention on the significance of the past as it relates to one particular event in the present—Joanna's murder.

Chapter 2 introduces Joe Christmas as an isolate. Byron Bunch describes his first appearance at the planing mill and his association with the other stranger, Brown. During the next two chapters, Hightower sits alone, then with Byron, who mentions the murder. At this point the novel still focuses on Byron's encounter with Lena. Chapter 5 initiates the abrupt narrative shift to the Christmas story. "It was after midnight. Though Christmas had been in bed for two hours, he was not yet asleep" (p. 95). This chapter dramatizes the few hours just prior to the murder when Christmas both experiences the fatality precedent to an action ("*Something is going to happen to me. I am going to do something,*" p. 97) and explains in advance his motives ("She ought not to started praying over me"). Chapter 6, with equal abruptness, begins the retrospective chronological narration of Christmas's life, and throughout this section of the novel, Lena and Hightower do not appear. The narration of Christmas's past ends with chapter 12 and the last scenes in this chapter build up to the moment of the murder, then shift to Christ-

mas's actions immediately following the murder out on the road—
the narrative omits the murder itself. It also omits the hours just
prior to the murder—because these have already been dramatized
back in chapter 5.

Both in its content and in its position in the narrative, chapter
five thus indicates that the murder of Joanna is the central dramatic
event prior to Christmas's death, the particular action toward which
the narration of Christmas's past builds, and it stresses Christmas's
motivation and psychological struggle just prior to the murder.[26]
His walk through Jefferson in the few hours before going back to the
house leads him through Freedman Town and represents in small
that longer walk on the lonely street that becomes the symbol of
Christmas's life. "Nothing can look quite as lonely as a big man
going along an empty street. Yet though he was not large, not tall,
he contrived somehow to look more lonely than a lone telephone pole
in the middle of a desert. In the wide, empty, shadow-brooded street
he looked like a phantom, a spirit, strayed out of its own world, and
lost" (p. 106). When Christmas entered Freedman Town, however,
"then he found himself." "On all sides, even within him, the bodiless
fecund-mellow voices of negro women murmured. It was as though
he and all other manshaped life about him had been returned to the
lightless hot wet primogenitive Female" (p. 107). He associates
blackness with femaleness, and subsequently runs from both. In a
moment, he associates all the streets of his betrayals (and implicitly
the street corner where he met Bobbie) with his present actions: "He
could see the street down which he had come, and the other street,
the one which had almost betrayed him; and further away and at
right angles, the far bright rampart of the town itself, and in the
angle between the black pit from which he had fled with drumming
heart and glaring lips. No light came from it, from here no breath,
no odor. It just lay there, black, impenetrable, in its garland of
Augusttremulous lights. It might have been the original quarry,
abyss itself" (p. 108). The meanings of "quarry"—source, bottomless
pit, and object of the hunt—all connote Christmas's dilemma in
these hours prior to the murder: he too contains within himself the
source of his conflict, yet he has been forced into it by a paradox
outside his individual control, and is both his own victim and society's. He certainly premeditates some kind of action, if not actual
murder, in these hours: "His way was sure" (p. 108). Joanna is the
single embodiment of the abyss within Joe's reach.

In the final outcome of the novel, Joanna's murder is subsidiary to
Christmas's lynching. After Joanna's murder, however, the
townspeople emerge as a community acting in concert. *Light in Au-*

gust examines the murder from the point of view of the townspeople as a necessary prelude to exploring why they lynch Christmas.[27] Unlike "Dry September" or "Red Leaves," in which the fictional worlds are limited to an essentially closed system of townspeople (the traveling drummers do not live in Jefferson, but none of them either enters the town or leaves it within the span of the story), *Light in August* focuses on a man who has never been a member of a community—and community, after chapter 12, becomes an obtrusive presence for the first time, both in the novel and in Christmas's life.

The first seven pages of chapter 13 recall in detail the language, situation, and source of conflict in "Dry September." The short story opens with a simile comparing the spread of rumor to "a fire in dry grass." Chapter 13 opens with a real fire: "Within five minutes after the countrymen found the fire, the people began to gather" (p. 271). The people emerge "as though out of thin air"—and begin to function as a community. Later, in a decided echo of the short story, they gather in front of the jail—"the clerks, the idle, the countrymen in overalls; the talk. It went here and there about the town, dying and borning again like a wind or a fire" (p. 330). The narrative summarizes their initial reaction: "Among them the casual Yankees and the poor whites and even the southerners who had lived for a while in the north, who believed aloud that it was an anonymous negro crime committed not by a negro but by Negro and who knew, believed, and hoped that she had been ravished too: at least once before her throat was cut and at least once afterward" (p. 272). The community's reaction lacks a focus at its inception in the novel; nor have they found a leader. As yet the men remain anonymous who, "with pistols already in their pockets began to canvass about for someone to crucify" (p. 272).

As a result of her murder, Joanna Burden becomes the symbol of a threat to community identity in much the same way as Minnie Cooper's rumored rape threatened the identity and security of the townspeople in "Dry September." The language Faulkner uses echoes the short story almost word for word: "And the women came too, the idle ones in bright and sometimes hurried garments, with secret and passionate and glittering looks and with secret frustrated breasts" (p. 273). They rally around Joanna as if she were a battle standard (*"Murdering a white woman the black son of a,"* p. 275) in spite of the fact that "none of them had ever entered the house. While she was alive they would not have allowed their wives to call on her" (p. 275). She had been "a foreigner, an outlander" (p. 272), although she was born and died in Jefferson.

When the sheriff arrives at the scene of the crime, he seizes a Negro and begins to question him. The deputy strikes the Negro twice with a strap and forces him to reveal that Brown and Christmas lived alone in a cabin in back of the house. The information saves the Negro from being lynched himself, but forces within the community become manifest and lead shortly to Brown's confession that Christmas is a Negro and Joanna's murderer. Faulkner's phrase for the unleashing of these forces is "an emotional barbecue" (p. 273).[28]

The same sentiments that reverberate through the barbershop in "Dry September" permeate *Light in August* as well. "It was as if the very initial outrage of the murder carried in its wake and made of all subsequent actions something monstrous and paradoxical and wrong, in themselves against both reason and nature" (p. 280). The atmosphere of McLendon's military defense, preventing the murder and violation of "mothers and wives and sisters" in "Dry September," becomes expanded in *Light in August* in Faulkner's characterization of Percy Grimm. Born too late to fight in World War I, until he discovered the "civilian-military act," Grimm was "like a man who had been for a long time in a swamp, in the dark. It was as though he not only could see no path ahead of him, he knew that there was none" (p. 426). It is not Christmas per se who gives Grimm's life new direction, but rather his crime that has enabled Grimm to achieve at last his position in the community as its civilian defender:

> Then suddenly his life opened definite and clear. . . . *He could now see his life opening before him, uncomplex and inescapable as a barren corridor, completely freed now of ever again having to think or decide, the burden* which he now assumed and carried as bright and weightless and martial as his insignatory brass: a sublime and implicit faith in physical courage and blind obedience, and a belief that the white race is superior to any and all other races and that the American uniform is superior to all men, and that all that would ever be required of him in payment for this belief, this privilege, would be his own life (p. 247, my italics)

As Cleanth Brooks writes, ". . . Percy Grimm is a man who needs desperately to be felt a part of the community. He needs it so much that he attempts to seize the community values by violence. He yearns to wear a uniform *marking* him as the community's representative and defender . . ." (my italics).[29]

Curiously, Faulkner uses comparable language to describe Percy Grimm's effect on Christmas. The two passages show that what Grimm and Christmas have in common is a desperate desire for an acknowledged position in the community. Chapter 14 dramatizes the beginning of the chase, then shifts to Christmas and the perspective of the fleeing scapegoat. He knows that they are hunting him with dogs, and he hears his pursuers track him to the cottonhouse where he exchanged his own shoes for a pair of brogans—"the black shoes, the black shoes smelling of negro" (p. 313).

> Looking down at the harsh, crude, clumsy shapelessness of them, he said "Hah" through his teeth. *It seemed to him that he could see himself being hunted by white men at last* into the black abyss which had been waiting, trying, for thirty years to drown him and into which now and *at last* he had actually entered, bearing now upon his ankles the definite and ineradicable gauge of its upward moving. . . . He breathes deep and slow, feeling with each breath himself diffuse in the neutral grayness, becoming one with loneliness and quiet that has never known fury or despair. *"That was all I wanted,"* he thinks, in a quiet and slow amazement. "That was all, for thirty years. That didn't seem to be a whole lot to ask in thirty years." (p. 313, my italics)

The passage recalls, and seems to contradict, the earlier moment in chapter 5, when Christmas leaves Freedman Town and finds himself among white people. He sees "the white faces intent and sharp," four people sitting around a card table, and thinks, also, "'That's all I wanted. That dont seem like a whole lot to ask'" (p. 108). It is the peace, sense of security, of "becoming one with loneliness" that the moments share in Christmas's longings, and yet, in chapter 14, the peace seems to *result* from Christmas's knowledge that he has become a quarry.

The days after the murder, and after Christmas has given direction to the chase by appearing in the Negro church, produce a period of clarity for him. He feels a sense of peace now that they are hunting him *at last,* now that, by running, he has externalized his inner sense of being isolated (his discreditability has become discredit, social stigma). The chase becomes for him a ritual similar to the race the body servant runs in "Red Leaves." He knows this, and he knows that his pursuers know it intuitively, because several people recognize him in broad daylight along the road outside of Jefferson, and do not capture him.

> "They recognized me too," he thinks. "Them, and that white woman. And the negroes where I ate that day. Any of them could have captured me, if that's what they want. Since that's what they all want: for me to be captured. But they all run first. They all want me to be captured, and then when I come up ready to say Here I am *Yes I would say Here I am I am tired I am tired of running of having to carry my life like it was a basket of eggs* they all run away. Like there is a rule to catch me by, and to capture me that way would not be like the rule says." (p. 319, Faulkner's italics).

Just as he knew his direction on the road from Freedman Town on his way to his confrontation with Joanna, he knows the rules for his capture. "Again his direction is straight as a surveyor's line, disregarding hill and valley and bog. Yet he is not hurrying. He is like a man who knows where he is and where he wants to go and how much time to the exact minute he has to get there in" (p. 320). Such a description of Christmas suggests a complete revolution in his thinking about himself as a result of the previous few days. No longer is he a man without direction, without identity. He has become the hunted, the victim, and he "is like a man who knows where he is" (p. 320). Christmas, like Grimm, has been "completely freed now of ever again having to think or decide" (p. 426).

The novel dramatizes the lynching as a chess game, in which both Grimm and Christmas act as pawns for some Player (pp. 437–39). In an echo of the chase in "Red Leaves," the two men look at one another, "almost face to face": "For an instant they glared at one another, the one stopped in the act of crouching from the leap, the other in midstride of running, before Grimm's momentum carried him past the corner" (p. 437). Even Grimm's emotional participation in his own action is suspended for a moment when he comes upon the cabin where he expects to find Christmas: "He knew now that he had lost a point. That Christmas had been watching his legs all the time beneath the house. He said, 'Good man'" (p. 437). The lynching, then, for Grimm and the townspeople, as well as for Christmas, partakes of a certain quality of ritual. As Pitavy writes, "Once they believe it, he [Christmas] becomes a Negro in their eyes, and they treat him as such. The community needs a scapegoat, and that this should be a Negro is reassuring: the ritual punishment purges the white community after the threat to its integrity, and confirms the code for and by which it lives. To doubt the justice of the code would be to doubt the identity of the community. . . ."[30]

Christmas and Grimm are individual manifestations of forces that forever conflict beneath the social surface and that, from time to time, emerge in moments of dramatic action, unpredictable in advance, yet, as well, completely and absolutely predetermined. The predetermined nature of these two men as forces that have erupted within the community suggests the way the Calvinist sensibility has informed Faulkner's narrative as well as his fictional community. The novel becomes "holistic," in the way Harry Henderson uses the term in his discussion of *The Scarlet Letter*.[31] As Peter Swiggart writes, "The two characters are driven by the same excess of puritan zeal even though the one figure is consistently self-righteous and the other marks himself as a deserving victim. . . . Together they act out the drama of the Southern puritan mind and its tragic dilemma. . . . Thus Joe Christmas becomes his own pursuer and Percy Grimm his own victim."[32]

Both murderer and Negro, Christmas has committed social transgressions that sufficiently motivate his lynching, but Faulkner suggests an additional explanation for the excessive violence Christmas ultimately receives. The townspeople speculate: "'He dont look any more like a nigger than I do. But it must have been the nigger blood in him. It looked like he had set out to get himself caught like a man might set out to get married. . . . If he had not set fire to the house, they might not have found out about the murder for a month.'" Part of this speaker's incredulity centers on the fact that Christmas could easily have escaped. But Christmas wanted to be caught, or, like the body servant, recognized the inevitability of his capture—and the morning he comes into Mottstown, he spends his time going to the barbershop, buying some new clothes, and walking up and down the street, waiting for people to recognize him. The talk continues:

> " . . . Halliday saw him and ran up and grabbed him and said, 'Aint your name Chistmas?' and the nigger said that it was. He never denied it. He never did anything. He never acted like either a nigger or a white man. That was it. That was what made the folks so mad. For him to be a murderer and all dressed up and walking the town like he dared them to touch him, when he ought to have been skulking and hiding in the woods, muddy and dirty and running. It was like he never even knew he was a murderer, let alone a nigger too." (p. 331)

The speaker cannot tolerate the ambiguity of either Christmas's behavior or the clothes he wears—the new white man's clothes and the second-hand Negro brogans too big for him—which suggest the conflict he has struggled with throughout his life. "'He never acted like either a nigger or a white man. That was it. That was what made the folks so mad.'" Christmas does not markedly manifest either his race or his crime, and it is this that increases the people's anger.

The passage supports the novel's interpretation of Christmas. Because he is only discreditable instead of visibly discredited, he needs to threaten the community severely before they can recognize him as an alien, before they will recognize him at all; and because the members of the community do not, cannot recognize him for what they think he is (black) even after they capture him, the threat to them is greater (it seems to come from inside, since Christmas seems to be white) and they react violently. Thus Percy Grimm not only murders Christmas; he castrates him too ("'Now you'll let white women alone, even in hell,'" p. 439). As Swiggart writes, "The crucifixion image which dominates this climactic scene derives its meaning less from Joe's martyrdom than from the violence of society's retribution. The men who watch the scene are confronted with their own need for violent expiation. . . ."[33] Yet as Vickery, who calls Grimm the "young priest" of the occasion, points out, "the elect and white of Jefferson castrate and slay the Negro according to ancient custom, but instead of purification, they are left with a sense of their own guilt and self-doubt."[34] We don't see much of the community after their catharsis, but "Dry September" teaches us that Vickery's conclusion must be accurate. Certainly McLendon in the short story is left with a sense of his *own* "guilt and self-doubt."

Christmas has learned to expect victimization and crucifixion almost from birth. When as a boy he is beaten by McEachern in the stable, he faces the man like "a post or tower upon which the sentient part of him mused like a hermit, contemplative and remote with ecstasy and selfcrucifixion" (p. 150).[35] But he does not free himself of the inward-impelling desire for movement and discredit, to achieve a permanent position, even of outcast, in the social framework, until the town of Jefferson, aiding in his search for self-realization, recognizes him as murderer and Negro and hunts him with dogs. As Alfred Kazin puts it, "this man is *born* an abstraction and is seeking to become a person. . . ." Christmas "attains in this first moment of selfhood, the martyrdom that ends it."[36] Faulkner himself said about Christmas that "He knew that he would never know what he was, and his only salvation in order to live with himself was to repudiate mankind, to live outside the human race. And he tried to do that but nobody would let him. . . ."[37] Nobody would let him because in this very act of trying "to live outside the human race," Christmas embodies the divided conscience of his society.[38] From the viewpoint of the community as well as the individual, discreditability is the worst stigma of all.

III

We see Christmas for the last time in the moment of his death. "He just lay there, with his eyes open and empty of everything save consciousness" (p. 439), and in that consciousness he finds peace. "For a long moment he looked up at them with peaceful and unfathomable and unbearable eyes." The imagery connotes resurrection, and the vision of Christmas that remains "will be there, musing, quiet, steadfast, not fading and not particularly threatful, but of itself alone serene, of itself alone triumphant" (p. 440). If Joanna's murder is the most significant dramatic event in the novel, Christmas's lynching is certainly the most significant symbolic event. Yet Faulkner's very emphasis on the quasi-spiritual significance of Christmas's death raises the much-debated critical problem of the novel's unity.[39] In particular, what is Gail Hightower's function in the novel, and why does Faulkner place the details of Christmas's death (chap. 19) before Hightower's history (chap. 20)? Again the novel's design aids our understanding. After Joanna's death, Faulkner explores the community's reaction; after Christmas's lynching, he explores Hightower's reaction. Faulkner's study of Grimm preceding the lynching articulates his examination of the communal impulse to violent action; his subsequent exploration of Hightower is a study of enlightened reaction, where Hightower, even in his name, becomes a register of symbolic significance for the reader.

Hightower's narrative of position contrasts with Christmas's narrative of process.[40] We see Hightower mainly, although not exclusively, sitting in his study window looking down on the street. Even the sign in front of his house Hightower himself refers to as "his monument" (p. 52). He indicates that he has long ago accepted what the townspeople did to him, telling Byron, "'They are good people. They must believe what they must believe, especially as it was I who was at one time both master and servant of their believing. And so it is not for me to outrage their believing nor for Byron Bunch to say that they are wrong. Because all that any man can hope for is to be permitted to live quietly among his fellows'" (p. 69). When Byron indirectly narrates Hightower's history in the opening chapters, it is *as* history that we are aware of it—because nothing in the novel's present moment interferes with Hightower's tranquillity until he hears about Joe Christmas.

Before the flashback to Christmas's childhood interrupts the Hightower narrative, it is clear (chaps. 3 and 4) that Hightower feels affected in some way by Christmas's ontological situation, before he even knows what Christmas has done. As Byron begins to report the fire and his encounter with Lena, one detail in his story moves Hightower. "'Part negro,' Hightower says. His voice sounds light, trivial, like a thistle bloom falling into silence without a sound, without any weight. He does not move. For a moment longer he does not move. Then there seems to come over his whole body, as if its parts were mobile like face features, that shrinking and denial, and Byron sees that the still, flaccid, big face is suddenly slick with sweat. But his voice is light and calm. 'What about Christmas and Brown and yesterday?' he says." (p. 83) When Byron finishes relating the event of "yesterday," Hightower is deeply affected. Byron sits, "watching across the desk the man who sits there with his eyes closed and the sweat running down his face like tears. Hightower speaks: 'Is it certain, proved, that he has negro blood? Think, Byron; what it will mean when the people—if they catch. . . . Poor man. Poor mankind'" (p. 93). Among all the outcast characters in *Light in August,* it is Hightower who speaks, Hightower who is deeply touched, because Hightower has confronted the lynch mob. His position, more than any of the others, approaches the Negro's on the spectrum of social exclusion. Neither his sacrilege nor his moral failings incensed the town as much as the suggestion that he has committed a crime against society—that "he was not a natural husband, a natural man, and that the negro woman was the reason" (p. 65). Hightower has experienced the power of social rumor, and his sweat indicates that his concern for Christmas goes deeper than empathy—as deep as fear.

When the narrative returns to Hightower after Joanna's murder, it finds him engaged in internal conflict. The tranquillity he possessed before he heard about Chistmas is gone. When he goes to the market, the earth seems to rock beneath him, and he thinks, "I wont! I wont! I have bought immunity. I have paid. I have paid'" (p. 292). Later, approaching "his sanctuary," his house, he repeats, "'I paid for it. I didn't quibble about the price. No man can say that. I just wanted peace; I paid them their price without quibbling'" (p. 293). Hightower feels involved with Joe Christmas before Byron ever approaches him with Mrs. Hines's appeal. The language of his denial, before meeting the Hineses and afterwards ("'It's not because I cant, dont dare to . . . it's because I wont! I wont! do you hear?,'" p. 370), suggests that Hightower is at some level reexperiencing his own excommunication as he witnesses Christmas's struggle, and that his refusal to take any part is an inability to understand his own past.

Not until Christmas dies does Hightower experience a clearer understanding. Hightower's own involvement in the lynching recalls Hawkshaw's attempt to stop McLendon in "Dry September." In the short story, Hawkshaw finds himself among the lynch mob (although not with them in principle) when they pick up Will Mayes. When Mayes strikes the members of the group, he strikes Hawkshaw, and Hawkshaw strikes him back. The ineffectiveness of his attempts to stop the lynching and his contradictory act of striking Mayes both lead Hawkshaw to jump out of the car. He is aware of the futility of his actions, and he retches beneath the moon. In *Light in August,* Hightower also finds himself among the lynchers, but when Christmas strikes him, he does not strike back. Instead, too late, he tries to protect him. The time when he might have been effective has passed, however, and he is permitted to make no sacrifices for Christmas. At the same time, his attempt suggests that he participates emotionally in Christmas's conflict.

Faulkner does not stress the act of Christmas's death as much as the necessity for Hightower to vicariously participate in it by witnessing. This explains why the description of Joe's death cannot be omitted as Joanna's is. Hightower stands with Percy Grimm at the crucifixion; and later in the evening, once again sitting at his study window, he begins to imaginatively relive his past. Because he has participated in crucifixion, first as victim, and now as implicated bystander, he begins to see how much guilt and responsibility he must bear for his own martyrdom. As he waits for the moment of sunset, when he expects to hear the galloping hooves, he watches the faces from his past moving before him on a wheel. The "wheel of thinking" begins to slow for him, "the power which propels it not yet aware" (p. 462), and Hightower begins to face his own unworthiness.

> He sees himself offer as a sop fortitude and forbearance and dignity, making it appear that he resigned his pulpit for a martyr's reasons . . . making it appear that he was being driven, uncomplaining, into that which he did not even then admit had been his desire since before he entered the seminary . . . allowing himself to be persecuted, to be dragged from his bed at night and carried into the woods and beaten with sticks, he all the while bearing in the town's sight and hearing, without shame, with that patient and voluptuos ego of the martyr, the air, the behavior, the *How long, O Lord* until, inside his house again and the door locked, he lifted the mask with voluptuous and triumphant glee: *Ah. That's done now. That's past now. That's bought and paid for now (p. 464)*[41]

Hightower's single desire, that which led him to the seminary, into marriage, and finally to Jefferson, is for detachment and supension, or a "high tower": "That was what the word seminary meant: quiet and safe walls within which the hampered and garmentworried spirit could learn anew serenity to contemplate without horror or alarm its own nakedness" (p. 453). Participating in Christmas's crucifixion by witnessing it catalyzes his contemplation of the self-horror and leads him into a kind of meditation.

Hightower's final catharsis occurs when he sees Christmas's face, and then one which he recognizes, finally, as Percy Grimm's—"Then it seems to him that some ultimate dammed flood within him breaks and rushes away" (p. 466). Hightower recognizes that he is both Christmas and Percy Grimm, both victim and accuser, and his realization leaves him "empty and lighter than a forgotten leaf and even more trivial than flotsam lying spent and still upon the window ledge which has no solidity beneath hands that have no weight" (p. 466).

It is necessary for Hightower to have witnessed before he gains understanding; Christmas's conflict becomes Hightower's (and the community's) vehicle for working out the meaning of communal exclusion. Christmas's death is justifiable because it leads Hightower to the moment of apocalyptic vision he has been waiting to have his entire life. Hightower has sat at his window before and seen his grandfather's cavalry rush by: "They have thundered past now and crashed silently on into the dusk; night has fully come" (p. 70). Earlier in the novel, the moment is not accompanied by vision. However, after Christmas's death, Hightower experiences a delay before he hears the hooves. "It is as though they had merely waited until he could find something to pant with, to be reaffirmed in triumph and desire with. . . ." (p. 466). Once he does hear them, they do not dissipate; "it seems to him that he still hears them: the wild bugles and the clashing sabres and the dying thunder of hooves" (p. 467).

In terms of the Hightower narrative, then, the significance of placing Christmas's death *prior* to Hightower's vision is clear. In order to understand fully the implications of the novel's design, we need to phrase the same question differently: why does Hightower's vision *succeed* Christmas's death? I have shown what meaning Christmas's crucifixion has for Hightower; what clarification, retrospectively, does Hightower's vision provide for understanding Christmas's death?

The relationship of meaning between the two narratives operates tautologically. Consider at least one other alternative Faulkner might have adopted: he might have reversed the order of chapters 19 and 20. Hightower's vision might have preceded Christmas's crucifixion in the narrative. Such an order, although it would retain the symbolic significance of the crucifixion for Hightower, would fail to stress the reciprocal significance of Hightower's vision for Christmas's death. Faulkner, then, risks anticlimax but with the effect of enlarging meaning, in spite of the fact that, as a result, critics in the past have failed to apprehend fully Hightower's function in the novel.

For Hightower demythologizes Christmas's crucifixion. Hightower's vision at the end of chapter 20 is not a religious revelation, what Beach Langston calls "his own limited 'imitation of Christ,'"[42] but rather an intense reliving of his grandfather's galloping hooves. In spite of the fact that Hightower is excommunicated from his

church, he is still presented as the most orthodox religious figure in
Light in August, and if any character is theologically and spiritually
prepared for a Christological vision, that person is Hightower. Of a
different nature entirely, his revelation acts as a corrective to a
merely symbolic Christian interpretation of Christmas's death. I do
not mean to imply that Faulkner avoids Christ-symbolism—this is
certainly not the case—but rather that his broader interpretation of
the Christian passion provide the framework for an exploration of
religion as a community tool.[43] It is not enough to state, as Hugh
Holman does, that the unity of *Light in August* is a product of
"Faulkner's uses of the Christ story."[44] It is not Faulkner who "uses"
the Christ story but the tradition of American community ritual
since the Puritans—whose "use" or "misuse" amounted to investing
social sanctions with religious significance. Part of Hightower's
function in the novel is to expose the community's use of religion to
provoke and excuse its own violent social fanaticism.

The Presbyterian church originated theories for the divine sanction of slavery during the religious controversies just prior to the
war, and, as William Cash points out in *The Mind of the South,*
certain issues took on religious significance for the southerner—
before and during the war, social symbols were made sacred. The
southern woman became one source of spiritual inspiration (consider McLendon's call to "war" in "Dry September"). As Cash expresses it, in the wake of northern accusations of southern miscege-
nation, the southern white woman became "the South's
Palladium"—"the standard for its rallying, the mystic symbol of its
nationality in the face of the foe. . . . And—she was the pitiful
Mother of God. Merely to mention her was to send strong men into
tears—or shouts. There was hardly a sermon that did not begin and
end with tributes in her honor, hardly a brave speech that did not
open and close with the clashing of shields and the flourishing of
swords for her glory. At the last, I verily believe, the ranks of the
Confederacy went rolling into battle in the misty conviction that it
was wholly for her that they fought."[45] Furthermore, when the war
was over, these sacred symbols continued to be catalysts for intense
emotional patriotism.

> Local patriotism was far from being dead in them, but nobody re-
> membered now that they had ever gone out to die merely for Virginia
> or Carolina or Georgia. In their years together, a hundred control
> phrases, struck from the eloquent lips of their captains in the smoke
> and heat of battle, had burned themselves into their brains—phrases
> which would ever after be to them as the sounding of trumpets and the
> rolling of drums, to set their blood to mounting, their muscles to
> tensing, their eyes to stinging, to call forth in them the highest loyal-

ties and the most active responses. And of these phrases the great master key was in every case the adjective Southern.[46]

In *Light in August,* elements of community identity are similarly imbued with sacred meaning. Hence the profusion of "ministers" of various kinds: McEachern the fundamentalist who acts as Christmas's spiritual guardian, preaching self-sacrifice, unquestioning devotion, and obedience—to McEachern; Joanna's father, who made the Negro his religion and preached abolition; Doc Hines, the minister of white supremacy, seizing the pulpit in Negro churches, "himself his own exhibit A" (p. 325); Percy Grimm, who ad-ministers community justice; Christmas himself, preaching no particular message, disrupting a Negro church service with shouts and anathema; and certainly Hightower, descendant of an avatar of heroism and glory (his grandfather killed in a chicken coop) and a rabid abolitionist (his father), who chooses the pulpit because he believes in more than his grandfather's legend—"He had believed in the church too, in all that it ramified and evoked" (p. 453). Lena Grove, herself not a minister, is looking for one.

Without exception, religion for each of these so-called ministers acts as an effective social defense, a preserving or sanctifying force for whatever personal conflict produces a need for bolstering principle or self-image. The clearest examples of the use of religion as a preserving element may be seen in Doc Hines, Joanna, and Hightower. Mrs. Hines tells how her husband came to be in jail the night Milly was born: "'He said he had to fight because he is littler than most men and so folks would try to put on him. . . . But I told him it was because the devil was in him. . . . And so he took it to himself then, because it was a sign'" (p. 352). Joanna sees herself as a savior, burdened with a black cross. She tells Joe, "'Escape it you cannot. The curse of the black race is God's curse. But the curse of the white race is the black man who will be forever God's chosen own because He once cursed him'" (p. 240). In other words, for Joanna, whom Faulkner describes as "the New England glacier exposed suddenly to the fire of the New England biblical hell,"[47] the black man's "curse" is his own humanity; the white man, attempting to deny *his,* is burdened with the black man as a symbol for the abnegation and denial. By installing herself as the spiritual advisor and private benefactress of the Negro colleges, Joanna protects herself from seeing her own "blackness," from recognizing her own repressed humanity. When it emerges, she ecstatically screams "'Negro! Negro!'" at Christmas—but she returns to prayer. Religion is her final defense: and significantly *because* she prays Christmas feels compelled to kill her. Hightower uses his pulpit to defend his calling to Jefferson and refers to his compulsion to seek the bulwark of religion as the spirit's "nakedness" (p. 453). The further this "nakedness" is removed from theology, the more violent its defense becomes. And Doc Hines is a raving fanatic. His preaching in the Negro churches does not even pretend to be consistent with any theology whatsoever.

In this context, the etymological distinction between "religion" and "theology" is as significant for Hightower as it was for Ishmael. "Theology" derives from Greek words meaning "the word of God," and has come to signify particular doctrine of particular gods. "Religion" has a much less specific origin. It means "to tie back, to bind back," to some source, some roots. For the fanatics in *Light in August,* and for the community that adopts violence in the name of God, religion involves binding, constricting, and protecting their root identity, their self-image ("'He said he had to fight because he is littler than most men'"), or their moral position (on the Negro). The violence that accompanies the personal fundamentalism of Hines and McEachern is manifest at a social level as well. Religion, not theology, becomes the principle of social exclusion and hence of community definition.[48]

At the same time, it becomes the *vehicle* for exclusion: it sanctions doing battle on the Lord's side—for McLendon and Percy Grimm. Religion *becomes* violence as well as the legal and political sanction for violence within the community that wishes to protect itself from internal conflict. Hightower is significant for Faulkner because he embraces theology rather than religion—he attempts to hide his nakedness behind his pulpit. However, it is not his sacrilege that provokes his excommunication but rather his reputed violation of "sacred" social code. When Hightower faces the Klan, theology yields to religious fanaticism. Hightower's significance for our understanding of community violence as it enacts Christmas's death is then clear: Hightower provides a vehicle by which Faulkner distinguishes between religion and theology, and religion becomes a social force.

Religion is the greatest barrier to Christmas's acceptance by society from his birth—because what the religious impulse refuses to tolerate more than anything else is ambiguity. When in doubt, society condemns. Anyone not clearly innocent is judged guilty. Salvation must be conclusively provided; damnation is inherent in the human condition. Thus, Christmas's moments of greatest violence are provoked by the religious impulse operating to sanction him: and he strikes McEachern, who would have him catechismically internalize the very forces that excommunicated him at birth; and he kills Joanna, because she wants him to join those same forces in prayer. He joins once—when he disrupts the Negro church service—and thus ironically makes use of the forces of exclusion for his own ends: knowing that society will never recognize him as a person, he is satisfied with being a marked man and a martyr in a community.

Gail Hightower thinks his own martyrdom has bought him immunity from further suffering. When he hears about Christmas, he begins to realize it has not. Hightower is forced to emerge from his sanctuary to listen to Byron, to feel compassion for Mrs. Hines, to deliver Lena's baby, and finally to speak out for Christmas. Hightower sees himself as paying again. Several times, referring especially to demands Byron makes on him, he says, "Perhaps this too is reserved for me." Once he says it, and the narrator replies, "But it is not all. There is one thing more reserved for him" (p. 392), referring to the witness that will be required of him at Christmas's execution. Hightower, then, is not permitted to be a martyr—just as he is not "permitted to live quietly among his fellows."

The night before Christmas's death, Hightower sits in his study window listening to the organ music from three churches in Jefferson. The passage is crucial to understanding *Light in August,* and it anticipates Ellison's treatment of "social" religion in *Invisible Man.*

> The organ strains come rich and resonant through the summer night, blended, sonorous, with that quality of abjectness and sublimation, as if the freed voices themselves were assuming the shapes and attitudes of crucifixions, ecstatic, solemn, and profound in gathering volume. Yet even then the music has still a quality stern and implacable, deliberate and without passion so much as immolation, pleading, asking, for not love, not life, forbidding it to others, demanding in sonorous tones death as though death were the boon, like all Protestant music. (p. 347)

The voices singing the music of the Protestant passion are "freed" by "assuming the shapes and attitudes of crucifixions." Each person in the congregation wants to be a martyr, hopes for crucifixion, because martyrdom ends quickly; it is only sainthood, absolute self-righteousness, that must be sustained for a lifetime. So they ask not for love, not for life, but for immolation, for death. Hightower listens: "he seems to hear within it the apotheosis of his own history, his own land, his own environed blood: that people from which he sprang and among which he lives who can never take either pleasure or catastrophe or escape from either, without brawling over it. Pleasure, ecstasy, they cannot seem to bear: their escape from it is in violence, in drinking and fighting and praying; catastrophe too, the violence identical and apparently inescapable" (p. 347). Hightower sees a society where the only pleasure is pain; where the only ecstasy is stasis; and where violence is therefore necessary to maintain these contradictions in oxymoronic equilibrium. Religion for the community of Jefferson becomes the point of balance; it is the only field of life where the pain and the stasis may be exalted, may be sung about, may be orgiastically and emotionally witnessed.

The epigraph to Flannery O'Connor's novel, *The Violent Bear It Away,* reads as follows:

"From the days of John the Baptist until now, the Kingdom of Heaven suffereth violence, and the violent bear it away." Matthew 11:12

Flannery O'Connor extends Faulkner's exploration of the reciprocal transmutation of religion to violence, and her epigraph clarifies Faulkner's own focus. The word *suffereth* has two Biblical senses: one certainly connotes the experience of pain; the other, however, means *to permit, or to encourage. Violent* is etymologically akin to two other English words, *to violate,* and the noun, *vim* (as in vim and vigor). These words derive from the Latin *vis,* meaning *strength,* and *The Oxford English Dictionary* also links the Greek *hiēsthai, to hurry,* and the Old english *wāth, pursuit.* The Bible verse directly links violence with religious fervor, strength of feeling, and extreme or urgent expressions of that feeling. Matthew states that Heaven "suffereth" this violence, which I interpret to mean "permits" and "bears" violence within itself. "And the violent bear it away." It is the violent one, the individual possessed by religious fervor, who carries the Kingdom of Heaven with(in) him.

"*'And so why should not their religion drive them to crucifixion of themselves and one another?'* he thinks" (p. 348). Hightower hears within the music "the declaration and dedication of that which they know that on the morrow they will have to do." He thinks of Joe Christmas, seems to hear them saluting not any god but "the doomed man in the barred cell." He knows they will do it gladly. "'Since to pity him would be to admit selfdoubt and to hope for and need pity themselves. They will do it gladly, gladly. That's why it is so terrible, terrible, terrible'" (p. 348). The need for the transcendental Absolute is felt as absolutely in Faulkner's South as it ever was in Puritan New England. Self-doubt cannot be admitted. And so the community will crucify gladly. It is "terrible" because they move farther away from the Absolute as they try to cling more closely to it.

Ilse Dusoir Lind states, "And yet Hightower's equation of Southern religion with Southern violence is not quite Faulkner's. . . . He makes this formulation early in his narrative; later he will progress to a better understanding of the Southern religious problem than this."[49] Hightower's statement appears "early in the narrative" in the sense that it appears before the dramatization of Christmas's death; but within the chronology of Hightower's narrative, it is the last time we see him alone before we see him again as a witness (the intervening conversation with the Hineses prepares for Hightower's defense of Christmas in the execution scene). Whether or not we want to "equate" Hightower's formulation with Faulkner's, *Light in August* certainly implies that Hightower is the only character who not only understands the social function of religion in the community, but is also allowed to transcend his place as excommunicant—whether for a moment of vision or for a lifetime is uncertain, and indeterminable from the text.

Some critics, Hugh Holman among them, claim that Hightower actually dies at the end of chapter 20. Others, myself included, interpret the scene as a moment of vision instead. Faulkner certainly does not make it clear that Hightower dies; nevertheless it is conceivable that he is no longer alive, at least symbolically—he thinks he is dying, after all; his hands become weightless; "the dust swirls skyward sucking, fades away into the night which has fully come"; and his head leans forward, "huge and without depth," upon "the twin blobs of his hands" (p. 467). Without testing the patience and credulity of the reader by narratively raising Hightower straight to heaven, Faulkner at the same time implies that something of this nature has happened.[50] Hightower has transcended; and whether the nature of his transcendance approaches that of the Eastern nirvana,[51] its literary prototype in Ishmael's transcendental masthead consciousness, or the Christian resurrection into heaven, Faulkner suggests that if Christmas is a martyr, Hightower is some kind of social saint. But not the Christian kind, where "saint" may also mean "savior"; Hightower is a saint because, unlike Christmas, whose agony is over in a moment, he "suffers" at the hands of society throughout his life. As a student once mentioned to me, in a different context, it is easier to be a martyr than a saint—assured the same glory "over yonder," the price *here* is quicker paid.[52]

V

In its total scope, *Light in August* is more than a community study. Joe Christmas, an individual who mirrors society's internal conflict, is balanced by Byron Bunch and Lena Grove, characters who live outside of society, who transcend the relative flux and change of human institutions—individuals who exist in the realm of the absolute, in the realm of the beauty and truth of Keats's "Ode on a Grecian Urn."[53]

Byron Bunch, whose very name ironically suggests an aggregate, lives his life separate from the community. When we first see him in the novel, he is working alone on Saturday afternoon at the planing mill. For the townspeople, he is a "man of mystery" (p. 44). Yet although Byron does not participate in the community of Jefferson, he comes to be a catalyst for community in its larger, more spiritual sense, drawing together the lives of Lena Grove, Hightower, Mrs. Hines, and Joe Christmas. Faulkner states, referring to Byron's position in Jefferson, "Man knows so little about his fellows" (p. 43). There are depths to Byron that the townspeople cannot fathom.

Byron is not a marked man. He is described as being "nondescript" (p. 44), someone who does not manifest his character as characteristic. His habits are his own, and most significant among these habits are his late-night talks with Hightower and his weekend rides thirty miles into the country where he "spends Sunday leading the choir in a country church—a service which lasts all day long" (p. 43). Faulkner does not stress Byron's religion; and Byron himself hides it from the community of Jefferson. In light of the blatant presence of religious fanaticism in the town and in the novel, the lack of emphasis comes to have the effect of underlining its importance. For Byron, who "'would injure no man'" (p. 50), who states to Hightower, "'It was a strange thing. I thought that if there ever was a place where a man would be where the chance to do harm could not have found him it would have been out there at the mill on a Saturday evening'" (p. 71), the religious impulse leads him again and again to action that is noble and absolute and inevitable.

For Faulkner, Byron represents an alternative to violence as a means of resolving conflict. Hightower, in a tone of irony and bitterness, his voice "high and thin," calls Byron "the guardian of public weal and morality. The gainer, the inheritor of rewards" (p. 344). If Hightower is bitter, however, Faulkner is not—for Byron acts as a social and spiritual mediator for the reader. Alone among the townspeople, Byron does not excommunicate Hightower and he does not care whether Christmas is black or white. Byron not only exists outside his community, but beyond the social domain as well: he refuses to acknowledge or participate in social expectations and proscriptions.

In addition, Byron acts primarily out of compassion and love for Lena. Byron's stable and consistent and impelling attraction for

Lena is a cosmic force. Lena is literally one center of creation in the novel as a pregnant woman; but she also becomes the focus of Byron's creative energy that sustains his action. "'I done come too far now,' he says, 'I be dog if I'm going to quit now.' . . . 'Aint nobody never said for you to quit,' she says" (p. 479). Byron is a religious man in that special sense of the word I discussed earlier: he is trying, through his love for Lena, to "bind [or bunch] himself back" to the source of creation. Such a spiritual impulse evokes no violence within Byron; and unlike the other women in the novel, Lena is innocently capable of pleasure, of laughter, or wonder. Byron and Lena possess the power of spirituality that remains hidden, of religion that is not a manifest part of individual or social identity, that does not become a tool of social exclusion but rather a means of appropriating life.

Light in August remains a novel that focuses on Joe Christmas and explores the process by which the religious impulse becomes transformed into violence. Faulkner's narrative frame—Lena's slow advance, "like something moving forever and without progress across an urn" (p. 5)—is his "attic shape," his artistic container, the "silent form" of the Keats poem. The central narratives (of Christmas and Hightower) explore as explorations or interpretations of these lines from Keats:

> What men or gods are these? What maidens loth?
> What mad pursuit? What struggle to escape?
> What pipes and timbrels? What wild ecstasy?

Yet these questions are generated by the urn's surface only. The deeper paradox of the Keats poem is suggested by these lines:

> Bold lover, never, never canst thou kiss,
> Though winning near the goal—yet do not grieve;
> She cannot fade, though thou hast not thy bliss,
> Forever wilt thou love and she be fair.

In the frozen circular tableau of the urn, Keats finds mad pursuit that will never gain the goal; struggle to escape that must always fail; yet beauty in the stasis of eternity—the goal and the struggle remain as life-supporting forces. Faulkner's novel contains no fair maidens, and is not concerned with the fading of female charm; but Faulkner derives the same level of truth from the stasis of struggle.[54]

Throughout *Light in August,* there are moments of conflict where time seems to stop momentarily and pursuer and pursued regard each other across a chasm. One such moment occurs when Byron watches from a distance as Brown jumps the train: "They see one another at the same moment: the two faces, the mild, nondescript, bloody one and the lean, harried, desperate one contorted now in a soundless shouting above the noise of the train, passing one another as though on opposite orbits and with an effect as of phantoms or apparitions" (p. 417). Another occurs during Grimm's pursuit of Christmas: "For an instant they looked at one another almost face to face. . . . For an instant they glared at one another, the one stopped in the act of crouching for the leap, the other in midstride of running" (p. 437). The visual effect of these moments is like that produced by the urn, where pursuer and pursued seem to regard each other, or struggle with each other, without resolution. Then dramatic action begins again, and following these moments, conflict becomes externalized, actualized; and in imagination as well as in reality the pursuer and the pursued coalesce, in the same way that, for Hightower, Percy Grimm's and Joe Christmas's faces seem to blend into each other. The distance symbolized by the urn dissolves, the individuals become part of cosmic process, and in the juxtaposition of opposites, some release occurs.

Harold Kaplan writes,

> The modern mind is dialectical to an extreme; it looks for division, it dramatizes opposition. For this emphasis, Faulkner's *Light in August* is a classic of the modern imagination as well as perhaps the most representative of his works. We have in it a series of oppositions which intensify drama to the point of freezing; hard blocks of force are held in arrest as if resolution could never come. The characters have almost allegorical simplicity of function in conflict, divided against each other and divided within themselves.[55]

The dynamic moments of the novel are Faulkner's attempts to explore the conflict between pursuer and pursued. This eternal struggle and conflict creates the effect of a closed circle for Christmas and Byron. Only in capture is the circle momentarily transcended on an individual basis. Thus violence acts to momentarily close the circle, as well as to creatively open it. At the surface, the pursuit is mighty and the resulting achievement is violence. At a greater distance, Lena keeps on moving across the urn, time is frozen, and the forces of birth and death, comedy and tragedy, become cosmic in scope. As Frank Baldanza points out, "Lena conducts the classic comic pursuit of her seducer just as relentlessly as nearly everyone else cooperates in the tragic pursuit of Joe. . . ."[56] Thus the final resolution of the novel becomes bedtime entertainment for the furniture dealer's wife—and the situation is about to involve her more directly than she knows: "'I just showed you once. You aint ready to be showed again, are you?'" (p. 472).

In one sense, Hawthorne's marking and Melville's cetology have no technical analogues in *Light in August*; there is no single symbol or subject that a narrator pursues, mantra-like, to arrive at significance in the work. Byron Bunch comes close to narrating the novel, but there is always some other presence there to say "Byron Bunch knows this" (p. 27). Yet what Byron finally knows is no substitute for the omniscience of an Ishmael. Unlike Hawthorne's narrator of "The Custom-House," and unlike Ishmael, who both move towards narrative omniscience but who remain within the limits of allegorical and analogical method, Faulkner's narrator never emerges in *Light in August* as a force of control. The text itself in its narrative design bears the full burden of pointing meaning in the novel.

When Christmas accepts his position as a socially discredited individual, when he "floats on the margin" of the community, Faulkner demonstrates what happens when a society is unable to tolerate ambiguity. The absence of a conspicuous narrator in *Light in August* suggests Faulkner's view of the role of prose fiction in such a society: the novel must demonstrate what Keats termed "negative capability." Hawthorne's retreat into allegory and Melville's tragedy of temporary vision do not provide means for the individual to transcend social and metaphysical isolation. Only a novel such as *Light in August,* which can allow us never to know the truth of Christmas's identity, which can create a vision, Hightower's, which points no allegorical or analogical meaning, and which can set Byron and Lena in perpetual motion without bringing them to rest, can truly be said to have achieved that "negative capability," to have passed beyond the limits of marking or symbolizing in the creation of a fictional world.

Faulkner's subject, social stigma, is sociological; but it is true that, as some critics have stated, *Light in August* is not a sociological novel.[57] Faulkner refuses to commit the crime he portrays. His very refusal to symbolize, to mark significance, to "stigmatize" his own characters, in effect, by making them carry allegorical burdens in addition to their historical and sociological ones, indicates the way in which American fiction can transcend its Puritan heritage. By refusing to insist on revealed meaning, the American narrator can counter our sociology with a vision of authentic community.

Notes

1. Anthologized in *American Literature: The Makers and the Making*, ed. Cleanth Brooks, R. W. B. Lewis, and Robert Penn Warren (New York: St. Martin's, 1973), pp. 104–5.

2. Erving Goffman, *Stigma* (Englewood Cliffs, N.J.: Prentice-Hall, 1963), p. 1.

3. Vickery, *The Novels of William Faulkner* (Baton Rouge: Louisiana State University Press, 1964), p. 67.

4. Ibid., p. 69.

5. Swiggart, "The Puritan Sinner: *Light in August*," chapter 8 in *The Art of Faulkner's Novels* (Austin: University of Texas Press, 1962), p. 133.

6. See, for example, William Van O'Connor, *The Tangled Fire of William Faulkner* (Minneapolis: University of Minnesota Press, 1954), p. 72. Alwyn Berland, in "*Light in August:* The Calvinism of William Faulkner," *Modern Fiction Studies*, 8 (Summer 1962, pp. 159–70, writes that Calvinism "endures in Faulkner's style . . .: violent, tortured, doom-ridden, apocalyptic. It endures, more curiously, in Faulkner's treatment of time. . . . [It] is revealed in two other important ways in *Light in August:* first, in the recurring theme of vengeful and fatalistic pursuit; second, in the almost universal coupling of sex and love with sin and destruction" (pp. 167–68).

7. Hyatt H. Waggoner, *William Faulkner: From Jefferson to the World* (Lexington: University of Kentucky Press, 1959), p. 101. He adds that Calvinism is "the chief intended antagonist in *Light in August*."

8. Pitavy, *Faulkner's Light in August*, tr. Gillian E. Cook (Bloomington: Indiana University Press, 1973), p. 98. Pitavy's book is probably the most comprehensive of critical studies on *Light in August* and is particularly useful for the annotated bibliography it provides.

9. Brooks, "Faulkner's Criticism of Modern America," *Virginia Quarterly Review*, 51 (Spring 1975), p. 55.

10. Lind, "The Calvinistic Burden of *Light in August*," *New England Quarterly*, 30 (September 1957), p. 308.

11. Cleanth Brooks supports this statement in "The Community and the Pariah," in *Twentieth Century Interpretations of Light in August*, ed. David L. Minter (Englewood Cliffs, N.J.: Prentice-Hall, 1969): "nearly all the characters in *Light in August* bear a special relation to the community. They are outcasts. . . . (p. 55). Pitavy writes, "In *Light in August*, the generally anonymous community is the background against which the essentially solitary people stand out. . . . (p. 113).

12. William Faulkner, *Light in August* (New York: Random House, 1932), p. 44. All further references to this work in this chapter appear in the text.

13. Pitavy disagrees with this interpretation of Byron, stating: "nor is he cut off from community, since, although he lives alone, he leads the choir in a country church every week" (p. 36).

14. Concerning Lena's isolation from community, there are variant interpretations. Pitavy writes that "the community accepts Lena, who, in spite of her pregnancy, does not challenge the social order . . ." (p. 109). Armstid's statement seems to contradict this. Cleanth Brooks states that Lena "leads a charmed life. Even the women who look upon her swollen body with evident disapproval press their small store of coins upon her, and the community in general rallies to help her" ("The Community and the Pariah," p. 57). Frank Baldanza, "The Structure of *Light in August*," *Modern Fiction Studies*, 113 (Spring 1967), to cite one example of the opposing view, writes: "Lena is isolated as a result of her indisguisably pregnant condition; but she is oblivious to the social disapproval of Mrs. Armstid and Mrs. Beard" (p. 70). My own view accords with Baldanza's.

15. Pitavy agrees here: "Joanna herself, devoted to the Negro cause, lives on the fringes of the community, just outside town, and the boys taunt her with the ultimate social insult: 'Nigger lover!'" (p. 108). John L. Longley, Jr., in *The Tragic Mask: A Study of Faulkner's Heroes* (Chapel Hill: University of North Carolina Press, 1963), compares Hightower and Joanna Burden, interestingly, to Captain Ahab and Chillingworth as examples of "the tragedy of isolation" (p. 228). Olga Vickery's description of the two characters is most interesting of all. She says that they represent "the two remaining categories [Joe Christmas represents the first], one geographical and the other religious, in terms of which the South establishes its identity. The Negro, the Yankee, the Apostate—these are the key figures in a society which defines itself by exclusion" (*The Novels of William Faulkner*, p. 75).

16. Pitavy writes, "In the end, when they had done all that was expected of them in this closed society . . ., and Hightower still remained, they ignored him as a unit of society and, paradoxically, felt at liberty to offer charity to this pariah now living outside their order" (p. 109).

17. Baldanza, p. 70.

18. Vickery, p. 68.

19. Pitavy questions whether or not Joe actually killed his foster father (p. 26). He thinks he did, however; he implies as much to Mrs. McEachern and says to himself, while Bobbie watches Max beat him up, *"Why, I committed murder for her"* (*Light in August*, p. 204).

20. Brooks, "Faulkner's Criticism of Modern America," p. 299.

21. As Carl Benson writes, "we discover that he has been adopted by a sadistic Calvinist, whose rigorous exactions of religious duties seem to Joe but a continuation, in slightly different terms, of the harsh treatment of the orphanage" (p. 547)

22. Vickery writes: "In a sense, the individual and the community are obverse reflections of each other. Yet because the reflection is obverse, each fails to recognize himself, and so reacts with instinctive fear and anger which ultimately lead him to destroy his own image. In short, each is the victim of the other" (p. 67). And Irving Howe, *William Faulkner* (New York: Random House, 1962), comments: *"Light in August* is the most socially inflected of Faulkner's novels, sensitive to the limitations and distortions society imposes on human conduct. In none of his other books is there such a full rendering of the force of dead institutions and dead matter as they exact their tyranny upon men. ... In *Light in August*, the limits of freedom are defined primarily through social co-ordinates, Christmas, in one important sense, being simply a function of his society ..." (pp. 211–12).

23. To recapitulate, Goffman defines stigma as the "situation of the individual who is disqualified from full social acceptance." He separates two characteristic and complementary patterns of stigma: "does the stigmatized individual assume his differentness is known about already or is evident on the spot, or does he assume it is neither known about by those present nor immediately perceivable by them? In the first case one deals with the plight of the *discredited*, in the second with that of the *discreditable*" (p. 4).

24. Swiggart, p. 138.

25. Lind, pp. 310–11.

26. Pitavy says about the connections of chapter 5 with chapters 6 through 12: "it touches on the same themes and images as are expanded and loaded with significance in the following chapters, and second, ... it prepares the ground for the lengthy plunge into Christmas's past and explains its necessity" (p. 16).

27. Pitavy emphasizes that "Christmas is not lynched, but killed by Percy Grimm" (p. 2). However, Grimm acts as the symbol of the community; he acts so that they do not have to act. As Joseph W. Reed, Jr., *Faulkner's Narrative* (New Haven: Yale University Press, 1973), points out, "When community personality meets with the force of an abstract ideal in Percy Grimm, everyone can embrace it ...—Grimm justifies their fears and at the same time can seem to represent a call to higher action, while still permitting them to retain their cherished modes of individual respectability and behavior. The macrocosm can become a whole by gaining in Grimm the will and force which they as individuals would never have known: with Grimm, the archetypal blind conscience, they can become as one for the pursuit of Christmas, the archetypal foe" (p. 134).

28. Referring to the entire passage in which this phrase appears, Reed comments interestingly, "The passage is a denunciation ... of the emptiness of man's usual workaday pursuits and the hypocritical excuse this emptiness provides for his madness in crowds. It is as bitter a reading of human motivation as is to be found in Faulkner, and it rules all of this book's prior references to community" (p. 137).

29. Brooks, "The Community and the Pariah," p. 62.

30. Pitavy, p. 94.

31. See chapter 2, note 25.

32. Swiggart, p. 145.

33. Ibid., p. 148.

34. Vickery, p. 74.

35. Swiggart writes: "Through his relation with the farmer, who is characterized by a Bible or catechism held in one hand and a strap in the other, Joe is given a taste of the expiating punishment for which he unconsciously yearns" (p. 132).

36. Kazin, "The Stillness of *Light in August,*" in *William Faulkner: Three Decades of Criticism,* ed. Frederick J. Hoffman and Olga W. Vickery (East Lansing: Michigan State University Press, 1960), pp. 252, 254.

37. *Faulkner in the University,* ed. Frederick L. Gwynn and Joseph L. Blotner (Charlottesville: University of Virginia Press, 1959), p. 118.

38. See Swiggart, p. 147.

39. Pitavy deals with this question in chapter 2 of *Faulkner's Light in August* and concludes, "the unity of the work and its meaning are the direct results of the much-maligned changeovers from plot to plot" (p. 45).

40. Pitavy asserts that "Faulkner appears to be less able to show a character's evolution than to reveal gradually a character already complete in his imagination, and who only appears to grow because the reader gains deeper knowledge of him as time goes on" (p. 83). On the surface, this would seem to explain the effect Faulkner gains by waiting until chapter 20 to narrate much of Hightower's past. However, it becomes clear that Hightower himself does not understand his own past until after Christmas's death. Therefore, by narrating it in chapter 20, Faulkner implies that Hightower's understanding, itself, is part of the present narration and development of the character.

41. Vickery writes, concerning Hightower's aborted "lynching": "As if recognizing that he has no place in Jefferson, that indeed his dream-world is threatened by it, Hightower deliberately provokes the violence which will ensure his isolation" (p. 78). Swiggart emphasizes that Hightower accepted "with delight a mock 'crucifixion' at the hands of a town mob" (p. 142). However, the evidence in this quoted passage from the novel that might support the interpretation that Hightower incited his own mob does not appear until chapter 20, during Hightower's moments of self-confession and self-recognition. This suggests to me that Hightower's view of that past moment in the narrative present of chapter 20 accords with Swiggart's view, but I see no indication that Hightower knew *then* that he was enjoying his "mock 'crucifixion.'"

42. Beach Langston, "The Meaning of Lena Grove and Gail Hightower in *Light in August,*" *Boston University Studies in English,* 5 (Spring 1961), p. 62.

43. Faulkner said, "sooner or later any writer is going to use something that has been used. And that Christ story is one of the best stories that man has ever invented, assuming that he did invent that story, and of course it will recur. Everyone that has had the story of Christ and the Passion as a part of his Christian background will in time draw from that. There was no deliberate intent to repeat it. That to me the people come first. The symbolism comes second" (*Faulkner in the University,* p. 117).

44. Hugh C. Holman, "The Unity of Faulkner's *Light in August,*" *PMLA,* 73 (March 1958), p. 155.

45. William J. Cash, *The Mind of the South* (New York: Vintage, 1942), p. 86.

46. Ibid., p. 104.

47. See Lind, p. 224.

48. Carl Benson, "Thematic Design in *Light in August,*" *South Atlantic Quarterly,* 53 (October 1954), talks about "the use and abuse of religion as related to the maintenance of community solidarity" (p. 552). William Van O'Connor writes, "Certainly it is mark of his genius that Faulkner can develop the terrible irony that it is out of the religion itself that the lynching comes . . ." (p. 86). And Pitavy states, "*Light in August* appears as a terrible denunciation of a religion which preaches the opposite of truth and the forgiveness of sins. . . . In fact, religion as it is seen in *Light in August* becomes an incitement to kill" (p. 116).

49. Lind, p. 328.

50. In *Faulkner in the University,* Faulkner said that Hightower "didn't die. . . . He had to endure, to live" and that he still had "the memory of his grandfather, who had been brave" (p. 75). On the question of whether Hightower dies, Pitavy writes in a footnote, "this is a vexed question. Ten or more critics agree that Hightower does in fact die. . . . Faulkner said that Hightower did not die. . . . However, does it really matter whether he dies or not? Neither supposition affects the character's conception or the overall impression of the book . . ." (p. 162). Among the critics who state that he dies are Beach Langston, "The Meaning of Lena Grove and Gail Hightower," and Carl Benson, "Thematic Design in *Light in August.*" Benson calls chapter 20 "the magnificent penultimate chapter—a chapter which, despite its strategic position and rhetorical splendor, has been generally neglected" (p. 543).

Dorothy Tuck, *Apollo Handbook of Faulkner* (New York: Crowell, 1964), supports my own interpretation. She writes: "Although there is no assurance that Hightower will now actively seek involvement with the living, or that he will no longer wait for the ghost-visited moment at twilight, his recognition of what he has been is a triumphantly positive achievement in which he gains stature as a kind of tragic figure rising from the shadows of an empty life" (p. 53).

51. See Langston.

52. He had attended the American Martyrs High School in Los Angeles and had learned this formulation from the priests there.

53. Olga Vickery supports the idea that Lena is not interested in finding a place in the community: "What she is looking for is security not respectability. Once Byron assumes this responsibility, she shows no great haste to marry and so to remove the social stigma from herself and her child" (p. 80).

54. For further comments on the relationship between the Keats poem and Faulkner's urn image, see Norman Holmes Pearson, "Lena Grove," *Shenandoah*, 3 (Spring 1952), pp. 3–7, or the excerpt from Pearson included in Minter, ed., *Twentieth Century Interpretations*.

55. Harold Kaplan, "The Inert and the Violent: *Light in August*," in *The Passive Voice: An Approach to Modern Fiction* (Athens: Ohio University Press, 1966), p. 111.

56. Baldanza, p. 70.

57. See, for example, O'Connor, p. 84, or Pitavy, p. 56.

6

Invisible Man: **The World in a Man-of-War**

My exploration of marked characters in American fiction ends with
the following discussion of Ralph Ellison's *Invisible Man*. There are
conspicuous omissions from my study, as I discussed in chapter 1;
however, only Ellison's novel attempts the epic scope Hawthorne,
Melville, and Faulkner achieve. *The Scarlet Letter, Moby-Dick,
Light in August,* and *Invisible Man* are all appropriately described
as quest narratives. The pursuit that begins with Hawthorne's
study of social exclusion, that Melville develops in his narrative of
Ishmael, who chooses to isolate himself in order to achieve omniscience, and that Faulkner explores as emblematic of a search for identity in Christmas's self-exclusion, reaches its most recent variation
in Ellison's novel, a twentieth-century fusion of the "heroic fugitive"
school of Negro writers of the early and mid-nineteenth century (the
most significant text is Frederick Douglass's autobiographical *Narrative* of 1845) and the heritage of the American transcendentalists,
which has gone "underground," like Ellison's narrator, since the
1840s.

Like Joe Christmas, Ellison's Invisible Man is a victim of society's
insistence on revealed meaning. What his stigma—that he is
black—reveals hides the person he thinks he is. The irony of the
novel is that invisibility becomes a stigma that Invisible Man embraces. However, his affirmation of invisibility is much more complex than Joe Christmas's choice to become a marked member of his
community. As Hightower's transcendence and Byron's love for
Lena ultimately show, the outcast's crucifixion may lead to social
transfiguration. That is, Christmas's martydom, in spite of its tragic
indictment of the community of Jefferson, contributes to comic resolution at the end of the novel. Christmas himself dies, but in the
aesthetic distance Faulkner achieves in Byron's eternal pursuit, he
suggests the possibility of redemption.

Like Faulkner, Ellison attempts to transcend the limitations Puritanism has imposed in American society. Ellison uses comedy to avoid imposing "revealed meaning" on chaos; like Faulkner's narrator, Invisible Man embraces ambiguity.[1] Yet Faulkner's vision yields to Ellison's insistence that humanity must precede community. Unlike Faulkner, Ellison has no vision of community to offer us. Yet in *Shadow and Act*, he accords Faulkner the highest praise when he states,

> Indeed, through his many novels and short stories, Faulkner fights out the moral problem which was repressed after the nineteenth century, and it was shocking for some to discover that for all his concern with the South, Faulkner was actually seeking out the nature of man. Thus we must turn to him for that continuity of moral purpose which made for the greatness of our classics. As for the Negro minority, he has been more willing perhaps than any other artist to start with the stereotype, accept it as true, and then seek out the human truth which it hides.[2]

The "human truth" for Ellison involves more than an individual's relation to the community; it requires recognition of those elements of personal identity that are "invisible" to society. In spite of Invisible Man's incessant search for "brotherhood," the novel focuses on the individual. As I will discuss in this chapter, Invisible Man's search for a badge of acceptance in a group allies him with Ahab; when he fails, he manages to become an Ishmael. In attempting to "join," he demonstrates Christmas's despair; when he goes underground at last, he learns the comic force of Byron's "religion," by which he "binds himself back" to his source.

Robert Bone writes, "The bursting forth of Negro personality from the fixed boundaries of Southern life is Ellison's essential theme. And it is this, at bottom, that attracts him to the transcendentalists. ... In broader terms, it may be said that Ellison's ontology derives from transcendentalism."[3] Ellison explores his narrator's relationship to American history and American literary history and indicates that the American identity remains an object of transcendental quest. In *Invisible Man*, naming is an analogue for marking: by emerging gradually from one experience after another with people who would keep him anonymous, the narrator earns his self-assigned name. Like Hawthorne, Melville, and Faulkner, Ellison too, as Robert Bone suggests, epitomizes the pervasive presence of the transcendental imagination in American fiction.

I

The Epilogue to *Invisible Man* ends with a question: "Who knows but that, on the lower frequencies, I speak for you?"[4] The Prologue begins with a statement: "I am an invisible man." It has become a critical cliché to interpret ends of literary works as recycling mechanisms, redirecting the reader back into the text. Ralph Ellison is conscious of this paradigm, and his narrator explicitly states in the Prologue, "the end is in the beginning" (p. 9). The beginning, the narrator's opening statement, is also his goal of affirmation and realization. If we view the closing question with the opening statement in mind, we are compelled to ponder how Ellison's narrator does indeed speak for us. To what extent does the reader become the protagonist; to what extent does he share the narrator's invisibility?[5]

It comes as a surprise to the literary critic to face such a question in response to the work, and perhaps his first inclination may be to avoid doing so. If he chooses instead to explore the novel's central theme—invisibility—he is partially foiled by Ellison's narrator, who insists on interpreting the novel for us in the Prologue-Epilogue frame. What is left to the critic but revelation and reiteration of the obvious? The narrator admits as much in the last paragraph of the Epilogue when he states,

> "Ah," I can hear you say, "so it was all a build-up to bore us with his buggy jiving. He only wanted us to listen to him rave!" But only partially true: Being invisible and without substance, a disembodied voice, as it were, what else could I do? What else but try to tell you what was really happening when your eyes were looking through? (p. 503)

He addresses us as contributors to his invisibility, as conspirators with those people who "refuse to see me": "When they approach me they see only my surroundings, themselves, or figments of their imagination—indeed, everything and anything except me" (p. 7). But he speaks also as a narrator to his readers, justifying his role as commentator and interpreter. And as such, he directs our attempts to explain "what was really happening" in the novel. His justification for blocking our literary critical attempts is enlightening: it is to compensate for his substancelessness, his "disembodied voice." Preventing, by answering, the critical question, *What* is the novel about?, the narrator forces the more personal question, *Who* is the novel about? If we succeed in reading the novel without asking this question, we run the risk of Ellison's invisibility. We become, likewise, a disembodied voice.

In what amounts to a theory of literary criticism, Ellison states in a footnote in *Shadow and Act*:

> Perhaps the ideal approach to the work of literature would be one allowing for insight into the deepest psychological motives of the writer at the same time that it examined all external sociological factors

> operating within a given milieu. For while objectively a social reality, the work of art is, in its genesis, a projection of a deeply personal process, and any approach that ignores the personal at the expense of the social is necessarily incomplete. (p. 27)

In what way is it possible to write about *Invisible Man* in terms of Ellison's own "theory" of literary criticism? Ellison stresses that personal and sociological motives operate "at the same time." It would not seem appropriate for the reader to catalog his own experiences of invisibility. To do so would be not to participate in Ellison's dialogue but to write another novel. What the narrator needs in order to achieve self-realization is a social and historical context. He decides to emerge from hibernation, to "come out" of the hole he is in, but not yet. The reader's half of the exchange must provide this context, must embody the voice. If the narrator's final appeal to our "lower frequencies" succeeds, he is out of his hole. We let him out, because we put him in. And we do the same for ourselves.

What context does the narrator demand? The range of possibilities for his "coming out" is as vastly protean as the range of possibilities the invisible man himself sees as the "next phase" of his conflict: "Until some gang succeeds in putting the world in a strait jacket, its definition is possibility. Step outside the narrow borders of what men call reality and you step into chaos—ask Rinehart, he's a master of it—or imagination" (p. 498). The "narrow borders of what men call reality" is a euphemism in the novel for history, as history is one reconstruction of chaos, one definition. The narrator reflects that Tod Clifton died for his right to "plunge outside of history . . . into nothingness, into the void of faceless faces, of soundless voices lying outside history" (p. 379). He looks about him on the subway at "men out of time, who would soon be gone and forgotten" (p. 381). Who would record and document the lives of these men like Clifton? "They were outside the groove of history, and it was my job to get them in, all of them" (p. 383). Thus it becomes Invisible Man's responsibility at Clifton's funeral "to put his integrity together again" (p. 387).

He states in his eulogy that Clifton "lost his hold on reality" (p. 395). Invisible Man translates Clifton's coffin into the ghetto "box," attempting to remind the mourners of *their* reality:

> "It has a cracked ceiling and a clogged-up toilet in the hall. It has rats and roaches, and it's far, far too expensive a dwelling. The air is bad and it'll be cold this winter. Tod Clifton is crowded and he needs the room. 'Tell them to get out of the box,' that's what he would say if you could hear him. 'Tell them to get out of the box and go teach the cops to forget that rhyme. Tell them to teach them that when they call you *nigger* to make a rhyme with *trigger* it makes the gun backfire.'" (p. 396)

When he finishes his speech he states, "as I took one last look I saw not a crowd but the set faces of individual men and women. . . . Tod Clifton was underground." The reconstruction of Clifton's history permits Invisible Man to see the individuality of faces in the crowd; each individual becomes a manifestation of the dead man, "our hope shot down." Similarly, by becoming such a manifestation of the narrator, in admitting the invisibility we share, we in turn pull him out of his box, his hole. The attempt involves nothing less than a rewriting of history, a new Reconstruction.

The gun that backfires is the grandfather's gun. The grandfather's deathbed advice, in the opening pages of the novel, creates a puzzle that the narrator discovers he must recreate in order to resolve: "'Son, after I'm gone I want you to keep up the good fight. I never told you, but our life is a war and I have been a traitor all my born days, a spy in the enemy's country ever since I give up my gun back in the Reconstruction'" (p. 29). But it becomes the reader's gun as well, and the reader's puzzle.

> Historically wars and revolutions form the background for the high periods of the novel, and civil wars, Hemingway has written, are the best wars for the writer. To which we would add, yes, because they have a way of continuing long after wars between nations are resolved; because, with the combatants being the same people, civil wars are never really won; and because their most devastating engagements are fought within the individual human heart.[6]

The combatants are the same people; the reader is one of the individual faces in the crowd at Clifton's death; history is *our* reconstruction; we are all invisible; and until we recognize our internal state of civil war, we are trapped underground.

In *Shadow and Act*, Ellison analyzes the effects of the Civil War on the American consciousness. In reading Whitman, Emerson, Thoreau, Hawthorne, Melville, and Mark Twain, "we are reminded that from 1776 to 1876 there was a conception of democracy current in this country that allowed the writer to identify himself with the Negro." For his nineteenth-century predecessors, "slavery (it was not termed a 'Negro problem' then) was a vital issue in the American consciousness, symbolic of the condition of Man, and a valid aspect of the writer's reality." In what Ellison terms "the counterrevolution of 1876, . . . the Negro issue [was] pushed into the underground of the American conscience and ignored" (p. 98). "I felt that except for the work of William Faulkner something vital had gone out of American prose after Mark Twain. . . . Whatever [the nineteenth-century novelists] thought of my people per se, in their imaginative economy the Negro symbolized both the man lowest down and the mysterious, underground aspect of human personality. In a sense the Negro was the gauge of the human condition as it waxed and waned in our democracy" (p. 104). The difference between the "underground of the American conscience," and that "underground aspect of human personality" in which "the Negro was the gauge of the human condition," is the difference between a cold hole and a warm hole. As the narrator of the novel's Prologue warns, "Now don't jump to the conclusion that because I call my home a 'hole' it is damp and cold like a grave; there are cold holes and warm holes. Mine is a warm hole . . . warm and full of light" (p. 9). Invisible Man prefers his state of hibernation to the version of American reality that would term his "hole" a grave.

R. W. B. Lewis acknowledges Invisible Man's position in the heritage of the American Adam, "the authentic . . . figure of heroic innocence and vast potentialities, poised at the start of a new history."[7] For Lewis, a study of the all-but-lost archetype of emancipation, innocence, and self-reliance may be one means of "hoisting" the American identity to a higher "plane of understanding." "We stand in need of more stirring impulsions, of greater perspectives and more penetrating controversies. Perhaps a review of that earlier debate can help us on our way. We can hardly expect to be persuaded any longer by this historic dream of the new Adam. But it can pose anew, in the classic way of illumination as it did in the nineteenth century, the picture of what might be against the knowledge of what is, and become once more a stimulus to enterprise and a resource for literature."[8] Invisible Man's lighted hole acts precisely as this kind of "classic illumination," and the only impetus to rebirth that is lacking is "a review of that earlier debate," the dialogue of Ellison's socially conscious literary criticism.

The novel urges, then, that the reader place Invisible Man back into history and provide his embodiment, his American context. It is to this end that the multitude of symbols and structures the novel provides must be interpreted. For the invisible man, "to be unaware of one's form is to live a death" (p. 10). To free ourselves from the same formlessness of invisibility, it is necessary to reintegrate our awareness of the historical, literary, and sociological aspects of the changing American identity that lead to Invisible Man's self-realization.

II

The first six chapters take place in the South, converting into "symbolic action" the necessity that the protagonist move North.[9] In a *Paris Review* interview reprinted in *Shadow and Act*, Ellison states:

In my novel the narrator's development is one through blackness to
light; that is, from ignorance to enlightenment: invisibility to visibility. He leaves the South and goes North; this, as you will notice in
reading Negro folktales, is always the road to freedom—the movement upward. You have the same thing again when he leaves his
underground cave for the open. (p. 173)

Historically, as Ellison suggests, the road North was "the road to
freedom"—for Frederick Douglass, Eliza, *Uncle Tom's Children*,
James Baldwin's Florence in *Go Tell It on the Mountain*, and Ellison's Brother Tarp, who reminds Invisible Man of his slave history
by giving him the filed chain link. With the gift, Invisible Man
inherits an obligation to become, himself, a link in the chain of black
emancipation. Tarp acted nobly and essentially: "'I lost my wife and
my boys and my piece of land. . . . I said no to a man who wanted to
take something from me'" (p. 335). By the same means, as he wrote
in his autobiographical *Narrative* of 1845, Frederick Douglass began
his escape from slavery—by physical resistance to Edward Covey.
"You have seen how a man was made a slave; you shall see how a
slave was made a man."[10] The same resistance ultimately per-
meates *Invisible Man* and other contemporary fiction. As Thomas
Vogler expresses it, "the novelists seem to agree that violence and
distortion must be the means of projecting a vision to which society
is hostile. They seem further to agree that the contemporary world
presents a continued affront to man, and that his response must
therefore be at least in part that of the rebel."[11] In the literal sense
of his name, however, Tarp acts as a "cover"—for emancipation has
become a false construct for the contemporary heroic fugitive. The
intellectual rebel no longer confronts a tangible bondage—as Ellison writes, "reality is difficult to come by."[12]

In retrospect, the narrator's "beautiful college" in green and white
becomes a "flower-studded wasteland" (p. 38). His memory of the
bronze statue of the Founder, "hands outstretched . . . above the face
of a kneeling slave," is altered by his later perception, in which he is
"unable to decide whether the veil is really being lifted, or lowered
more firmly in place" (p. 37). Yet he realizes that at one time, in his
pastoral innocence, he was unable to hear the "stagnant stillness"
for the humming of bees and the sound of mockingbirds. Part of the
pastoral nostalgia that Invisible Man feels for the South he owes to
that historical road, open to the slave, that is no longer open to him.
Filing a chain link, real as well as symbolic action, literally frees.
When external conflict becomes internalized, "repressed," as Ellison
would have it, reality becomes pastoralized and man, "invisible."

The South, as the narrator remembers it, is only a beautiful place
for those who lack consciousness, and retrospectively it bears the

burden for his suffering. "Since then I've sometimes been overcome with a passion to return into that 'heart of darkness' across the Mason-Dixon line, but then I remind myself that the true darkness lies within my own mind, and the idea loses itself in the gloom. Still the passion persists. Sometimes I feel the need to reaffirm all of it, the whole unhappy territory and all the things loved and unlovable in it, for all of it is part of me. Till now, however, this is as far as I've ever gotten, for all life seen from the hole of invisibility is absurd" (p. 501). What is "absurd" about the South, for Invisible Man, is not the "darkness" but the unreality. He sees his college as defined totally in terms of black and white—even to the white line on the highway that separates the college from the "trash" section of town—and more important, as totally defined. For example, Norton implies that Invisible Man may choose his "fate" from among a multitude of possibilities: "'If you become a good farmer, a chef, a preacher, doctor, singer, mechanic—whatever you become, and even if you fail, you are my fate'" (p. 44). In fact Norton's very catalog, omitting artist, intellectual, statesman, teacher, and capitalist, also expresses the limitations of that fate.

What Vogler calls the "vestigial aura of Edenic simplicity"[13] which Ellison, like Faulkner, attributes to the South, is the simplicity of definition, the American Adam's ability to create "language itself by naming the elements of the scene about him."[14] Invisible Man is named, defined, categorized—in the South by Norton and Bledsoe, in the North by the Brotherhood—until he begins to "awake" from the nightmare of (his own) history. Yet even though he claims as his own the power that for so long worked against him, he does not find the strength to emerge from his hole. He leaves the South in order to extend his range of possibilities but ends still choosing definition (even if, this time, it is self-definition) as a substitute for reality—"Until some gang succeeds in putting the world in a strait jacket, its definition is possibility" (p. 498). Leaving the South is only useful as a metaphor for liberation. The North (controlled by the Nortons, Emersons, and Brother Jacks) falsifies and demythologizes the metaphor for Invisible Man. In viewing the South with pastoral eyes, as a region from which he has "escaped" and to which he cannot return, Invisible Man fails to perceive how clearly he carries his own "south" within him into Harlem.

The theme of escape from the South runs through white as well as black fiction, and includes William Styron's Peyton Loftis, Eudora Welty's King MacLain in *The Golden Apples*, and Faulkner's Quentin Compson, whose attempt to come to terms with his Southern heritage leads to suicide. Quentin protests to Shreve in *Absalom,*

Absalom!, "'Gettysburg. . . . You can't understand it. You would have to be born there.'"[15] The articulation of this theme in *Invisible Man* and all of southern fiction poses a challenge to northern readers, who were not "born there." Unlike Invisible Man, northern readers do not have open to them even a symbolic avenue of escape. Keats's "negative capability" comes close to characterizing the move North as Faulkner and Ellison explore it, and historically, Keats's expression finds no more appropriately American symbol than the myth of the Mason-Dixon line. As Invisible Man puts it, "In the South everyone knew you, but coming North was a jump into the unknown" (p. 431).

It is one of the ironic attractions of southern literature and black literature, for many of us, that we can get outside the southern and black experience precisely *because* we were born outside it. We can look at it because we are not it. But the semantics of this distinction may trap us, blind us as it does the Indians in "Red Leaves." Faulkner realized that definition is only possible through negation, what Erich Neumann called "the acceptance of the shadow."[16] In "Red Leaves," the Negro body servant experiences what life means by becoming a heroic fugitive from death. Quentin Compson goes North to find out his southern identity, and, unable to affirm it, succeeds at least in denying his denial. Shreve asks him, at the end of *Absalom*, why he hates the South. The passion of ambivalence Quentin reveals—"'I dont hate it! I dont hate it!'"[17]—cannot be understood by Shreve; but it *is* understood by Ralph Ellison, who would suggest that the North/South dichotomy is only part of the "American" experience. By the intuitive logic of this argument, it should be easier for the northerner and the white reader to realize the affirmation Quentin and Invisible Man just fail to achieve. We need only direct our attention—we need only *look*—in order to see and thus restore the narrator and ourselves to visibility: "I am invisible, understand, simply because people refuse to see me" (p. 7).

A problem emerges. Given our refusal to see, is it possible for Invisible Man, one representative of a mass of white and black individuals, to achieve by moving North an alternative identity that will endure for an individual, a group, or a race? Ellison offers the blues as a lyrical expression of personal catastrophe, and states, "They fall short of tragedy only in that they provide no solution, offer no scapegoat but the self."[18] Ellison's alternative to a redemption that depends on the recognition of his visibility lies in self-sacrifice. He defines "humanism" as "man's basic attitude toward a social order which he accepts, and individualism his basic attitude toward one he rejects."[19] Individualism becomes a means of affirmation, but its price is great: there is "no scapegoat but the self." Moving North becomes a move to anonymity: "How many days could you walk the streets of the big city without encountering anyone who knew you, and how many nights?" (p. 431). But it also cuts him off from community. Ellison explains,

> The pre-individualistic black community discourages individuality out of self-defense. Having learned through experience that the whole group is punished for the actions of the single member, it has worked out efficient techniques of behavior control. . . .
> Personal warmth is accompanied by an equally personal coldness, kindliness by cruelty, regard by malice. And these opposites are as quickly set off against the member who gestures toward individuality as a lynch mob forms at the cry of rape.[20]

"The horrible thing," Ellison stresses, "is that the cruelty is also an expression of concern, of love."

III

It is not surprising, in the attempt to depict a society where "there is in progress between black and white Americans a struggle over the nature of reality,"[21] that naturalism should not be an effective or even an appropriate mode of aesthetic discourse. Ellison explains, in part, his choice of allegorical mode: "I was forced to conceive of a novel unburdened by the narrow naturalism which has led, after so many triumphs, to the final and unrelieved despair which marks so much of our current fiction."[22] As a novelist Ellison confronts the problem his narrator expresses in the Prologue: "Responsibility rests upon recognition, and recognition is a form of agreement" (p. 16). Invisible Man justifies here his own withdrawal from "social responsibility" when he goes underground—the terms of "agreement" between himself and his society have not been mutually acceptable. It is not "final and unrelieved despair" that Ellison's narrator avoids when he avoids naturalism, but a presentation of reality that might be subject to "agreement."[23]

To understand this, it is only necessary to review controversies over two novels about black protagonists, Richard Wright's *Native Son* and William Styron's *The Confessions of Nat Turner*. Ellison summarizes the complaints against *Native Son* in *Shadow and Act:* "I felt that Wright was overcommitted to ideology. . . . You might say that I was much less a social determinist. But I suppose that basically it comes down to a difference in our concepts of the individual. I, for instance, found it disturbing that Bigger Thomas had none of the finer qualities of Richard Wright, none of the imagination, none of the sense of poetry, none of the gaiety. And I preferred

Richard Wright to Bigger Thomas" (p. 16). This statement amounts to an attack on the novel's presentation of reality and recalls an earlier criticism by James Baldwin, "Everybody's Protest Novel": "The failure of the protest novel lies in its rejection of life, the human being, the denial of his beauty, dread, power, in its insistence that it is his categorization alone which is real and which cannot be transcended."[24] Irving Howe, in his famous essay "Black Boys and Native Sons," defends Richard Wright. "How could a Negro put pen to paper, how could he so much as think or breathe, without some impulsion to protest, be it harsh or mild, political or private, released or buried? The 'sociology' of his existence formed a constant pressure on his literary work, and not merely in the way this might be true for any writer, but with a pain and ferocity that nothing could remove."[25] He goes on to attribute the success of "younger novelists," Baldwin and Ellison, in moving "beyond Wright's harsh naturalism and toward more supple modes of fiction" to the fact that "Wright has been there first, courageous enough to release the full weight of his anger."[26]

Robert Bone agrees with Baldwin's statement when he writes, "Protest fiction, by portraying sociological types, holds its readers at a distance from the human person."[27] In Wright's insistence that it is "categorization alone which is real and which cannot be transcended," to use Baldwin's words, he expresses the problem of naturalism where there is disagreement over the nature of reality. Allegory automatically forces the reader to "transcend" social categories in order to determine the significance of the work. Allegory is symbolic, comprised of representative men. Therefore in writing allegory, Ellison compels even his white readers to "transcend" the very "reality" they would not have otherwise agreed upon long enough to ponder its meaning.

It is clear how this works if we consider one contrast between Joe Christmas and Invisible Man. Howe writes about Wright's Bigger Thomas, "only through violence does he gather a little meaning in life, pitifully little."[28] The same statement holds true when applied to Joe Christmas, even though Faulkner's novel does not begin to approach the harshness of Wright's. When Christmas is castrated by Percy Grimm, the novel soars to its "unbelievable crescendo"[29] in a catharsis of pain. The closest Invisible Man comes to castration is his dream about it at the end of the novel, and even there, as I will discuss later in this chapter, Ellison uses castration not referentially but symbolically, as an image of blinding.

Similar conflict inspires the essays in *Nat Turner: Ten Black Writers Respond*. John Oliver Killens sums up the collective thesis of these essays, calling Styron's "pretense" to adopt Turner's point of view "a colossal error, one that required tremendous arrogance."[30] "This is all just a way of saying that the story of Nat Turner is still to be written, and it will be up to a black man to write *this* great American tragedy."[31] Naturalism becomes an epistemological tool in the struggle over the nature of white and black reality, as if the vehemence of argument served as a catalyst for social change.

Ellison denies the assumption and rejects naturalism. However, this artistic repudiation places limitations on Ellison's narrator-protagonist. "You ache," he says in the Prologue, "with the need to convince yourself that you do exist in the real world" (p. 7). We might ask whether or not the protagonist of the novel, in achieving a new identity, succeeds in convincing himself of his reality. More important, does he convince anyone else? The problem of naturalism for the narrator and the protagonist's ache for reality become part of the same dilemma. "'I too have become acquainted with ambivalence. . . . That's why I'm here,'" Invisible Man writes in the Prologue. He proposes this ambivalence, underground, as a solution to his conflict in the real world. Paradoxically, just as he discovers his southern identity in the North—"I yam what I am" (p. 231)—so he resolves his anonymity by making visible his invisibility. The protagonist's struggle becomes the narrator's allegory: "I am an invisible man."

To the extent that the narrator's fictional world articulates ambivalence—as he states in the Epilogue, "too much of your life will be lost, its meaning lost, unless you approach it as much through love as through hate" (p. 501)—the particular characters within it become less free to do the same. The protagonist encounters other people as symbols, refusing or unable to see them as less phantom-like than himself, as Clifton's funeral and his emotional transactions with Mary Rambo or Brother Trap indicate. Ellison says in the *Paris Review* interview, "I felt that such a man as this character would have been incapable of a love affair; it would have been inconsistent with his personality."[32] There is more than the lack of a love affair that strikes the reader—there is a lack of love, constraining the protagonist and inhibiting the narrator. His depiction of characters becomes "black and white." Only after Clifton achieves mythical proportions for Invisible Man does he elicit the protagonist's "love." The narrator chooses "symbolic action" as method and response to his lack of reality.

As *The Scarlet Letter* demonstrates, at the moment when questions of art become real confrontations (when Chillingworth views Dimmesdale's naked breast but Hawthorne's narrator averts *his* eyes), Hawthorne withdraws into allegory. In so doing, Hawthorne expresses his Puritanism, his need for a container, for a scaffolding on which to rest his narrative. Ellison's choice of allegory is not quite a withdrawal. Ellison needs aesthetic distance and he also does not believe white readers will accept *his* naturalistic version of reality. In order to prevent disagreement, Ellison transcends the literal and embraces the allegorical mode. Allegory, for Ellison as much as for Hawthorne, if for different reasons, becomes a form of artistic "underground."[33]

IV

In his allegorical interpretation of his protagonist's behavior, the narrator of *Invisible Man* attempts to break out of his isolation. Erving Goffman's distinction, in *Stigma*, between persons who feel visibly "discredited" and those who feel relatively invisible but still "discreditable" provides a model for interpreting this isolation sociologically as well as historically. As Goffman implies, visual discredit limits social behavior in a predictable and therefore manageable way; whereas the individual who remains only discreditable attempts to "pass" but chronically experiences the fear that his stigma will be recognized and his behavior then limited. To the extent that he "passes," we might call him successfully invisible: he wears a mask of social ease to cover up real or imaginary, social or psychic "dis-ease."[34] Even the most visibly marked individual is not stigmatized in every social group, however—especially when the group itself holds a particular stigma as its principle of organization. Thus Richard Wright is not born with the knowledge of his "blackness" because he is born into an all-black community. He learns it as he learns, in *Black Boy*, that he is stigmatized in the presence of whites. There is something "wrong" with him. Wright's friends, Griggs in particular, try to teach him that playing the "nigger" role is a more "manageable" and physically safer way of dealing with the white world.

Quentin Compson summarized the complexity of the problem in *The Sound and the Fury:*

> When I first came East I kept thinking You've got to remember to think of them as coloured people not niggers, and if it hadn't happened that I wasn't thrown with many of them, I'd have wasted a lot of time and trouble before I learned that the best way to take all people, black or white, is to take them for what they think they are, then leave them alone. That was when I realized that a nigger is not a person so much as a form of behaviour; a sort of obverse reflection of the white people he lives among.[35]

A "nigger" is an "obverse reflection" in the sense that his behavior conforms to white expectations; "nigger" behavior makes visible those human qualities that "white people" do not choose to recognize in themselves. It is ironically by reflecting white expectations that the "nigger" displays most clearly what the "white" wishes to remain hidden. In suggesting this paradox, Quentin suggests the realization that will reverse the obverse: and, as Ellison's protagonist learns, in recognizing that "nigger" is a form of behavior, a social role, he becomes a person.

It is clear that the more the "nigger" role is overplayed, the more *visible* it is, the more it earns the player a measure of anonymity, of invisibility. Melville explored this in *Benito Cereno*, where the artful subservience of Babo and Atufal hides their actual command over the *San Dominick* from Captain Delano of the *Bachelor's Delight*. Any assertion of individual decency, responsibility, or intelligence may serve to differentiate one Negro from his fellows and put him next in line for real or ritual lynching. These human qualities, then, must be hidden if not completely denied, in order to prevent the individuality of the Negro from becoming visible to whites.[36] In the novella, when Don Benito's friend Aranda describes the Negroes as "tractable," he ironically indicates the potential success of the blacks' plan for revolt from the slavery to which they are being transported. The black's "brain, not body, had schemed and led the revolt, with the plot"[37] and the *San Dominick* only fails in its mutiny because of the superior arms of Captain Delano's crew.

Just as it is for Will Mayes in Faulkner's "Dry September," for the nineteenth-century Negro in the South, individuality was a death warrant. The man who rebelled against the acceptance of stigma, who refused to accept the subordination of his own identity into the shadow of blackness, could hope only to go North, where he might lose his stigma. Melville's literary analogue is the shipboard mutiny. The shadow the Negro casts on Don Benito, even after he has been saved, symbolizes the failure of all men to escape bondage, even when they have proven themselves morally and intellectually superior to the bonds that physically constrain them. Similarly, Ellison's novel explodes the myth of the North as the road to freedom; for it is in New York that the protagonist first begins to experience invisibility.

In Goffman's terms, Invisible Man does not lose his stigma in the move North but rather undergoes a transformation from discredit to discreditability—from a position of social certainty to one of insecurity. In this way Invisible Man shares the experience of both Hester and Dimmesdale, and resembles Joe Christmas in his inability, in the North, to be certain who he is. At his southern college, implicitly accepting his discredit (without "seeing" that he was doing so), he enjoyed the security and protection of the Founder's benevolence (as well as the limits of vision the blindfold symbolizes). He first begins to recognize his invisibility when Bledsoe, in forcing him to leave, denies this security. The concept of invisibility "embodies the complex psychological dilemmas of men without a sense of vital group identity, whose sense of individual human identity is often denied by the dominant society."[38] Learning the distinction between "group identity" and "individual human identity" is one means of overcoming the split Goffman's stigmatized individual experiences, between his "virtual social identity" (our expectations of his character, appearance, and occupation) and his "actual social identity" (the category and attributes he could in fact be proved to possess).[39] Ellison's protagonist, at the beginning of chapter 1, does not recognize the distinction. His role as an ambitious student who wants to follow Bledsoe's example provides him with his "vital group identity." He equates his personal responsibility with his social responsibility, equates his identity with his social role. The narrator, retrospectively, attributes this equation to Invisible Man's blindness.

As an ambitious student, Invisible Man wants recognition; he wants to distinguish himself in Bledsoe's eyes from the mass of his schoolmates, and his assignment to act as chauffeur for Mr. Norton becomes his "golden" opportunity to do so. Thus his crime originates in his desire for visibility; and, ironically, he achieves "recognition" from Bledsoe, even though he doesn't understand his expulsion this way. The punishment results not from his action—as Norton explains, "nor was the boy responsible" (p. 94)—but from the visibility he acquires in performing it. Unlike the escaping slave, Invisible Man does not see his move North as an escape—because he does not *choose* to act. Both Bledsoe and, in effect, his historical situation make his choice for him.

Invisible Man's social exclusion is a kind of "lynching"; Bledsoe cuts him off from the opportunity to distinguish himself. Such distinction presupposes membership in a group. Thus, once in the North, even after Bledsoe's letter to Emerson destroys his dream of reintegration with his college, Invisible Man continues to associate the pursuit of identity with membership and distinction in an organization—Men's House, the union meeting at Liberty Paints, finally the Brotherhood. He doesn't realize that the only membership card he can hope to receive is the mark of exclusion, the stigma of social difference.

At the opening smoker, the protagonist merited the audience's laughter when he used the phrase "social responsibility," which he envisions as "social equality" and which they translate as "you've got to know your place at all times" (pp. 32–33).[40] In the last meeting with the Brotherhood, he explains that he acted on his own "personal responsibility" (p. 400) in deciding to hold a public funeral for Tod Clifton; Brother Jack replies, "You were not hired to think" (p. 405). The social yields to the personal for the narrator by the end; Invisible Man tries to separate his identity from his social role. Thus, although his desire throughout the novel to become an integral part of a community seems to reflect his "social responsibility," his failure to do so becomes his path to self-discovery. He wants to "join" an established unity because he has not yet become aware that the strength and power that originate in union lie within himself. His isolation is metaphysical as well as social.

V

In an interview with Allen Geller, Ellison agreed to term Invisible Man "an example of a social rebel," but stated that "'he doesn't have that level of conscious revolt'" that might make him, like Ahab, a metaphysical rebel.[41] At the same time, in *Shadow and Act*, Ellison states that the novel expresses Invisible Man's "restlessness of spirit, . . . an American condition that transcends geography, sociology, and past condition of servitude" (p. 57). Ellison's debt to Melville has been more often attributed to *The Confidence Man* than other works, but it may also be read within the tradition of *Moby-Dick* and Ishmael's own "restlessness of spirit." Ellison's interpretation to the contrary, his own narrator moves beyond Ahab's exploration of the metaphysical.

In *Moby-Dick* Ahab fails to see himself as viewing the world from *behind* a mask, but rather sees the world itself—"all visible objects"—as the mask. Unlike Ishmael, who accepts the existence of the metaphysical in the physical world, for Ahab, all outward manifestations are unreasoning walls that must be thrust beyond. Thus the external world, which the white whale symbolizes for Ahab, limits his vision. He hates "that inscrutable thing" precisely because it is inscrutable, cannot be scrutinized, can only be made visible by destroying it and destroying himself in the process.

The character in *Invisible Man* who most closely resembles Ahab in his hatred is not the protagonist but rather Ras the Exhorter. For Ras, as for Ahab, white symbolizes evil; and Clifton and Invisible Man are two of evil's agents. His view prevents him from seeing beyond the wall, so that the protagonist is as invisible to Ras as he is to the Brotherhood. In the triumphant action that places him in immediate jeopardy and motivates his descent underground, Invisible Man confronts Ras on the streets of Harlem at the culmination of the riot. Ras spots him, as if he has been looking for him, shouts "'Betrayer!'" and "flung, of all things, a spear" (p. 482). The spear may be the African symbol of Ras's chosen identity—as Vogler points out, "Ras" may be pronounced "race"—but it is also Ahab's harpoon. Ahab tries to kill the whale moments before his own death: "'*Thus*, I give up the spear!'"[42]

Invisible Man recognizes the double futility of Ras's action and his own passive "agreement."

> I stood there, knowing that by dying, that by being hanged by Ras on this street in this destructive night I would perhaps move them one fraction of a bloody step closer to a definition of who they were and of what I was and had been. But the definition would have been too narrow; I was invisible, and hanging would not bring me to visibility, even to their eyes, since they wanted my death not for myself alone but for the chase I'd been on all my life; because of the way I'd run, been run, chased, operated, purged—although to a great extent I could have done nothing else, given their blindness (didn't they tolerate both Rinehart and Bledsoe?) and my invisibility. . . . And I knew that it was better to live out one's one absurdity than to die for that of others, whether for Ras's or Jack's. (pp. 483–84)

The "stricken whale" carries Ahab, the *Pequod*, and all its crew except Ishmael into the vortex. Faulkner's body servant and Joe Christmas run their captors' race. Invisible Man dodges the spear, refusing to be drawn into Ras's absurdity and instead of continuing to run, he throws it right back:

> So when Ras yelled, "Hang him!" I let fly the spear and it was as though for a moment I had surrendered my life and begun to live again, watching it catch him as he turned his head to shout, ripping through both cheeks, and saw the surprised pause of the crowd as Ras wrestled with the spear that locked his jaws. (p. 484)

The impulsive and decisive act sends Invisible Man underground as he flees from capture, and it makes his narrative necessary, as a means of further exploration and understanding. In this action Invisible Man cannot be compared to Ahab, but rather tries to achieve the "transcendence" of an Ishmael.

Ellison denies the metaphysical implications of Invisible Man's search because, as he states in the interview, "This is not a God-constructed world. I don't think God constructed society. I think it's man-made."[43] In spite of Ellison's remarks, Invisible Man resembles a twentieth-century version of Ishmael. Ishmael chooses a masthead distance; Ellison's protagonist climbs the ghetto steps and the stage podium—his variation of Ras's ladder— and ends even further removed, ends underground. Like the dramatic chapters of *Moby-Dick* and Ishmael's withdrawal as omniscient narrator, the "symbolic action" of *Invisible Man* achieves metaphysical distance for Ellison's narrator. Both Ishmael and Invisible Man have earned self-designated names that express their namelessness. Both recognize that their invisibility is the price of vision; and both see their search as motivated by internal need for light.

In the Prologue to *Invisible Man*, the narrator compares his own search to the whaleman's search for light, and states that the blackness of invisibility puts you "glory, glory, Oh my Lawd, in the WHALE'S BELLY" (p. 13). Like Jonah, Invisible Man tried for a long time to avoid his mission by not recognizing it. And like Ishmael, he fuses his social search with his soul's search: "I carried my sickness and though for a long time I tried to place it in the outside world, the attempt to write it down shows me that at least half of it lay within me" (pp. 497–98). It may not be a God-constructed world. As Ellison suggest, it may be only the social equivalent of the Leviathan that a man may now pursue. But within their different historical spheres, Ishmael and Invisible Man end by confronting the same problem. Ishmael's moment of transcendence is only temporary: when he is picked up by the "errant" Rachel, he is pulled back into the physical world with its old problems and no new solutions. Invisible Man does not let himself get picked up by the *Rachel* (or her counterpart, Mary Rambo); yet, as he contemplates returning above ground, he faces a question he cannot answer: does he return to a world that is *all* model, that may be adequately explained by sociologists, that cannot "see" his invisibility and thus make possible his humanity; or has he achieved permanent realization, which goes beyond Ishmael's limits, in the recognition that because society *is* man-made, man can make a better one?

VI

Invisible Man's search for a brotherhood is a social variation on Ishmael's metaphysical struggle for a focus that will engage his subjectivity. Robert Bone calls Ellison's heritage picaresque and Invisible Man's journey not a "religious quest or pilgrimage, but a journey toward experience, adventure, personal freedom":[44]

> In the South everyone knew you, but coming North was a jump into the unknown. ... You could actually make yourself anew. ... All boundaries down, freedom was not only the recognition of necessity, it was the recognition of possibility. And sitting there trembling I caught a brief glimpse of the possibilities posed by Rinehart's multiple personalities and turned away. It was too vast and confusing to con-

template. Then I looked at the polished lenses of the glasses and
laughed. I had been trying simply to turn them into a disguise but
they had become a political instrument instead. (p. 431)

By wearing Rinehart's glasses, Invisible Man enacts his invisibility;
he is taken for someone he is not. His own invisibility, his greatest
mask, becomes his political instrument; his personal freedom lies in
the ability to be a phantom. What society does not recognize, it
cannot control; and it does not recognize an invisible man.

Invisible Man thus affirms invisibility because he has transformed it, underground, and by his art, from a symptom of personal
disorder to a symbol of social rebellion;[45] it becomes his modus vivendi, where the self may correspond to no definition of identity but
its own.[46] This affirmation leads to his personal transcendence of
social problems but fails to link his new identity as an invisible man
with a program for social behavior. How does naming oneself or
pointing out moral issues ease his reintegration? Where is the social
potential and the ontological realism of "symbolic action"?

This is the question with which the novel ends. And, without an
answer to it, Invisible Man remains underground. In *Shadow and
Act*, Ellison talks about "that intensity of personal anguish . . . any
and everything in this life which plunges the talented individual
into solitude while leaving him the will to transcend his condition
through art" (p. 130): "My goal was not to escape, or hold back, but
to work through; to transcend, as the blues transcend the painful
conditions with which they deal. . . . if there is anything 'miraculous' about the book it is the result of hard work undertaken in the
belief that the work of art is important in itself, that it is a social
action in itself" (p. 137).[47] Ellison asserts that art is social action by
implicitly recognizing that the vision of the artist and the vision of
the stigmatized are intimately related.

The "joke" at the center of *Invisible Man* is the conclusion that, in
order for the narrator to achieve integration with his society, he
must become visible again. By enacting invisibility, he resumes the
stigma that originally protected him against lynching. But his new
visibility would be self-conscious strategy. "Before that I lived in the
darkness into which I was chased, but now I see. I've illuminated the
blackness of my invisibility—and vice versa. And so I play the invisible music of my isolation. . . . Could this compulsion to put invisibility down in black and white be thus an urge to make music of
invisibility?" (p. 16). His experience as a discreditably invisible man
gives him the "second sight" of the visibly stigmatized and leads to
his "attempt to write it down" (p. 497).

Out of invisibility comes the artist's vision. In the closing scene, Invisible Man in a waking dream sees himself castrated by Jack, Emerson, Bledsoe, and Norton.

> But now they came forward with a knife, holding me; and I felt the bright red pain and they took the two bloody blobs and cast them over the bridge. . . .
>   And I looked up through a pain so intense now that the air seemed to roar with the clanging of metal, hearing, HOW DOES IT FEEL TO BE FREE OF ILLUSION. (pp. 492–93)

The image of the "bloody blobs" develops the image of Jack's "two eyes in the bottom of a glass" and the full impact of blinding-as-castration fills the dream. At the same time, his castration becomes Jack's blinding as well as his own, and he shouts,

> "there hang not only my generations wasting upon the water—. . .
>   But your sun . . .
>   And your moon . . .
>   Your universe, and that drip-drop upon the water you hear is all the history you've made, all you're going to make. Now laugh, you scientists. Let's hear you laugh!"
>   And I awoke in the blackness. (pp. 493–94)

Invisible Man resembles White-Jacket here in his realization that, without his straitjacket, he can "see" more. And, as Earl Rovit writes, "In accepting himself as the Invisible Man he assumes the historic role which Emerson unerringly assigned to the American poet; he becomes 'the world's eye'—something through which one sees, even though it cannot itself be seen."[48] From his position as a man-of-war, a man-at-war, upon his arrival in the North, he becomes "the world's eye."

But out of vision comes visibility, and in this transformation art becomes social action. This is the "compulsion to put invisibility down in black and white"—the compulsion to make it visible and symbolically act it out in order to externalize it, then transcend it. As the black woman in the Prologue redefines freedom, "'I guess now it ain't nothing but knowing how to say what I got up in my head. But it's a hard job, son. Too much is done happen to me in too short a time. Hit's like I have a fever'" (p. 14). The myth of the road North is gone; Brother Tarp's physical flight to freedom is no longer an option for Invisible Man. "Knowing how to say" replaces the file as the narrator's political instrument. Unlike Ahab, Invisible Man need not destroy the evil that is white in order to strike through the mask. Like Ishmael, he reconstructs his journey to omniscient invisibility and begins to create a new myth.

To reconstruct mystery is to take possession of the powers of language: "Stephen's problem, like ours, was not actually one of creating the uncreated conscience of his race, but of creating the *uncreated features of his face*. Our task is that of making ourselves individuals. The conscience of a race is the gift of its individuals who see, evaluate, record" (p. 307).[49] Such creation is possible in fiction, which formulates experience. As Ellison writes, "the function, the psychology of artistic selectivity is to eliminate from art form all those elements of experience which contain no compelling significance."[50] Ellison's fiction marks this "compelling significance" and, like the scapegoat, brings to visibility hidden human truths, not to conform to reality, like *The Scarlet Letter*, but to *re*form it. Thus the fiction writer usurps the power of the social group—he stigmatizes for his own ends, destroying the Light and Power Monopoly of the lynch mob by stealing its catharsis. At the same time he provides a formula for reconstructing reality. For Ellison, the search for identity "is *the* American theme." In art, "the identity of fictional characters is determined by the implicit realism of the form, not by their relation to tradition; they are what they do or do not do. Archetypes are timeless, novels are time-haunted."[51] In *Invisible Man*, where identity is a problem, to take control of the creation of realism would be to alter reality in the process, and the novel is "implicitly realistic" because the narrator's choice of allegory has been socially determined: the escaping slave is an archetype; an invisible man is a new creation, or at least a new reconstruction. But Ellison avoids strict literary realism. At the end, his narrator does not say much about what it means to be an American. Perhaps his greatest accomplishment is his attempt, in the tradition of his predecessors, to write "the great American novel." For it is the attempt that *defines* what is American about this book.[52] "As Henry James suggested, being an American is an arduous task, and for most of us, I suspect, the difficulty begins with the name."[53]

The final solution to the narrator's dilemma remains the reader's acceptance of his own responsibility. It is not up to Invisible Man to emerge from his hole; we must join him there. The artist and the minority member confront the whole world. Until illumination becomes universal, we shall all be on the same train; and like Mr. Norton's, ours does not get to Centre Street without passing through the Golden Day. *Invisible Man* is Ellison's attempt to turn the literary mark into social password. By asserting that "black is beautiful," the formerly stigmatized minority member gains control of his own stigma. "I carried my sickness, and though for a long time I tried to place it in the outside world, the attempt to write it down shows me that at least half of it lay within me" (p. 498). For the narrator, writing eases his condition by revealing to him his own position; and, even if that position is not yet affirmed "outside" his hole, "in spite of myself, I've learned some things" (p. 501).

Ellison talks about the "special role" American fiction has played "in the development of the American nation. It had had to play that role, had had to concern itself with certain uniquely American tasks even in those instances in which it was not read (or not widely read, and I think here of *Moby-Dick*). And this for a number of reasons. One, as a literary form the novel has been primarily concerned with charting changes within society and with changes in personality as affected by society. . . ."[54] In this quotation, Ellison implies that the classic American novelist supposes an ideal reader, as by writing a book for such an individual might, should the book acquire readers, create an entire society of such people. The novelist changes the world the novel portrays, then, by changing the novel. He or she does this, I have tried to argue throughout this book, because the making of fictions, as Hawthorne, Melville, and Faulkner all knew, makes things visible that might have remained hidden. Fiction is Ellison's new "mark," both the vehicle of his discovery and the record of its accomplishment; the "second sight" of the stigmatized and the "inner vision" of the artist become yoked towards new integration.

Notes

1. As Earl Rovit writes, Ellison's comic art "will inevitably probe the masks of identity and value searching relentlessly for some deeper buried reality, . . . while accepting the fundamental necessity for masks and the impossibility of ever discovering an essential face beneath a mask. That is to say, this comic stance will accept with the same triumphant gesture both the basic absurdity of all attempts to impose meaning on the chaos of life, and the necessary converse of this, the ultimate significance of absurdity itself." (From "Ralph Ellison and the American Comic Tradition," *Wisconsin Studies in Contemporary Literature* 1 (1960): 34–42. Copyright 1960 by the Board of Regents of the University of Wisconsin System. (Reprinted in *Twentieth Century Interpretations of Invisible Man*, ed. John M. Reilly [Englewood Cliffs: Prentice-Hall, 1970], p. 57. All references to this work are to the reprint edition.)

2. Ellison, *Shadow and Act*, (New York: Random House, 1964), p. 43. All further references clearly to *Shadow and Act* and not to the novel appear in the text.

3. Bone, "Ralph Ellison and the Uses of Imagination," in Reilly, pp. 27–28. Bone goes on to say: "One senses in his work an unseen reality behind the surfaces of things. Hence his fascination with guises and disguises, with the con man and the trickster. Hence the felt dichotomy between visible and invisible, public and private, actual and fictive modes of reality. His experience as a Negro no doubt reinforces his ironic awareness of 'the joke that always lies between appearance and reality,' and turns him toward an inner world that lies beyond the reach of insult or oppression. This world may be approached by means of the imagination; it is revealed during the transcendent moment in jazz or the epiphany in literature. *Transcend* is thus a crucial word in Ellison's aesthetic."

4. Ralph Ellison, *Invisible Man* (New York, 1952), p. 503. All further references to this work in this chapter appear in the text.

5. My intention in this chapter is not to interpret the symbolism of discrete characters and incidents in the novel, but rather to speak to larger questions. There is a substantial body of criticism devoted to such interpretation and much of it has been anthologized. See in particular John M. Reilly, ed., *Twentieth Century Interpretations of Invisible Man*; John Hersey, ed., *Ralph Ellison: A Collection of Critical Essays* (Englewood Cliffs, N.J.: Prentice-Hall, 1974); and Joseph F. Trimmer, ed., *A Casebook on Ralph Ellison's Invisible Man* (New York: Crowell, 1972). Trimmer's *Casebook* contains a lengthy bibliography. For the "larger questions" surrounding the novel, Ellison's own *Shadow and Act* is the best introduction.

6. *Shadow and Act*, p. 66.

7. R. W. B. Lewis, *The American Adam* (Chicago: University of Chicago Press, 1955), p. 1.

8. Ibid., p. 9.

9. See Ellison's formulation of the fiction writer's effort in *Shadow and Act*, p. xix.

10. Frederick Douglass, *Narrative*, ed. Benjamin Quarles (Cambridge: Belknap Press, 1960), p. 97.

11. Thomas A. Vogler, "*Invisible Man:* Somebody's Protest Novel," *Iowa Review*, 1 (Spring 1970), p. 66.

12. *Shadow and Act*, p. xix.

13. Vogler, p. 67.

14. Lewis, p. 5.

15. William Faulkner, *Absalom, Absalom!* (New York: Random House, 1936), p. 361.

16. Erich Neumann, *Depth Psychology and a New Ethic*, trans. Eugene Rolfe (London, 1969), pp. 81–94 ff. Neumann writes, "The recognition and acceptance of the shadow presupposes more than a mere willingness to look at one's dark brother—and then to return him to a state of suppression, where he languishes like a prisoner in a gaol. It involves granting him freedom and a share in one's life" (p. 81).

17. *Absalom, Absalom!*, p. 378.

18. See the end of "Richard Wright's Blues," in *Shadow and Act*, p. 94.

19. Ibid., p. 33.

20. Ibid., pp. 90–91.

21. Ibid., p. 26. The phrase is a paraphrase of Richard Wright.

22. Ibid., p. 104. Irving Howe, "Black Boys and Native Sons" (anthologized in Trimmer) scoffs at Ellison's statement—"as if one could *decide* one's deepest and most authentic response to society!" (p. 159). Howe says that Richard Wright would have said "that only through struggle could men with black skins, and for that matter, all the oppressed of the world, achieve their humanity" (p. 159).

23. Robert Bone supports this point. In order to place Ellison in his twentieth-century tradition, he writes, "What is involved is a rejection of the naturalistic novel and the philosophical assumptions on which it rests. . . . [O]ne idea emerges with persistent force: *Man is the creator of his own reality.* If a culture shapes its artists, the converse is equally the case: The American novel is in this sense a conquest of the frontier; as it describes our experience, it creates it. This turn toward subjectivity, this transcendence of determinism, this insistence on an existential freedom, is crucial to Ellison's conception of the artist. It finds concrete expression in his work through the devices of masking and naming" (in Reilly, p. 29).

24. James Baldwin, *Notes of a Native Son* (Boston: Beacon Press, 1955), p. 23.

25. Howe, p. 151.

26. Ibid., p. 152.

27. Bone, p. 31.

28. Howe, p. 154.

29. William Faulkner, *Light in August* (New York: Random House, 1932), p. 440.

30. John Oliver Killens, "The Confessions of Willie Styron," in *William Styron's Nat Turner: Ten Black Writers Respond,* ed. John Henrik Clarke (Boston: Beacon Press, 1968), p. 36.

31. Ibid., p. 44.

32. *Shadow and Act,* p. 180.

33. Ellison's recently published fiction affirms his continuing choice of allegorical method. The narrator of "Cadillac Flambé," because he happens to carry a tape recorder, captures the exact words of LeeWillie Minifees as he proceeds to set fire to his "Coon Cage Eight." The other characters who appear in the story—the narrator, the senator, the people on the lawn, the police—act as audience, stage props, or technical crew for LeeWillie's spectacle. In a fictional conflagration not unlike Hawthorne's "Earth's Holocaust," the narrator allegorically interprets Minifees's action as "almost metaphysical" (*American Review 16* [New York: Bantam, 1973], pp. 249–69).

34. Erving Goffman, *Stigma* (Englewood Cliffs, N.J.: Prentice-Hall, 1963), pp. 4–19.

35. William Faulkner, *The Sound and the Fury* (New York: Random House, 1929), p. 106.

36. On Ellison's remarks concerning the suppression of individuality within the black community, Bone writes: "As soon, however, as this forbidden impulse seeks expression, an intolerable anxiety is aroused. Threatened by his own unfolding personality as much as by the whites, the Negro learns to camouflage, to dissimulate, to retreat behind a protective mask" (in Reilly, p. 29). See also Richard Kostelanetz, "The Politics of Ellison's Booker: *Invisible Man* as Symbolic History," in Trimmer, pp. 281–305, for a discussion of Booker T. Washington's prescriptions for conduct, both within the black community and in dealing with the white world.

37. *Benito Cereno*, in *Selected Tales and Poems by Herman Melville*, ed. Richard Chase (New York: Rinehart, 1950), p. 90.

38. T. M. Lieber, "Ralph Ellison and the Metaphor of Invisibility in Black Literary Tradition," *American Quarterly*, 24 (March 1972), p. 86.

39. Goffman, p. 2.

40. With reference to the way the Negro community discouraged individuality, Kostelanetz makes the following statement about Invisible Man's "social equality": "Challenged by the audience, he quickly reverts to the traditional unrevolutionary phase. Ellison here illustrates that as the speaker's censor relaxes, his true desires are revealed; but as soon as he remembers the power of Southern authority, he immediately represses his wish" (p. 9).

41. Allen Geller, "An Interview with Ralph Ellison," *Tamarack Review*, No. 32 (Summer 1964), p. 12.

42. *Moby-Dick*, p. 468.

43. Geller, p. 14.

44. Bone, in Reilly, p. 27.

45. Critics have stressed the usefulness of the narrator's art as a means of his self-realization. Robert Bone speaks of Ellison's novel as "an act of ritual naming, the novelist as a 'moralist-designate' who *names* the central moral issues of his time" and thus accepts the burden of his given name—Emerson (p. 31). Thomas Vogler views artistic activity as a process of self-examination, where Invisible Man "is forced, in the darkness of his hole, to explore the contents of the briefcase which are the real clues to his identity and the only source of light" (p. 71).

46. T. M. Lieber writes, "All men, unless their identity corresponds completely to someone else's image of reality, are at least partially invisible in Ellison's terminology" (p. 99).

47. Joel Porte says about Hawthorne: "Hawthorne can never really leave Salem, just as Hester can never quit the Boston of her tale, because the strength of the romance artist is based on his reviving and coming to terms with past pain" (*The Romance in America: Studies in Cooper, Poe, Hawthorne, Melville, and James* [Middletown, Conn.: Wesleyan University Press, 1969], p. 100). The quotation is applicable to Ellison in his use of the blues as an analogue for his own attempt in *Invisible Man*.

48. In Reilly, p. 59.

49. Rovit supports my argument. By the epilogue, he writes, "the hero has created the features of his face from the malleable stuff of his own experience. He who accepts himself as 'invisible' has ironically achieved a concrete tangibility, while those characters in the novel who seemed to be 'visible' and substantial men (Norton, Brother Jack, and even Tod Clifton) are discovered to be really 'invisible' since they

are self-imprisoned captives of their own capacities to see and be seen in stereotyped images" (Ibid., p. 58).

50. *Shadow and Act,* p. 82.

51. Ibid., p. 57.

52. Whether he succeeds or not, the attempt places him in the classic American tradition. As Robert H. Moore writes, "even if we concern ourselves with those American writers who were *not* novelists, we see that the makers of American literature had been also concerned with spelling out that which was peculiarly *American* about the American experience . . ." ("On Invitation Rites and Power: Ralph Ellison Speaks at West Point," *Contemporary Literature,* 15 [Spring 1974], p. 172). And as William J. Schafer states, "Ellison's novel . . . is above all an *American* novel. . . . It simply extends and develops Richard Wright's aphorism, 'The Negro is America's metaphor'" ("Ralph Ellison and the Birth of the Anti-Hero," in Trimmer, *Casebook,* p. 225).

53. *Shadow and Act,* p. 166.

54. Moore, p. 172.

Postscript

I state somewhat facetiously at the end of my first chapter that the logical question with which to end this study involves some understanding of the concept of non-marked characters in American fiction. To phrase the question another way would be to conclude a study of social stigma with a study of the similarities that connect nonstigmatized individuals in American fictional communities. If American writers could make fictions without marking, in the special sense in which I have defined the term, then our literature would not reflect the way the Puritans conceived our world and the way the transcendental imagination retains their habit of mind. Analogously, if we could get at the ways in which we are alike without assigning stigma, then we would become a different culture and we would have a different literature.

Marking in my own approach to American literature is both an interpretative epistemology and a focus or vehicle, a "mantra" of sorts, for which I have examined these classic works of American fiction. I have read the works in this study by marking their significance, and in every case, what has pointed the significance of the work is, itself, a mark of some kind. Therefore I have marked or noticed what it is in these novels that the narratives themselves mark or notice about the world they portray. I believe that in the self-conscious application of the very principle of Puritan inner scrutiny to literary works, I have been able to show how Hawthorne, Melville, Faulkner, and Ellison, in spite of their Puritan heritage, demonstrate a way of seeing that Puritanism obscured.

As Charles Feidelson writes of the Puritans, "the symbolizing *process* was constantly at work in their minds. . . . Every passage of life, enmeshed in the vast context of God's plan, possessed a delegated meaning."[1] Since it was the very intention of Puritan meditation to make things manifest, perhaps we might conclude that America's "manifest destiny" has covered over vital aspects of our culture. However, as the four authors in my study indicate in their work, in spite of this fact, or perhaps because of it, the destiny of American fiction has become the necessity to reveal those non-manifest mysteries that symbolize the essence of who we are. The act of marking or stigmatizing, which our history has shown to be so destructive in our social behavior, is constructive in fiction because it throws into relief the existence of those mysteries. American fiction points the meaning of our nonmanifest destiny.

It is understandable that the four authors whose works have been the subject of this book should characterize so large a movement in our literature. The experience of living outside a community one has drawn his identity from creates a sense of dislocation, leads to Goffman's discreditability. And the single central fact in each of these men's lives is social exclusion, whether by chance or by choice. Hawthorne was indeed "guillotined" as Surveyor of the Customs; Melville did test his own "landlessness" before he became a fiction writer; Faulkner inhabited a region that had marked itself in civil war and was an eccentric within that region; and Ellison has experienced what it means to be black in America. The fact that eccentrics or members of one minority group or another have created our best fiction suggests a truth that the Puritans did not know, namely, that social exclusion, more than strengthening the identity of the group, gives the scapegoat vision. At the same time, ironically, it is the very process of exclusion that defines what is American. The Puritans therefore, like Faulkner's Indians in "Red Leaves," taught us how to define ourselves by the things we are not. Feidelson writes, "The intellectual stance of the conscious artist in American literature has been determined very largely by problems inherent in the method of the Puritans. The isolation of the American artist in society, so often lamented, is actually parallel to the furtive and unacknowledged role of artistic method in the American mind; both factors began in the seventeenth century with the establishment of Puritan philosophy and of a society that tried to live by it."[2]

What Feidelson terms the "symbolistic imagination" and what I have described as the process of marking that characterizes the "transcendental imagination" are analogous ideas. Certainly symbol making involves marking, and what a fiction writer marks in his narrative easily becomes symbolic. What the concept of marking further demonstrates is the congruence of seemingly different but actually related mental acts, all of which form a series of analogies by which our fiction writers portray the American experience. The

Puritan meditation of inner scrutiny, their practice of social exclusion, the transcendentalists' metaphysics, Calvinist theology, the lynching of Negroes in the South, and the literary method of our classic fiction writers all share a common epistemology. Marking does more than reflect the resonances of a symbol within a literary work or a culture; it is not metaphor but methodology that links American literature and society.

Ralph Ellison sums it all up neatly in his "Conversation" with Ishmael Reed:

> The people who won their revolution by throwing the British off their backs and who declared that they were rejecting the hierarchical divisions of the past in the name of democracy began their experiment loaded down with hypocrisy and wrapped up to their wigs in facile self-righteousness.
>
> They declared themselves the new national identity, "American," but, as social beings, they were still locked in the continuum of history, and as language-users they were still given to the ceaseless classifying and grading of everything from stars and doodle bugs to tints of skin and crinks of hair, they had to have a standard by which they could gauge the extent to which their theories of democracy were being made manifest, both in the structure of the new society and in the lives of its citizens.
>
> Theoretically, theirs was a "classless" society, so what better (or easier) way of establishing such a standard than to say, "Well, now here we have all these easily identifiable blacks who're already below the threshold of social mobility—why not use them? They're not even human by our standards, so why not exploit them as the zero point on our scale of social possibility? Why not designate to *them* the negative ground upon which our society shall realize its goals? . . ."
>
> This is to telescope a hell of a lot of history and sociology, but you can see what I'm driving at. . . .[3]

In this study of social stigma, I have tried to do the same, to telescope (literary) history and sociology. In the process I have articulated one model of American thought. If at times my model interferes with the reader's appreciation of the literary work, I can only claim the good intention of trying to elucidate familiar literature in a way that will encourage yet another rereading. With the discipline of a meditator, I have tried to return again and again to my focus on the mark with only one goal in mind: that I, like Hawthorne, Melville, Faulkner, and Ellison, might transcend my own finite ability to look for America, might allow these great artists, as Doc Hines prophesies God will do for Joe Christmas, to "put on" their knowledge and share their vision of our "non-manifest" destiny.

Notes

1. Charles Feidelson, *Symbolism and American Literature* (Chicago: University of Chicago Press, 1953), pp. 78–79.

2. Ibid., p. 89.

3. *New York Times,* July 9, 1977, p. C-17.

Index